D0084301

EXCEL® MODELING IN CORPORATE FINANCE
Fifth Edition

CRAIG W. HOLDEN
Professor of Finance
Kelley School of Business
Indiana University

Boston Columbus Indianapolis New York San Francisco Upper Saddle River
Amsterdam Cape Town Dubai London Madrid Milan Munich Paris Montreal Toronto
Delhi Mexico City Sao Paulo Sydney Hong Kong Seoul Singapore Taipei Tokyo

To Kathryn, Diana, and Jimmy

Editorial Project Manager: Erin McDonagh
Editorial Assistant: Elissa Senra-Sargent
Managing Editor: Jeff Holcomb
Production Project Manager: Karen Carter
Operations Specialist: Carol Melville

Cover Designer: Suzanne Duda
Media Project Manager: Melissa Honig
Printer/Binder: Edwards Brothers Malloy Jackson Road
Cover Printer: Phoenix Color/Hagerstown

Credits and acknowledgments borrowed from other sources and reproduced, with permission, in this textbook appear on the appropriate page within text.

Microsoft and/or its respective suppliers make no representations about the suitability of the information contained in the documents and related graphics published as part of the services for any purpose. All such documents and related graphics are provided "as is" without warranty of any kind. Microsoft and/or its respective suppliers hereby disclaim all warranties and conditions with regard to this information, including all warranties and conditions of merchantability, whether express, implied or statutory, fitness for a particular purpose, title and non-infringement. In no event shall Microsoft and/or its respective suppliers be liable for any special, indirect or consequential damages or any damages whatsoever resulting from loss of use, data or profits, whether in an action of contract, negligence or other tortious action, arising out of or in connection with the use or performance of information available from the services.

The documents and related graphics contained herein could include technical inaccuracies or typographical errors. Changes are periodically added to the information herein. Microsoft and/or its respective suppliers may make improvements and/or changes in the product(s) and/or the program(s) described herein at any time. Partial screen shots may be viewed in full within the software version specified.

Microsoft® and Windows® are registered trademarks of the Microsoft Corporation in the U.S.A. and other countries. This book is not sponsored or endorsed by or affiliated with the Microsoft Corporation.

Copyright © 2015, 2012, 2009 by Pearson Education, Inc. All rights reserved.
Manufactured in the United States of America. This publication is protected by Copyright, and permission should be obtained from the publisher prior to any prohibited reproduction, storage in a retrieval system, or transmission in any form or by any means, electronic, mechanical, photocopying, recording, or likewise. To obtain permission(s) to use material from this work, please submit a written request to Pearson Education, Inc., Permissions Department, One Lake Street, Upper Saddle River, New Jersey 07458, or you may fax your request to 201-236-3290.

Many of the designations by manufacturers and sellers to distinguish their products are claimed as trademarks. Where those designations appear in this book, and the publisher was aware of a trademark claim, the designations have been printed in initial caps or all caps.

10 9 8 7 6 5 4 3

ISBN 10: 0-205-98725-7
ISBN 13: 978-0-205-98725-2

CONTENTS

DOWNLOADABLE CONTENTS

Excel Modeling in Corporate Finance Fifth Edition.pdf
Ready-To-Build spreadsheets available in both XLSX
and XLS file formats:
Ch 01 Single Cash Flow - Ready-To-Build.xlsx
Ch 02 Annuity - Ready-To-Build.xlsx
Ch 03 NPV Using Constant Discounting - Ready-To-Build.xlsx
Ch 04 NPV Using General Discounting - Ready-To-Build.xlsx
Ch 05 Loan Amortization - Ready-To-Build.xlsx
Ch 06 Lease vs Buy - Ready-To-Build.xlsx
Ch 07 Bond Valuation - Ready-To-Build.xlsx
Ch 08 Estimating the Cost of Capital - Ready-To-Build.xlsx
Ch 09 Stock Valuation - Ready-To-Build.xlsx
Ch 10 Firm and Project Valuation - Ready-To-Build.xlsx
Ch 11 The Yield Curve - Ready-To-Build.xlsx
Ch 12 U.S. Yield Curve Dynamics - Ready-To-Build.xlsx
Ch 13 Capital Structure - Ready-To-Build.xlsx
Ch 14 Project NPV - Ready-To-Build.xlsx
Ch 15 Cost-Reducing Project - Ready-To-Build.xlsx

Preface

For more than 30 years, since the emergence of Lotus 1-2-3 and Microsoft Excel® in the 1980s, spreadsheet models have been the dominant vehicles for finance professionals in the business world to implement their financial knowledge. Yet even today, most Corporate Finance textbooks have very limited coverage of how to build Excel models. This book fills that gap. It teaches students how to build financial models in Excel. It provides step-by-step instructions so that students can build models themselves (active learning), rather than being handed already-completed spreadsheets (passive learning). It progresses from simple examples to practical, real-world applications. It spans nearly all quantitative models in corporate finance, including nearly all niche areas of corporate finance.

My goal is simply to *change finance education from limited treatment of the most basic Excel models to comprehensive treatment of both simple and sophisticated Excel models*. This change will better prepare students for their future business careers. It will increase student evaluations of teacher performance by enabling more practical, real-world content and by allowing a more hands-on, active learning pedagogy.

Fifth Edition Changes

The Fifth Edition adds great new corporate finance content:

- Real options, including project valuation with abandonment options, expansion options, contraction options, chooser options, and compound options
- Lease vs. buy decisions, including car and corporate applications
- Taxable vs. traditional vs. Roth savings plans

All of the real-world data, including financial statements, bond prices, the yield curve, asset returns, exchange rates, and options prices, have been updated.

Ready-To-Build Spreadsheets

This product includes **Ready-To-Build spreadsheets**, which can be downloaded from the Pearson web site. The spreadsheets are available in both "**XLSX**" and "**XLS**" file formats. By default, the screen shots and instructions in the book are based on **Excel 2013**. For the items explained in this book, there are no significant differences relative to Excel 2010. There are few places where there are differences relative to Excel 2007. In those instances, "Excel 2007 Equivalent" boxes have been added in the margin to explain how to do the equivalent step in Excel 2007.

The instruction boxes on the Ready-To-Build spreadsheets are *bitmapped images* so that the formulas cannot just be copied to the spreadsheet. Both the instruction boxes and arrows are *objects*, so that they can easily be deleted when the spreadsheet is complete. Just select the boxes and arrows and press delete. This leaves a clean spreadsheet for future use.

Ready-To-Build Spreadsheets for every chapter provide:

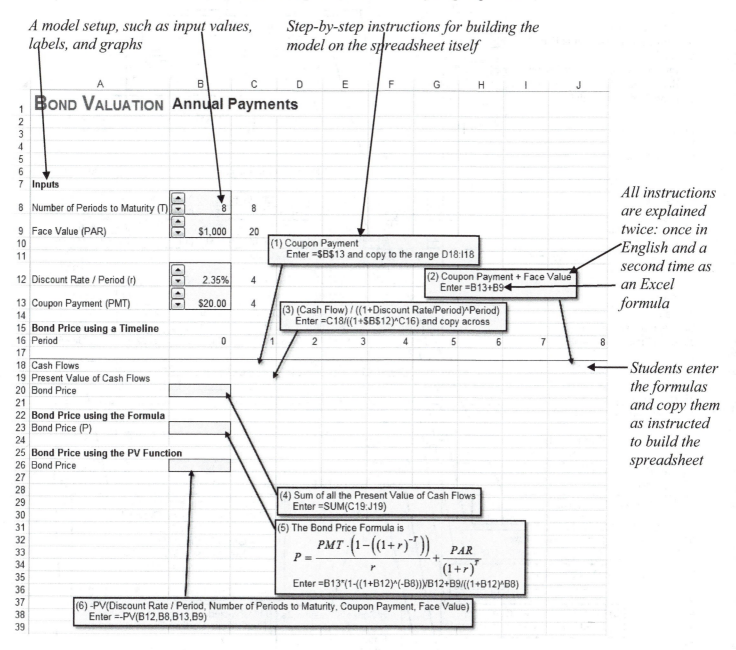

A model setup, such as input values, labels, and graphs

Step-by-step instructions for building the model on the spreadsheet itself

All instructions are explained twice: once in English and a second time as an Excel formula

Students enter the formulas and copy them as instructed to build the spreadsheet

BOND VALUATION **Annual Payments**

7 **Inputs**

8 Number of Periods to Maturity (T) — 8 — 8

9 Face Value (PAR) — $1,000 — 20

12 Discount Rate / Period (r) — 2.35% — 4

13 Coupon Payment (PMT) — $20.00 — 4

15 **Bond Price using a Timeline**

16 Period — 0 — 1 2 3 4 5 6 7 8

18 Cash Flows

19 Present Value of Cash Flows

20 Bond Price

22 **Bond Price using the Formula**

23 Bond Price (P)

25 **Bond Price using the PV Function**

26 Bond Price

(1) Coupon Payment
Enter =$B$13 and copy to the range D18:I18

(2) Coupon Payment + Face Value
Enter =B13+B9

(3) (Cash Flow) / ((1+Discount Rate/Period)^Period)
Enter =C18/((1+$B$12)^C16) and copy across

(4) Sum of all the Present Value of Cash Flows
Enter =SUM(C19:J19)

(5) The Bond Price Formula is

$$P = \frac{PMT \cdot \left(1 - \left((1+r)^{-T}\right)\right)}{r} + \frac{PAR}{(1+r)^{T}}$$

Enter =B13*(1-((1+B12)^(-B8)))/B12+B9/((1+B12)^B8)

(6) -PV(Discount Rate / Period, Number of Periods to Maturity, Coupon Payment, Face Value)
Enter =-PV(B12,B8,B13,B9)

Spin buttons, option buttons, and graphs facilitate visual, interactive learning

	A	B	C	D	E	F	G	H
1	**FIRM AND PROJECT VALUATION**			**Five Equivalent Methods**				
2								
3	**Inputs**							
				(1) Sales Revenue - Expenses Enter =C15-C16 and copy across				
4	Valuation Object	Valuation Object: ⦿ Firm ○ Project	1					
5	Date 0 Proj Investment or Firm Cap	$800.00		(2) Gross Earnings - Depreciation Enter =C17-C18 and copy across				
6	Tax Rate	40.0%						
7	Unlevered Cost of Equity Capital	10.0%		(3) Debt(t-1) * Cost of Riskfree Debt Enter =B80*$B$8 and copy across				
8	Riskfree Rate=Cost of Riskfree Debt	3.0%						
9	Infinte Horizon Growth Rate	5.0%		(4) EBIT - Interest Expense Enter =C19-C20 and copy across				
10	Include Infinite Horizon?	Infinite Horizon: ⦿ Yes ○ No	1					
11								
12	**Cash Flows**							**2nd Stage:**
13				First Stage: Finite Horizon				**Infin Horiz**
14	Date		0	1	2	3	4	5	6
15	Revenues			$650.00	$690.00	$720.00	$755.00	$775.00	$840.00
16	Expenses			$410.00	$435.00	$445.00	$470.00	$470.00	$475.00
17	Gross Earnings			$240.00	$255.00	$275.00	$285.00	$305.00	$365.00
18	Depreciation			$60.00	$60.00	$60.00	$60.00	$60.00	$60.00
19	Earnings Bef Interest & Tax (EBIT)			$180.00	$195.00	$215.00	$225.00	$245.00	$305.00
20	Interest Expense			$7.50	$7.65	$7.80	$7.95	$8.10	$8.25
21	Earnings Before Tax			$172.50	$187.35	$207.20	$217.05	$236.90	$296.75
22	Taxes			$69.00	$74.94	$82.88	$86.82	$94.76	$118.70
23	Earnings			$103.50	$112.41	$124.32	$130.23	$142.14	$178.05
24	Add Back Depreciation			$60.00	$60.00	$60.00	$60.00	$60.00	$60.00
25	Cash Flow from Operations			$163.50	$172.41	$184.32	$190.23	$202.14	$238.05
26								
27	New Invest in Plant and Equipment			($60.00)	($60.00)	($60.00)	($60.00)	($60.00)	($92.50)
28	After-Tax Salvage Value							$0.00	
29	New Invest in Working Capital			($10.00)	($10.00)	($10.00)	($10.00)	($10.00)	($10.00)
30	Cash Flows from Investments			($70.00)	($70.00)	($70.00)	($70.00)	($70.00)	($102.50)
31								
32	New Borrowing (Repayment)			$5.00	$5.00	$5.00	$5.00	$5.00	$13.75
33								
34	Free Cash Flow to Equity (FCFE)			$98.50	$107.41	$119.32	$125.23	$137.14	$149.30
35	= Dividends			$98.50	$107.41	$119.32	$125.23	$137.14	$149.30

(5) (Earnings Before Tax) * (Tax Rate) Enter =C21*$B$6 and copy across

(6) Earnings Before Tax - Taxes Enter =C21-C22 and copy across

(7) Depreciation Enter =C18 and copy across

(8) Earnings + Depreciation Enter =C23+C24 and copy across

(9) If Include Infinite Horizon = Yes, Then -Infinite Horizon Growth Rate * Book Value of Equity(T) - Gross Earnings(T+1) - New Invest in Working Capital(T+1) - New Borrowing(T+1) Else 0 Enter =IF(C10=1,-B9*G81-H18-H29-H32,0)

(10) Sum of Investments Cash Flows Enter =SUM(C27:C29)

(11) If Include Infinite Horizon = Yes, Then Infinite Horizon Growth Rate * Debt(T) Else 0 Enter =IF(C10=1,B9*G80,0)

(12) Cash Flow from Operations + Cash Flow from Investments + New Borrowing (Repayment) Enter =C25+C30+C32 and copy across

(13) Free Cash Flow to Equity Enter =C34 and copy

Many spreadsheets use real-world data

	A	B	C	D	E	F	G	H	I	J
1	**CORPORATE FINANCIAL PLANNING**				**Full-Scale Estimation**					
2	**Nike, Inc.**	5/31/2010	5/31/2011	5/31/2012	5/31/2013	5/31/2014	5/31/2015	5/31/2016	Ave. %	
3	**Financial Plan**	Actual	Actual	Actual	Actual	Forecast	Forecast	Forecast	of Sales	
4	**Key Assumptions**								(1) Forecast key assumptions Enter forecast values in the range F5:H10 (done for you)	
5	Sales Growth Rate		5.8%	16.0%	8.5%	9.0%	10.0%	11.0%		
6	Tax Rate	24.2%	24.1%	25.0%	24.7%	24.0%	24.0%	24.0%		
7	Int Rate on Short-Term Debt	0.12%	0.04%	0.09%	0.05%	0.10%	0.15%	0.20%		
8	Int Rate on Long-Term Debt	1.17%	0.71%	0.39%	0.58%	0.70%	0.80%	0.90%		
9	Dividend Payout Rate	26.9%	26.3%	28.8%	29.1%	28.0%	29.0%	30.0%		
10	Price / Earnings	18.4	18.6	21.6	22.2	21.0	21.0	21.0		
11										
12				(2) Gross Margin - SG&AE + Non-Op Inc - Depreciation Enter =B16-B18+B19-B20 and copy across						
13	**Income Statement (Mil.$)**									
14	Sales	$19,014.0	$20,117.0	$23,331.0	$25,313.0	$27,591.2	$30,350.3	$33,688.8		
15	Cost of Goods Sold	$10,213.6	$10,915.0	$13,183.0	$14,279.0	$15,236.4	$16,760.0	$18,603.6		
16	Gross Margin	$8,800.4	$9,202.0	$10,148.0	$11,034.0	$12,354.8	$13,590.3	$15,085.2		
17										
18	Selling, Gen & Adm Expenses	$6,326.4	$6,361.0	$7,051.0	$7,766.0	$8,677.0	$9,544.7	$10,594.6		
19	Non-Operating Income	$42.9	$21.0	($58.0)	$18.0	$10.5	$11.6	$12.8		
20	Depreciation	$0.0	$0.0	$14.0	$14.0	$8.0	$8.7	$9.7		
21	EBIT	$2,516.9	$2,862.0	$3,025.0	$3,272.0	$3,680.4	$4,048.4	$4,493.7		
22										
23	Interest Expense	$0.0	$0.0	$0.0	$0.0	$8.53	$2.93	$3.51		
24	Taxes	$610.2	$690.0	$756.0	$808.0	$881.2	$970.9	$1,077.7		
25	Extraordinary Items	$0.0	$39.0	$46.0	($21.0)	$21.2	$23.4	$25.9		
26	Net Income	$1,906.7	$2,133.0	$2,223.0	$2,485.0	$2,769.3	$3,051.2	$3,386.6		
27	Shares Outstanding (Millions)	968.0	936.0	916.0	894.0	894.0	894.0	894.0		
28	Earnings Per Share	$1.97	$2.28	$2.43	$2.78	$3.10	$3.41	$3.79		

What is Unique about This Book

There are many features that distinguish this book from any other:

- **Plain Vanilla Excel.** Other books on the market emphasize teaching students programming using Visual Basic for Applications (VBA) or using macros. By contrast, this book does nearly everything in plain vanilla Excel. Although programming is liked by a minority of students, it is seriously disliked by the majority. Excel has the advantage of being a very intuitive, user-friendly environment that is comprehensible to all. It is fully capable of handling a wide range of applications, including quite sophisticated ones. Further, the only assumption is that your students already know the basics of Excel, such as entering formulas in a cell and copying formulas from one cell to another. All other features of Excel (such as built-in functions, Data Tables, Solver, etc.) are explained as they are used.

- **Build from Simple Examples to Practical, Real-World Applications.** The general approach is to start with a simple example and build up to a practical, real-world application. In many chapters, the previous Excel model is carried forward to the next, more complex model. For example, the chapter on binomial option pricing carries forward Excel models as follows: (a.) single-period model with replicating portfolio, (b.) eight-period model with replicating portfolio, (c.) eight-period model with risk-neutral probabilities, (d.) eight-period model with risk-neutral probabilities for American or European options with discrete dividends, (e.) full-scale, fifty-period model with risk-neutral probabilities for American or European options with discrete dividends. Whenever possible, this book builds up to full-scale, practical applications using real data. Students are excited to learn practical applications that they can actually use in their future jobs. Employers are excited to hire students with Excel modeling skills, who can be more quickly productive.

- **Supplement for All Popular Corporate Finance Textbooks.** This book is a supplement to be combined with a primary textbook. This means that you can keep using whatever textbook you like best. You don't have to switch. It also means that you can take an incremental approach to incorporating Excel modeling. You can start modestly and build up from there.

- **A Change in Content, Too.** Excel modeling is not merely a new medium, but an opportunity to cover some unique content items that require computer support to be feasible. For example, the full-scale estimation Excel model in Corporate Financial Planning uses three years of historical 10K data on Nike, Inc. (including every line of their income statement, balance sheet, and cash flow statement), constructs a complete financial system (including linked financial ratios), and projects these financial statements three years into the future. The chapter on Estimating the Cost of Capital uses 10 years of monthly returns for individual stocks, U.S. Fama-French portfolios, and country ETFs to estimate the cost of capital using the Static CAPM based on the Fama-MacBeth method and to estimate the cost of capital using the APT or Intertemporal CAPM based on the Fama-MacBeth method. The Excel model to estimate firm valuation or project valuation demonstrates the equivalence of the Free Cash Flow to Equity, Free Cash Flow to the Firm, Residual Income, Dividend Discount Model, and the Adjusted Present Value technique, not just in the perpetuity case covered by some textbooks, but for a fully general two-stage project with an arbitrary set of cash flows over an explicit forecast horizon, followed by an infinite horizon growing perpetuity. As a practical matter, all of these sophisticated applications require Excel.

Conventions Used in This Book

This book uses a number of conventions.

- **Time Goes Across the Columns and Variables Go Down the Rows.** When something happens over time, I let each column represent a period of time. For example, in life-cycle financial planning, date 0 is in column B, date 1 is in column C, date 2 is in column D, etc. Each row represents a different variable, which is usually labeled in column A. This manner of organizing Excel models is common because it is how financial statements are organized.

- **Color Coding.** A standard color scheme is used to clarify the structure of the Excel models. The Ready-To-Build spreadsheets available for download use: (1) yellow shading for input values, (2) no shading (i.e., white) for throughput formulas, and (3) green shading for final results ("the bottom line"). A few Excel models include choice variables with blue shading.

- **The Timeline Technique.** The most natural technique for discounting cash flows in an Excel model is the timeline technique, where each column corresponds to a period of time. As an example, see the section labeled "Bond Price using a Timeline" in the figure below.

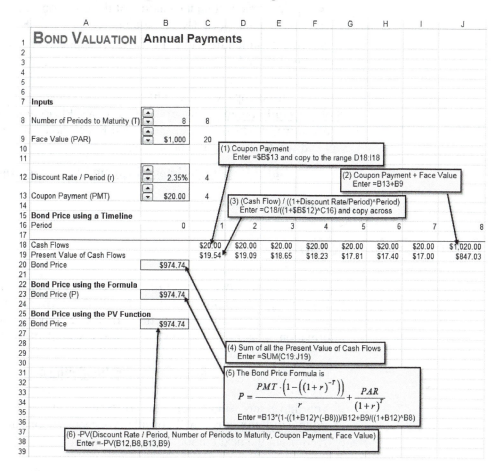

- **Using as Many Different Techniques as Possible.** In the figure above, the bond price is calculated using as many different techniques as possible. Specifically, it is calculated three ways: (1) discounting each cash flow on a time line, (2) using the closed-form formula, and (3) using Excel's PV function. This approach makes the point that all three techniques are equivalent. This approach also develops skill at double-checking these calculations, which is a very important method for avoiding errors in practice.

- **Symbolic Notation Is Self-Contained.** Every spreadsheet that contains symbolic notation in the instruction boxes is self-contained (i.e., all symbolic notation is defined on the spreadsheet).

Craig's Challenge

I challenge the reader of this book to dramatically improve your finance education by personally constructing all of the Excel models in this book. This will take you about 10–20 hours depending on your current Excel modeling skills. Let me assure you that it will be an excellent investment. You will:

- gain a practical understanding of the core concepts of Corporate Finance
- develop hands-on Excel modeling skills
- build an entire suite of finance applications, which you will fully understand

When you complete this challenge, I invite you to e-mail me at **cholden@indiana.edu** to share the good news. Please tell me your name, school, (prospective) graduation year, and which Excel modeling book you completed. I will add you to a web-based honor roll at:

http://www.excelmodeling.com/honor-roll.htm

We can celebrate together!

Excel Modeling Books

This book is one of two *Excel Modeling* books by Craig W. Holden, published by Pearson. The other book is *Excel Modeling in Investments*. Both books teach value-added skills in constructing financial models in Excel. Complete information about my *Excel Modeling* books is available at my web site:

http://www.excelmodeling.com

If you have any suggestions or corrections, please e-mail them to me at **cholden@indiana.edu**. I will consider your suggestions and will implement any corrections in the next edition.

Suggestions for Faculty Members

There is no single best way to use *Excel Modeling in Corporate Finance*. There are as many different techniques as there are different styles and philosophies of teaching. You need to discover what works best for you. Let me highlight several possibilities:

1. **Out-of-class individual projects with help.** This is a technique that I have used and it works well. I require completion of several short Excel modeling projects of every individual student in the class. To provide help, I schedule special "help lab" sessions in a computer lab during which time my graduate assistant and I are available to answer questions while students do each assignment in about an hour. Typically about half the questions are Excel questions and half are finance questions. I have always graded such projects, but an alternative approach would be to treat them as ungraded homework.

2. **Out-of-class individual projects without help.** Another technique is to assign Excel modeling projects for individual students to do on their own out of class. One instructor assigns seven Excel modeling projects at the beginning of the semester and has individual students turn in all seven completed Excel models for grading at the end of the semester. At the end of each chapter are problems that can be assigned with or without help. Faculty members can download the completed Excel models and answers to end-of-chapter problems at **http://www.pearsonhighered.com/holden**. See your local Pearson representative to gain access.

3. **Out-of-class group projects.** A technique that I have used for the last fifteen years is to require students to do big Excel modeling projects in groups. I have students write a report to a hypothetical boss that intuitively explains their method of analysis, key assumptions, and key results.

4. **In-class reinforcement of key concepts.** The class session is scheduled in a computer lab or students are asked to bring their laptop computers to class. I explain a key concept in words and equations. Then I turn to a 10–15 minute segment in which students open a Ready-To-Build spreadsheet and build the Excel model in real-time in the class. This provides real-time, hands-on reinforcement of a key concept. This technique can be done often throughout the semester.

5. **In-class demonstration of Excel modeling.** The instructor can perform an in-class demonstration of how to build Excel models. Typically, only a small portion of the total Excel model would be demonstrated.

6. **In-class demonstration of key relationships using Spin Buttons, Option Buttons, and Charts.** The instructor can dynamically illustrate comparative statics or dynamic properties over time using visual, interactive elements. For example, one spreadsheet provides a "movie" of 43 years of U.S. term structure dynamics. Another spreadsheet provides an interactive graph of the sensitivity of bond prices to changes in the coupon rate, yield-to-maturity, number of payments/year, and face value.

I'm sure I haven't exhausted the list of potential teaching techniques. Feel free to send an e-mail to **cholden@indiana.edu** to let me know novel ways in which you use this book.

Acknowledgments

I thank Katie Rowland, Tessa O'Brien, Mark Pfaltzgraff, David Alexander, Jackie Aaron, P.J. Boardman, Mickey Cox, Maureen Riopelle, and Paul Donnelly of Pearson for their vision, innovativeness, and encouragement of *Excel Modeling in Corporate Finance*. I thank Erin McDonagh, Karen Carter, Amy Foley, Nancy Fenton, Susan Abraham, Mary Kate Murray, Ana Jankowski, Lori Braumberger, Holly Brown, Debbie Clare, Cheryl Clayton, Kevin Hancock, Josh McClary, Bill Minic, Melanie Olsen, Beth Ann Romph, Erika Rusnak, Gladys Soto, and Lauren Tarino of Pearson / Prentice Hall for many useful contributions. I thank Robert Taggart of Boston College for his significant contribution to the Firm and Project Valuation chapter and for his appendix to the "Reconciling the Residual Income Method with Other Approaches to Valuing Firms or Projects" chapter. I thank Professors Alan Bailey (University of Texas at San Antonio), Zvi Bodie (Boston University), Jack Francis (Baruch College), David Griswold (Boston University), Carl Hudson (Auburn University), Robert Kleiman (Oakland University), Mindy Nitkin (Simmons College), Steve Rich (Baylor University), Tim Smaby (Penn State University), Noah Stoffman (Indiana University), Charles Trzcinka (Indiana University), Sorin Tuluca (Fairleigh Dickinson University), Marilyn Wiley (Florida Atlantic University), and Chad Zutter (University of Pittsburgh) for many thoughtful comments. I thank my dad, Bill Holden, and my graduate students Michael Kulov, Sam Singhania, Harry Bramson, Brent Cherry, Scott Marolf, Heath Eckert, Ryan Brewer, Ruslan Goyenko, Wendy Liu, and Wannie Park for careful error-checking. I thank Jim Finnegan and many other students for providing helpful comments. I thank my family, Kathryn, Diana, and Jimmy, for their love and support.

About The Author

CRAIG W. HOLDEN

 Craig W. Holden is a Professor of Finance at the Kelley School of Business at Indiana University. His M.B.A. and Ph.D. are from the Anderson School at UCLA. He is the winner of many teaching and research awards, including a Fama/DFA Prize. His research on market microstructure has been published in leading academic journals. He has written *Excel Modeling in Investments* and *Excel Modeling in Corporate Finance*. The Fifth Editions in English are published by Pearson and there are International, Chinese, and Italian editions. He has chaired 20 dissertations, been a member or chair of 58 dissertations, serves as the Secretary-Treasurer of the *Society for Financial Studies*, serves as an associate editor of the *Journal of Financial Markets*, and serves on the program committees of the *Western Finance Association* and the *European Finance Association*. He chaired the department undergraduate committee for thirteen years, chaired the department doctoral committee for four years, chaired three different schoolwide committees for a combination of six years, and currently serves for a third year on the campus tenure advisory committee. He has led several major curriculum innovations in the finance department. More information is available at Craig's home page: **www.kelley.iu.edu/cholden**.

PART 1 TIME VALUE OF MONEY

Chapter 1 Single Cash Flow

1.1 Present Value

Problem. A single cash flow of $1,000.00 will be received in 5 periods. For this cash flow, the appropriate discount rate / period is 6.0%. What is the present value of this single cash flow?

Solution Strategy. We will calculate the present value of this single cash flow in three equivalent ways. First, we will calculate the present value using a time line, where each column corresponds to a period of calendar time. Second, we use a formula for the present value. Third, we use Excel's **PV** function for the present value.

Excel 2013

FIGURE 1.1 Excel Model for Single Cash Flow - Present Value.

	A	B	C	D	E	F	G	H	I	J
1	SINGLE CASH FLOW	Present Value								
2										
3	Inputs									
4	Single Cash Flow	$1,000.00	20							
5	Discount Rate / Period	6.0%	6							
6	Number of Periods	5	5							
7										
8										
9										
10										
11										
12										
13										
14	Present Value using a Time Line									
15	Period	0		1	2	3	4	5		
16	Cash Flows							$1,000.00		
17	Present Value							$747.26		
18										
19	Present Value using the Formula									
20	Present Value	$747.26								
21										
22	Present Value using the PV Function									
23	Present Value	$747.26								
24										
25										
26										
27										
28										
29										

Chart: **Single Cash Flow - Present Value** (y-axis $0.00 to $1,400.00, x-axis Period 0 to 5) — Cash Flows, Present Value

(1) The single cash flow occurs in the final period
Enter =B4

(2) (Cash Flow) / (1+Discount Rate/Period) ^ Period)
Enter =G16/((1+$B$5)^G15)

(3) (Cash Flow) / ((1 + Discount Rate/Period) ^ Period)
Enter =B4/((1+B5)^B6)

(4) -PV(Discount Rate / Period, Number of Periods, 0, Single Cash Flow)
Enter =-PV(B5,B6,0,B4)

The Present Value of this Single Cash Flow is $747.26. Notice you get the same answer all three ways: using the time line, using the formula, or using the PV function!

1.2 Future Value

Problem. A single cash flow of $747.26 is available now (in period 0). For this cash flow, the appropriate discount rate / period is 6.0%. What is the period 5 future value of this single cash flow?

Solution Strategy. We will calculate the future value of the single cash flow in three equivalent ways. First, we will calculate the future value using a time line, where each column corresponds to a period of calendar time. Second, we use a formula for the future value. Third, we use Excel's **FV** function for the future value.

Excel 2013   **FIGURE 1.2 Excel Model for Single Cash Flow - Future Value.**

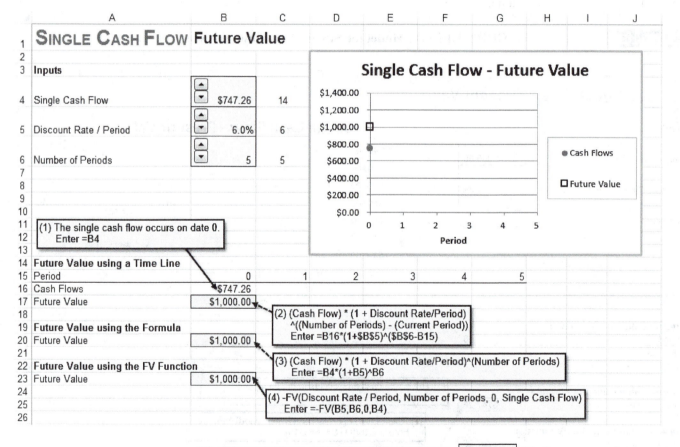

The Future Value of this Single Cash Flow is $1,000.00. Notice you get the same answer all three ways: using the time line, using the formula, or using the FV function!

Comparing Present Value and Future Value, we see that they are opposite operations. That is, one operation "undoes" the other. The Present Value of $1,000.00 in period 5 is $747.26 in period 0. The Future Value of $747.26 in period 0 is $1,000.00 in period 5.

Problems

1. A single cash flow of $1,673.48 will be received in 4 periods. For this cash flow, the appropriate discount rate / period is 7.8%. What is the present value of this single cash flow?

2. A single cash flow of $932.47 is available now (in period 0). For this cash flow, the appropriate discount rate / period is 3.9%. What is the period 4 future value of this single cash flow?

Chapter 2 Annuity

2.1 Present Value

Problem. An annuity pays $80.00 each period for 5 periods. For these cash flows, the appropriate discount rate / period is 6.0%. What is the present value of this annuity?

Solution Strategy. We will calculate the present value of this annuity in three equivalent ways. First, we will calculate the present value using a time line, where each column corresponds to a period of calendar time. Second, we use a formula for the present value. Third, we use Excel's **PV** function for the present value.

Excel 2013

FIGURE 2.1 Excel Model for Annuity - Present Value.

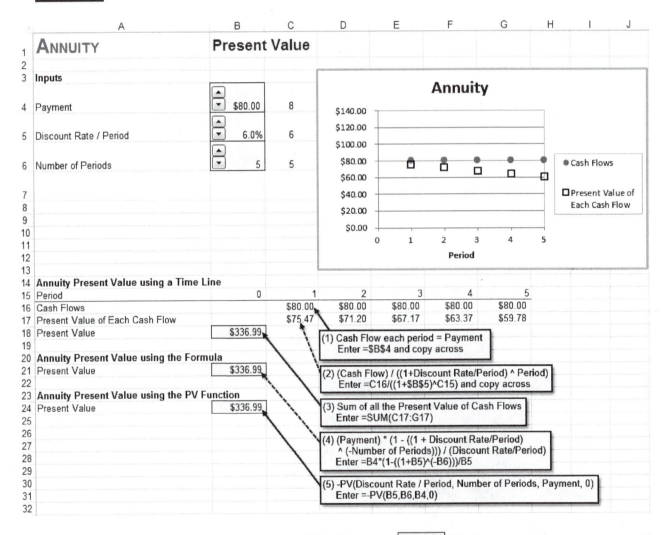

The Present Value of this Annuity is $336.99. Notice you get the same answer all three ways: using the time line, using the formula, or using the PV function.

2.2 Future Value

Problem. An annuity pays $80.00 each period for 5 periods. For these cash flows, the appropriate discount rate / period is 6.0%. What is the period 5 future value of this annuity?

Solution Strategy. We will calculate the future value of this annuity in three equivalent ways. First, we will calculate the future value using a time line, where each column corresponds to a period of calendar time. Second, we use a formula for the future value. Third, we use Excel's **FV** function for the future value.

Excel 2013

FIGURE 2.2 Excel Model for Annuity - Future Value.

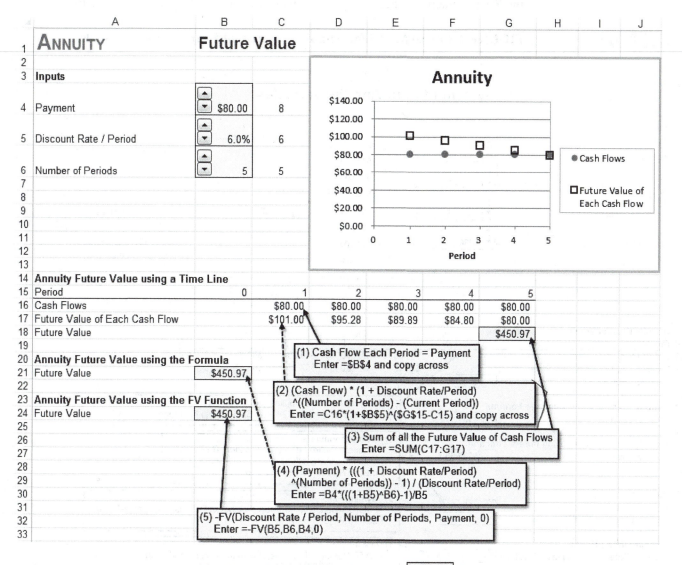

The Future Value of this Annuity is $450.97. Notice you get the same answer all three ways: using the time line, using the formula, or using the FV function.

2.3 System of Four Annuity Variables

Problem. There is a tight connection between all of the inputs and output to annuity valuation. Indeed, they form a system of four annuity variables: (1) Payment, (2) Discount Rate / Period, (3) Number of Periods, and (4) Present Value. Given any three of these variables, find the fourth variable.

Solution Strategy. Given any three of these variable, we will use as many equivalent ways of solving for the fourth variable as possible. The Annuity – Present Value spreadsheet solves for the present value using a Timeline, a formula, and the **PV** function. Building on that spreadsheet, add the Payment using the formula and **PMT** function. Then add the Discount Rate / Period using the **RATE** function. Then add the Number of Periods, using the **NPER** function.

Excel 2013

FIGURE 2.3 Excel Model for Annuity - System of Four Annuity Variables.

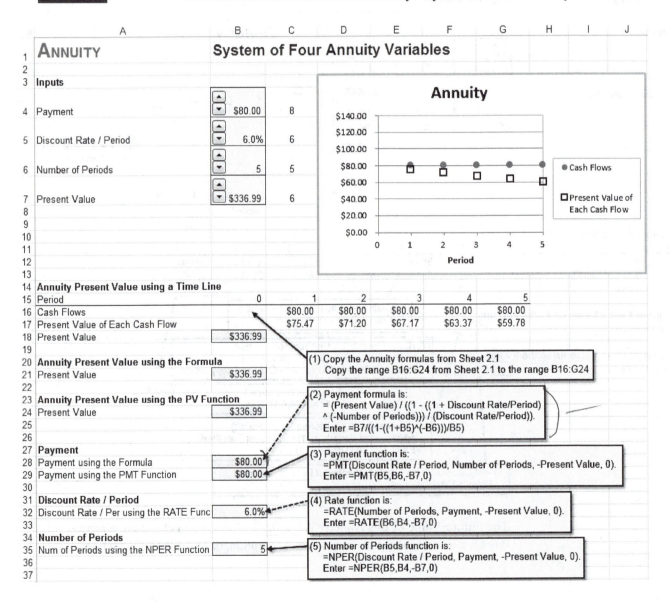

We see that the system of four annuity variables is internally consistent. The four outputs in rows **13** through **32** (Present Value = $336.99, Payment = $80.00, Discount Rate / Period = 6.0%, and Number of Periods = 5) are identical to the four inputs in rows **4** through **7**. Thus, any of the four annuity variables can be calculated from the other three in a fully consistent manner.

Problems

1) An annuity pays $142.38 each period for 6 periods. For these cash flows, the appropriate discount rate / period is 4.5%. What is the present value of this annuity?

2) An annuity pays $63.92 each period for 4 periods. For these cash flows, the appropriate discount rate / period is 9.1%. What is the period 5 future value of this annuity?

3) Consider a system of four annuity variables.

   (a) An annuity pays $53.00 each period for 4 periods. For these cash flows, the appropriate discount rate / period is 7.0%. What is the present value of this annuity?

   (b) An annuity pays each period for 10 periods, the appropriate discount rate / period is 7.0%, and the present value is $142.38. What is the payment each period?

   (c) An annuity pays $173.00 each period for 13 periods, and the present value is $513.94. What is the discount rate / period of this annuity?

   (d) An annuity pays $40.00 each period, the appropriate discount rate / period is 6.0%, and the present value is $168.49. What is the number of periods?

Chapter 3 NPV Using Constant Discounting

3.1 Nominal Rate

Problem. A project requires a current investment of $100.00 and yields future expected cash flows of $21.00, $34.00, $40.00, $33.00, and $17.00 in periods 1 through 5, respectively. All figures are in thousands of dollars. For these expected cash flows, the appropriate nominal discount rate is 8.0%. What is the net present value of this project?

Solution Strategy. We will calculate the net present value of this project in two equivalent ways. First, we will calculate the net present value using a time line, where each column corresponds to a period of calendar time. Second, we use Excel's **NPV** function for the net present value.

Excel 2013

FIGURE 3.1 NPV Using Constant Discounting – Nominal Rate.

	A	B	C	D	E	F	G	H	I	J
1	NPV USING CONSTANT DISCOUNTING				Nominal Rate					
2	(in thousands of $)									
3										
4	Inputs									
5										
6										
7										
8	Outputs									
9	Nominal Discount Rate	8.0%								
10										
11										
12										
13										
14	Net Present Value using a Time Line									
15	Period	0	1	2	3	4	5			
16	Cash Flows	($100.00)	$21.00	$34.00	$40.00	$33.00	$17.00			
17	Present Value of Each Cash Flow	($100.00)	$19.44	$29.15	$31.75	$24.26	$11.57			
18	Net Present Value	$16.17								
19										
20	Net Present Value using the NPV Function									
21	Net Present Value	$16.17								
22										
23										
24										
25										
26										

(2) (Cash Flow) / (1 + Discount Rate) ^ Period)
    Enter =B16/((1+$B$9)^B15) and copy across

(3) Sum of all the Present Value of Cash Flows
    Enter =SUM(B17:G17)

(4) (Current Investment) + NPV(Discount Rate, Future Cash Flows)
    Enter =B16+NPV(B9,C16:G16)

The Net Present Value of this project is $16.17. Notice you get the same answer both ways: using the time line or using the NPV function.

3.2 Real Rate

Problem. A project requires a current investment of $100.00 and yields future expected cash flows of $21.00, $34.00, $40.00, $33.00, and $17.00 in periods 1 through 5, respectively. All figures are in thousands of dollars. The inflation rate is 3.0%. For these expected cash flows, the appropriate Real Discount Rate is 4.854%. What is the net present value of this project?

Solution Strategy. We begin by calculating the (nominal) discount rate from the inflation rate and the real discount rate. The rest of the net present value calculation is the same as the Net Present Value - Constant Discount Rate Excel model.

Excel 2013   **FIGURE 3.2 NPV Using Constant Discounting – Real Rate.**

The inflation rate of 3.0% and the real discount rate of 4.854%, combine to yield a nominal discount rate of 8.0%, which is the same as before. Therefore, the Net Present Value of this project is $16.17, which is the same as before.

Problems

1. A project requires a current investment of $189.32 and yields future expected cash flows of $45.19, $73.11, $98,54, $72.83, and $58.21 in periods 1 through 5, respectively. All figures are in thousands of dollars. For these expected cash flows, the appropriate discount rate is 6.3%. What is the net present value of this project?

2. A project requires a current investment of $117.39 and yields future expected cash flows of $38.31, $48.53, $72.80, $96.31, and $52.18 in periods 1 through 5, respectively. All figures are in thousands of dollars. The inflation rate is 2.7%. For these expected cash flows, the appropriate Real Discount Rate is 8.6%. What is the net present value of this project?

Chapter 4 NPV Using General Discounting

4.1 Nominal Rate

Problem. A project requires a current investment of $100.00 and yields future expected cash flows of $21.00, $34.00, $40.00, $33.00, and $17.00 in periods 1 through 5, respectively. All figures are in thousands of dollars. For these expected cash flows, the appropriate nominal discount rates are 8.0% in period 1, 7.6% in period 2, 7.3% in period 3, 7.0% in period 4, and 7.0% in period 5. What is the net present value of this project?

Solution Strategy. We will calculate the Net Present Value of this project using a Time Line. This is the *only* possible way to calculate the project NPV in the general case where the discount rate changes over time. Excel's **NPV** function cannot be used because it is limited to the special case of a constant discount rate. There is no simple formula for NPV, short of typing in a term for each cash flow.

FIGURE 4.1 NPV Using General Discounting – Nominal Rate.

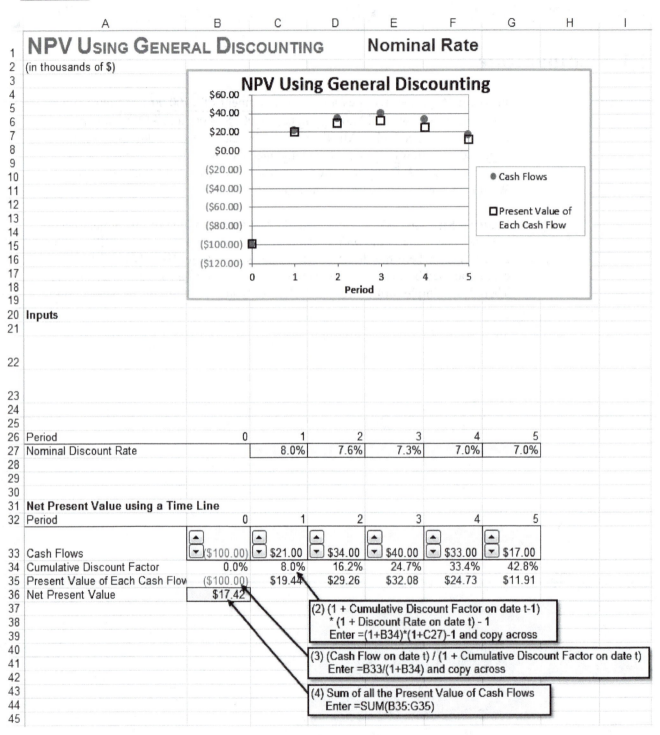

The Net Present Value of this project is $17.42.

4.2 Real Rate

Problem. A project requires a current investment of $100.00 and yields future expected cash flows of $21.00, $34.00, $40.00, $33.00, and $17.00 in periods 1 through 5, respectively. All figures are in thousands of dollars. The forecasted inflation rate is 3.0% in period 1, 2.8% in period 2, 2.5% in period 3, 2.2% in period 4, and 2.0% in period 5. For these expected cash flows, the appropriate REAL discount rate is 4.854% in period 1, 4.669% in period 2, 4.683% in period 3, 4.697% in period 4, and 4.902% in period 5. What is the net present value of this project?

Solution Strategy. We begin by calculating the (nominal) discount rate for each period from the inflation rate in each period and corresponding real discount rate. The rest of the net present value calculation is the same as the Net Present Value - General Discount Rate Excel model.

Excel 2013   **FIGURE 4.2 NPV Using General Discounting – Real Rate.**

	A	B	C	D	E	F	G	H	I	J
1	**NPV USING GENERAL DISCOUNTING**				**Real Rate**					
2	(in thousands of $)									
20	**Inputs**									
21	Period		0	1	2	3	4	5		Add to All Periods
22	Inflation Rate			3.0%	2.8%	2.5%	2.2%	2.0%		0.0%
23	Real Discount Rate			4.854%	4.669%	4.683%	4.697%	4.902%		0.0%
24										
25	**Outputs**									
26	Period		0	1	2	3	4	5		
27	Nominal Discount Rate			8.0%	7.6%	7.3%	7.0%	7.0%		
28										
29				(1) (1 + Inflation Rate) * (1 + Real Discount Rate) - 1						
30				Enter =(1+C22)*(1+C23)-1 and copy across						
31	**Net Present Value using a Time Line**									
32	Period		0	1	2	3	4	5		
33	Cash Flows		($100.00)	$21.00	$34.00	$40.00	$33.00	$17.00		
34	Cumulative Discount Factor		0.0%	8.0%	16.2%	24.7%	33.4%	42.8%		
35	Present Value of Each Cash Flow		($100.00)	$19.44	$29.26	$32.08	$24.73	$11.91		
36	Net Present Value		$17.42							

The Net Present Value of this project is $17.42 , the same as above.

You can experiment with different inflation rates or real discount rates by clicking the corresponding spin button for each period. Alternatively you can raise or lower the inflation rates or real discount rates for *all periods* by clicking on the spin button in the range **J22:J23**.

This Excel model can handle *any* pattern of discount rates. For example, it can handle the special case of a constant inflation rate at 3.0% and a constant real discount rate at 4.854% .

Excel 2013

FIGURE 4.3 NPV Using General Discounting – Real Rate.

	A	B	C	D	E	F	G	H	I	J
1	NPV Using General Discounting				Nominal and Real Rates					
2	(in thousands of $)									
20	**Inputs**									
21	Period		0	1	2	3	4	5		Add to All Periods
22	Inflation Rate			3.0%	3.0%	3.0%	3.0%	3.0%		0.0%
23	Real Discount Rate			4.854%	4.854%	4.854%	4.854%	4.854%		0.0%
24										
25	**Outputs**									
26	Period		0	1	2	3	4	5		
27	Nominal Discount Rate			8.0%	8.0%	8.0%	8.0%	8.0%		
28										
29				(1) (1 + Inflation Rate) * (1 + Real Discount Rate) - 1						
30				Enter =(1+C22)*(1+C23)-1 and copy across						
31	**Net Present Value using a Time Line**									
32	Period		0	1	2	3	4	5		
33	Cash Flows		($100.00)	$21.00	$34.00	$40.00	$33.00	$17.00		
34	Cumulative Discount Factor		0.0%	8.0%	16.6%	26.0%	36.0%	46.9%		
35	Present Value of Each Cash Flow		($100.00)	$19.44	$29.15	$31.75	$24.26	$11.57		
36	Net Present Value		$16.17							

The Net Present Value of this project is $16.17 , which is the same answer as the previous chapter on NPV Using Constant Discounting. The general discount rate Excel model is the most general way to do discounting and is the most common approach that we will use in the rest of this book.

Problems

1. A project requires a current investment of $54.39 and yields future expected cash flows of $19.27, $27.33, $34.94, $41.76, and $32.49 in periods 1 through 5, respectively. All figures are in thousands of dollars. For these expected cash flows, the appropriate nominal discount rates are 6.4% in period 1, 6.2% in period 2, 6.0% in period 3, 5.7% in period 4, and 5.4% in period 5. What is the net present value of this project?

2. A project requires a current investment of $328.47 and yields future expected cash flows of $87.39, $134.97, $153.28, $174.99, and $86.41 in periods 1 through 5, respectively. All figures are in thousands of dollars. The forecasted inflation rate is 3.4% in period 1, 3.6% in period 2, 3.9% in period 3, 4.4% in period 4, and 4.7% in period 5. For these expected cash flows, the appropriate REAL discount rate is 7.8% in period 1, 7.1% in period 2, 6.5% in period 3, 6.0% in period 4, and 5.4% in period 5. What is the net present value of this project?

Chapter 5 Loan Amortization

5.1 Basics

Problem. To purchase a house, you take out a ⟨30⟩ year mortgage. The present value (loan amount) of the mortgage is ⟨$300,000⟩. The mortgage charges an interest rate / year of ⟨8.00%⟩. What is the annual payment required by this mortgage? How much of each year's payment goes to paying interest and how much to reducing the principal balance?

Solution Strategy. First, we use Excel's **PMT** function to calculate the annual payment of a 30 year annuity (mortgage). Then we will use a time line and simple recursive formulas to split out the payment into the interest component and the principal reduction component.

Excel 2013

FIGURE 5.1 Excel Model for Loan Amortization - Basics.

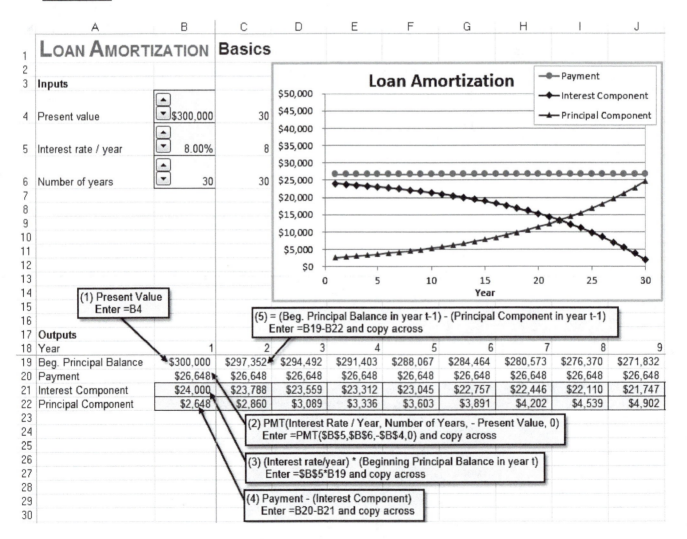

The Annual Payment is $26,648. The figure below shows the final years of the time line for the loan.

Excel 2013 **FIGURE 5.2 Final Years of the Time Line of Loan Amortization - Basics.**

	A	B	Z	AA	AB	AC	AD	AE	AF
17	**Outputs**								
18	Year	1	25	26	27	28	29	30	31
19	Beg. Principal Balance	$300,000	$123,192	$106,399	$88,262	$68,675	$47,521	$24,674	($0)
20	Payment	$26,648	$26,648	$26,648	$26,648	$26,648	$26,648	$26,648	
21	Interest Component	$24,000	$9,855	$8,512	$7,061	$5,494	$3,802	$1,974	
22	Principal Component	$2,648	$16,793	$18,136	$19,587	$21,154	$22,847	$24,674	

The principal balance drops to zero in year 31 after the final payment is made in year 30. The loan is paid off! It doesn't matter whether the zero amount in cell AF10 displays as positive or negative. The only reason it would display as negative is due to round off error in the eighth decimal or higher, which is irrelevant for our purposes.

The Interest Component depends on the size of the Beg. Principal Balance. In year 1 the interest component starts at its highest level of $24,000 because the Beg. Principal Balance is at its highest level of $300,000. The interest component gradually declines over time as the Principal Balance gradually declines over time. The interest component reaches its lowest level of $1,974 as the Beg. Principal Balance reaches its lowest level of $24,674. The principal repayment component is the residual part of the payment that is left over after the interest component is paid off. In year 1 when the interest component is the highest, the principal component is the lowest. Even though you made a payment of $26,648 in year 1, only $2,648 of it went to paying off the principal! The principal payment gradually increases over time until it reaches its highest level of $24,674 in year 30.

5.2 Sensitivity Analysis

Problem. Examine the same 30 year mortgage for $300,000 as in the previous section. Consider what would happen if the interest rate / year dropped from 8.00% to 7.00%. How much of each year's payment goes to paying interest vs. how much goes to reducing the principal under the two interest rates?

Solution Strategy. Construct a data table for the interest component under the two interest rates. Construct another data table for the principal component under the two interest rates. Create a graph of the two interest components and two principal components.

FIGURE 5.3 Excel Model for Loan Amortization – Sensitivity Analysis.

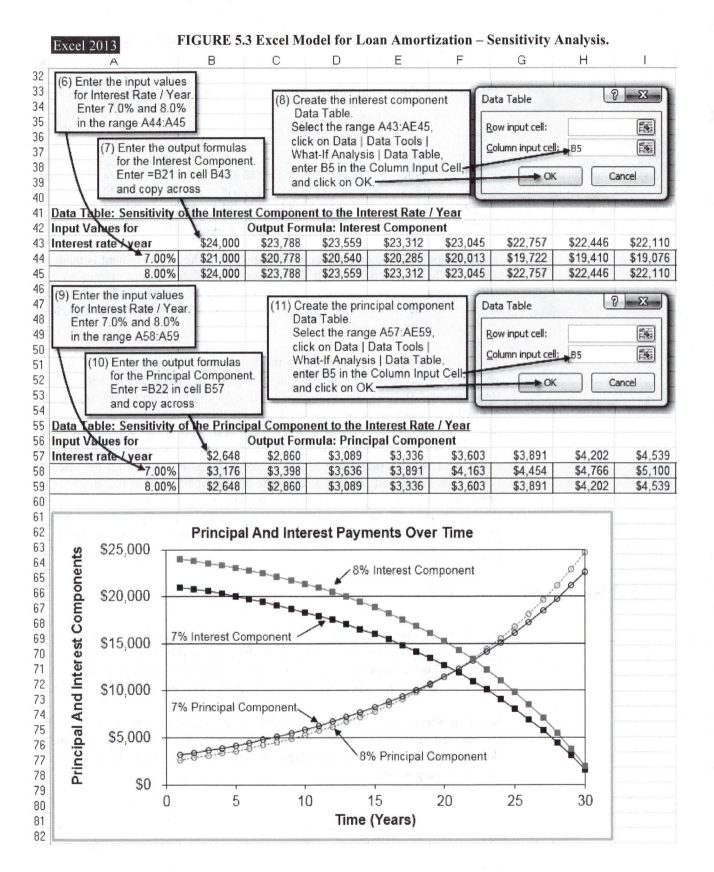

Excel 2013

	A	B	C	D	E	F	G	H	I
32	(6) Enter the input values								
33	for Interest Rate / Year.								
34	Enter 7.0% and 8.0%								
35	in the range A44:A45								
36									
37	(7) Enter the output formulas								
38	for the Interest Component.								
39	Enter =B21 in cell B43								
40	and copy across								
41	**Data Table: Sensitivity of the Interest Component to the Interest Rate / Year**								
42	**Input Values for**			**Output Formula: Interest Component**					
43	**Interest rate / year**	$24,000	$23,788	$23,559	$23,312	$23,045	$22,757	$22,446	$22,110
44	7.00%	$21,000	$20,778	$20,540	$20,285	$20,013	$19,722	$19,410	$19,076
45	8.00%	$24,000	$23,788	$23,559	$23,312	$23,045	$22,757	$22,446	$22,110
46									
47	(9) Enter the input values								
48	for Interest Rate / Year.								
49	Enter 7.0% and 8.0%								
50	in the range A58:A59								
51	(10) Enter the output formulas								
52	for the Principal Component.								
53	Enter =B22 in cell B57								
54	and copy across								
55	**Data Table: Sensitivity of the Principal Component to the Interest Rate / Year**								
56	**Input Values for**			**Output Formula: Principal Component**					
57	**Interest rate / year**	$2,648	$2,860	$3,089	$3,336	$3,603	$3,891	$4,202	$4,539
58	7.00%	$3,176	$3,398	$3,636	$3,891	$4,163	$4,454	$4,766	$5,100
59	8.00%	$2,648	$2,860	$3,089	$3,336	$3,603	$3,891	$4,202	$4,539

(8) Create the interest component Data Table. Select the range A43:AE45, click on Data | Data Tools | What-If Analysis | Data Table, enter B5 in the Column Input Cell, and click on OK.

Data Table

Row input cell:
Column input cell: B5
OK   Cancel

(11) Create the principal component Data Table. Select the range A57:AE59, click on Data | Data Tools | What-If Analysis | Data Table, enter B5 in the Column Input Cell, and click on OK.

Data Table

Row input cell:
Column input cell: B5
OK   Cancel

Principal And Interest Payments Over Time

8% Interest Component
7% Interest Component
7% Principal Component
8% Principal Component

Time (Years)

From the graph, we see that the Interest Component is much lower at 7% than it is at 8%. Indeed you pay $3,000 less in interest ($21,000 vs. $24,000) in year 1. The difference in interest component gradually declines over time. The principal component stays nearly the same over time. The principal component is slightly more frontloaded at 7% than at 8%. That is, $528 *more* of your payment goes to principal in year 1 at 7% than at 8%. Then it switches and $2,080 *less* of your payment goes to principal in year 30.

Problems

1. To purchase a house, you take out a 30 year mortgage. The present value (loan amount) of the mortgage is $217,832. The mortgage charges an interest rate / year of 9.27%. What is the annual payment required by this mortgage? How much of each year's payment goes to paying interest and how much to reducing the principal balance?

2. In purchasing a house, you need to obtain a mortgage with a present value (loan amount) of $175,000. You have a choice of: (A) a 30 year mortgage at an interest rate / year of 9.74% or (B) a 15 year mortgage at an interest rate / year of 9.46%. What is the annual payment required by the two alternative mortgages? How much of each year's payment goes to paying interest and how much to reducing the principal balance by the two alternative mortgages? Which mortgage would you prefer?

3. Consider a 30 year mortgage for $442,264 as in the previous section. What would happen if the interest rate / year dropped from 9.21% to 7.95%. How much of each year's payment goes to paying interest and how much goes to reducing the principal under the two interest rates?

Chapter 6 Lease Vs. Buy

6.1 Car

Problem. You are trying to decide whether to lease a car for four years or buy a new car now and sell it four years later. The annual lease payment would be $4,100 with payments made at the *beginning* of each year. The new car price is $32,000 now. Four years later, it will be worth $21,000. The appropriate discount rate for this project is 8.0%. Should you lease or buy?

Solution Strategy. Compute the present value of the lease payments. Compute the present value of the purchase cost now and the sales revenue (which is a negative cost) four years later.

Excel 2013   **FIGURE 6.1 Lease Vs. Buy - Car.**

	A	B	C	D	E	F	G
1	LEASE VS. BUY	Car	(1) Lease payment Enter =$B$7 and copy across				
2							
3	Inputs		(2) Cash Flow / ((1 + Discount Rate)^Year) Enter =B7/((1+$B$4)^B6) and copy to the ranges C8:E8 and B13:F13				
4	Discount Rate	8.0%					
5							
6	Lease	0	1	2	3		
7	Lease Payment	$4,100	$4,100	$4,100	$4,100		
8	Present Value of Each Cash Flow	$4,100	$3,796	$3,515	$3,255		
9	Present Value of Lease Cost	$14,666					
10							
11	Buy	0	1	2	3	4	
12	Purchase Price and Residual Value	$32,000				($21,000)	
13	Present Value of Each Cash Flow	$32,000	$0	$0	$0	($15,436)	
14	Present Value of Buy Cost	$16,564	(3) Sum of the Present Values Enter =SUM(B8:F8) and copy to B14				
15							
16							

The present value of the lease payments is $14,666. The present value of the purchase cost now and sales revenue later is $16,564. So in this case, it is less expensive to lease.

6.2 Corporate

Problem. A corporation is trying to decide whether to lease a machine for five years and pay the residual purchase cost to buy the machine in the last year of the lease or buy the machine now. The annual lease payment would be $4,100 with payments made at the *beginning* of each year. The residual purchase cost would be $12,600 to be paid at the *beginning* of the fifth year. The lease payments are standard business expenses that reduce the corporation's tax liability accordingly. $45,700 can be borrowed from the bank to buy the machine now. Annual loan payments would be made for 5 years at a 6% interest rate. The machine can be fully depreciated in a straight line manner over 5 years. Both the loan interest payment and the depreciation provide tax shields against a corporate tax rate of 40%. The appropriate discount rate for both alternatives is the *after-tax* cost of debt, where the corporation's cost of debt is assumed to be the same as the loan rate. Should the corporation lease or buy?

Solution Strategy. Compute the present value of the after-tax lease payments and the residual purchase cost. Compute the present value of the loan payments and the tax shields on the loan interest payments and depreciation.

Excel 2013

FIGURE 6.2 Lease Vs. Buy - Corporate.

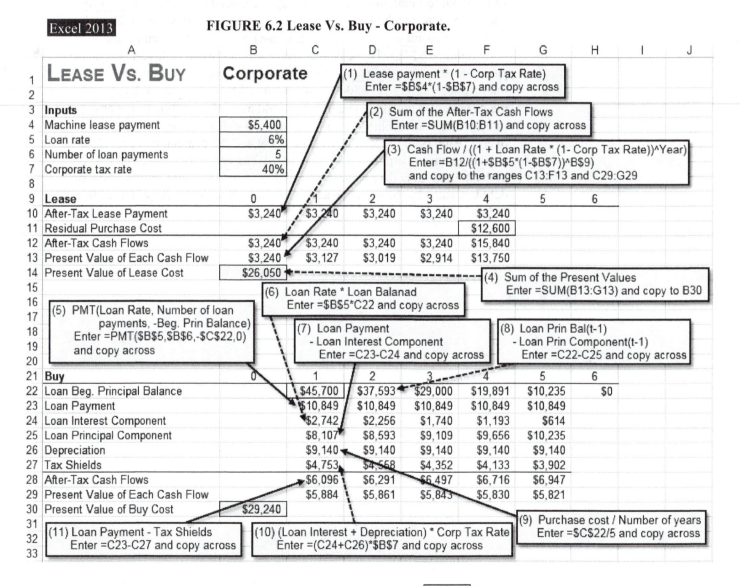

The present value of the lease cost is $26,050. The present value of the buy cost is $30,366. So in this case, the corporation should lease.

Problems

1. You are trying to decide whether to lease a car for four years or buy a new car now and sell it four years later. The annual lease payment would be $6,300 with payments made at the *beginning* of each year. The new car price is $47,000 now. Four years later, it will be worth $33,000. The appropriate discount rate for this project is 7.2%. Should you lease or buy?

2. A corporation is trying to decide whether to lease a machine for five years and pay the residual purchase cost to buy the machine in the last year of the lease or buy the machine now. The annual lease payment would be $8,700 with payments made at the *beginning* of each year. The residual purchase cost would be $25,200 to be paid at the *beginning* of the fifth year. The lease payments are standard business expenses that reduce the corporation's tax liability accordingly. $89,300 can be borrowed from the bank to buy the machine now. Annual loan payments would be made for 5 years at a 5% interest rate. The machine can be fully depreciated in a straight line manner over 5 years. Both the loan interest payment and the depreciation provide tax shields against a corporate tax rate of 40%. The appropriate discount rate for both alternatives is the *after-tax* cost of debt, where the corporation's cost of debt is assumed to be the same as the loan rate. Should the corporation lease or buy?

PART 2 VALUATION

Chapter 7 Bond Valuation

7.1 Annual Payments

Problem. On October 17, 2013, an 8 year Treasury Bond with a face value of $1,000.00, paying $20.00 in coupon payments per year had a discount rate per year (yield) of 2.35%. Consider a bond that paid a $35.00 coupon payment once per year. What is price of this annual payment bond?

Excel 2013

FIGURE 7.1 Bond Valuation – Annual Payments.

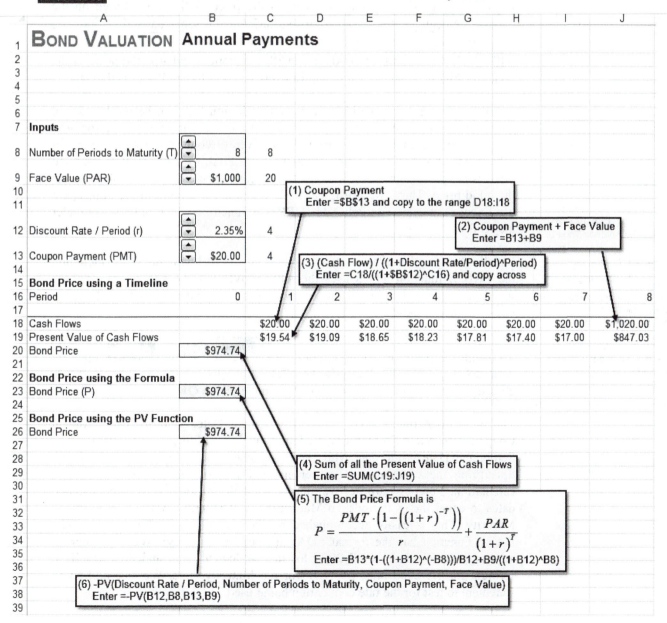

Solution Strategy. We calculate the bond price in three equivalent ways. First, we will calculate the bond price as the present value of the bond's cash flows. Second, we use a formula for the bond price. Third, we use Excel's PV function for a bond price.

The resulting annual bond price is $974.74. Notice you get the same answer all three ways: using the cash flows, using the formula, or using the PV function!

7.2 EAR, APR, and Foreign Currencies

Problem. On October 17, 2013, a 4 year Treasury Bond with a face value of $1,000 and an annual coupon rate of 1.88% had a yield to maturity of 1.08%. This bond makes 2 (semi-annual) coupon payments per year and thus has 8 periods until maturity. What is the price of this bond based on the Effective Annual Rate (EAR) convention? What is the price of this bond based on the Annual Percentage Rate (APR) convention? On the same date, the following exchanges rates were observed: $1.00 = ¥6.0996, $1.00 = €0.7389, and $1 = IDR 61.45. Under both the EAR and APR conventions, what is the price of the bond in Chinese Yuan (¥), European Euros (€), and in Indian Rupees (IDR)?

Solution Strategy. We will create an option button that can be used to select either the EAR or APR rate convention. The choice of rate convention will determine the discount rate / period. For a given discount rate / period, we will calculate the bond price in four equivalent ways. First, we will calculate the bond price as the present value of the bond's cash flows. Second, we use a formula for the bond price. Third, we use Excel's PV function for a bond price. Fourth, we use Excel's Analysis ToolPak Add-In **PRICE** function, which only works under the APR convention.

Excel's Analysis ToolPak contains several advanced bond functions, including the **PRICE** function which uses the APR convention. To access any of these functions, you need to install the Analysis ToolPak. Otherwise you will get the error message #NAME?.

Excel 2007 Equivalent

To install the Analysis ToolPak in Excel 2007, click on , click on Excel Options at the bottom of the drop-down window, click on **Add-Ins**, highlight **Analysis TookPak** in the list of Inactive Applications, click on **Go**, check the **Analysis ToolPak**, and click on **OK**.

To install the Analysis ToolPak, click on File, click on Options, click on **Add-Ins**, highlight the **Analysis ToolPak** in the list of Inactive Applications, click on **Go**, check the **Analysis ToolPak**, and click on **OK**.

The bond price function is =PRICE(Settlement Date, Maturity Date, Annual Coupon Rate, Yield To Maturity, Redemption Value, Number of Payments). The Settlement Date is the date when you exchange money to purchase the bond. Specifying the exact day of settlement and maturity allows a very precise calculation. For our purpose, we simply want the difference between the two dates to equal the (8 Periods To Maturity) / (2 Payments / Year) = 4 Years To Maturity. This is easily accomplished by the use of the DATE function. The DATE Function has the format =DATE(Year, Month, Day). We will enter an arbitrary starting date of 1/1/2000 for the Settlement Date and then specify a formula for 1/1/2000 plus T / NOP for the Maturity Date. We also add an IF statement to test for the rate convention being used.

FIGURE 7.2 Bond Valuation – EAR, APR, & Foreign Currencies.

	A	B	C	D	E	F	G	H	I	J
1	BOND VALUATION	EAR, APR, & Foreign Currencies				Currency: US Dollar			Exch Rate $1.00 =	$1.00
2										
3	Inputs									
4	Rate Convention	○ EAR ⦿ APR	2	Annual Percentage Rate						
5	Annual Coupon Rate	1.88%	2							
6	Yield to Maturity (Annualized)	1.08%	2							
7	Number of Payments / Year	2	2							
8	Number of Periods to Maturity (T)	8	8							
9	Face Value (PAR)	$1,000	20							
10										
11	Outputs									
12	Discount Rate / Period (r)	0.5%								
13	Coupon Payment (PMT)	$9								
14										
15	Bond Price using a Timeline									
16	Period	0	1	2	3	4	5	6	7	8
17	Time (Years)	0.0	0.5	1.0	1.5	2.0	2.5	3.0	3.5	4.0
18	Cash Flows		$9.40	$9.40	$9.40	$9.40	$9.40	$9.40	$9.40	$1,009.40
19	Present Value of Cash Flows		$9.35	$9.30	$9.25	$9.20	$9.15	$9.10	$9.05	$966.83
20	Bond Price	$1,031.24								
21										
22	Bond Price using a Formula									
23	Bond Price	$1,031.24								
24										
25	Bond Price using a Function									
26	Bond Price	$1,031.24								
27										
28	Bond Price using the PRICE Function (under APR)									
29	Bond Price	$1,031.24								

The resulting semi-annual bond price is $1,031.24 under APR and $1,031.35 under EAR. Notice you get the same answer all ways: using the cash flows, using the formula, using the PV function, or using the PRICE function under APR!

It is interesting to link two graphs: (1) bond pricing by yield to maturity and (2) bond pricing by calendar time. The former is done with a Data Table and the later with the PV formula.

Excel 2013   **FIGURE 7.3 Bond Valuation – EAR, APR, & Foreign Currencies.**

	A	B	C	D	E	F	G	H	I	J
52										
53	(6) If Rate Convention = EAR,									
54	Then (1+Yield To Maturity)^(1 / (Number of Payments / Year)) - 1									
55	Else (Yield To Maturity) / Number of Payment / Year)									
56	Enter =IF($C$4=1,((1+C60)^(1/$B$7))-1,C60/$B$7) and copy across									
57										
58	(7) The Output Formula is the Bond Price									
59	Enter =B26									
60	Yield to Maturity (Annualized)		1.0%	2.0%	3.0%	4.0%	5.0%	6.0%	7.0%	8.0%
61										
62	**Data Table: Sensitivity of Bond Price to Discount Rate / Period**									
63					Input Values for Discount Rate / Period					
64	Output Formula:		0.5%	1.0%	1.5%	2.0%	2.5%	3.0%	3.5%	4.0%
65	Bond Price	$1,031	$1,034	$995	$958	$922	$888	$855	$824	$794
66										
67	Data Table		(8) Create the bond price Data Table.							
68			Select the range B64:V65, click on							
69	Row input cell: B12		Data | Data Tools | What-If Analysis | Data Table,							
70			enter B12 in the Row Input Cell,							
71	Column input cell:		and click on OK.							
72										
73	OK Cancel									
74										
75										
76	**Bond Pricing By Calendar Time**									
77	Calendar Time (Years)	0	0.5	1	1.5	2	2.5	3	3.5	4
78	Time to Maturity (Years)	4	3.5	3	2.5	2	1.5	1	0.5	0
79	Number of Periods to Maturity (T)	8	7	6	5	4	3	2	1	0
80	Bond Price of Coupon Bond	$1,031	$1,027	$1,024	$1,020	$1,016	$1,012	$1,008	$1,004	$1,000
81	Bond Price of Par Bond	$1,000	$1,000	$1,000	$1,000	$1,000	$1,000	$1,000	$1,000	$1,000
82										
83				(9) (Time to Maturity) * (Number of Payments / Year)						
84				Enter =B78*$B$7 and copy across						
85										
86	(10) -PV(Discount Rate / Period, Number of Periods to Maturity, Coupon Payment, Face Value)									
87	Enter =-PV($B$12,B79,$B$13,$B$9) and copy across									
88	(11) -PV(Discount Rate / Period, Number of Periods to Maturity, (Discount Rate / Period) * (Face Value), Face Value)									
89	Enter =-PV($B$12,B79,$B$12*$B$9,$B$9) and copy across									

These graphs allow you to change the inputs and instantly see the impact on the bond price by yield to maturity and by calendar time. This allows you to perform instant experiments on the bond price, such as the following:

- What happens when the annual coupon rate is increased?
- What happens when the yield to maturity is increased?
- What happens when the number of payments / year is increased?
- What happens when the face value is increased?
- How does the price of coupon bond change over time when it is at a premium (above par) vs. at a discount (below par)?

What happens when the annual coupon rate is decreased to the point that it equals the yield to maturity? What happens when it is decreased further?

Excel 2013   **FIGURE 7.4 Bond Valuation – EAR, APR, & Foreign Currencies.**

	G	H	I	J	K	L	M
1	Currency:	Chinese Yuan	Exch Rate $1.00 =	¥6.1			
2						Currency Number	1
3						(Select from below)	
4						1 = Chinese Yuan	¥ 6.0996
5	1 / (Number of Payments / Year)) - 1 mber of Payment / Year)					2 = European Euro	€ 0.7349
6	37))-1,B6/B7)					3 = Indian Rupee	IDR 61.45
7	(Number of Payments / Year)					4 = US Dollar	$1.00

This spreadsheet has foreign currency conversion built into it. Cell **M2** is the currency selection cell. The default is currency 4, which is US Dollars. If you enter 1 in cell **M2**, then the spreadsheet converts to Chinese Yuan.

Excel 2013   **FIGURE 7.5 Bond Valuation – EAR, APR, & For. Cur. – Chinese Yuan.**

	A	B	C	D	E	F	G	H	I	J	L	M
1	**BOND VALUATION**	**EAR, APR, & Foreign Currencies**					Currency:	Chinese Yuan	Exch Rate $1.00 =	¥6.1		
2											Currency Number	1
3	**Inputs**										(Select from below)	
4	Rate Convention	○ EAR ◉ APR	2	Annual Percentage Rate							1 = Chinese Yuan	¥ 6.0996
5	Annual Coupon Rate	1.88%	2	(1) If Rate Convention = EAR, Then (1+Yield To Maturity)^(1 / (Number of Payments / Year)) - 1 Else (Yield To Maturity) / Number of Payment / Year) Enter =IF(C4=1,((1+B6)^(1/B7))-1,B6/B7)							2 = European Euro	€ 0.7349
6	Yield to Maturity (Annualized)	1.08%	2								3 = Indian Rupee	IDR 61.45
7	Number of Payments / Year	2	2	(2) Coupon Rate * Face Value / (Number of Payments / Year) Enter =B5*B9/B7							4 = US Dollar	$1.00
8	Number of Periods to Maturity (T)	8	8	(3) Period / (Number of Payments / Year) Enter =B16/$B$7 and copy across								
9	Face Value (PAR)	¥6,099.6	20									
10				(4) Copy the Timeline, Formula, and Function from the previous sheet Copy the range B18:J26 from the previous sheet to B18								
11	**Outputs**											
12	Discount Rate / Period (r)	0.5%										
13	Coupon Payment (PMT)	¥57.3										
14												
15	**Bond Price using a Timeline**											
16	Period	0	1	2	3	4	5	6	7	8		
17	Time (Years)	0.0	0.5	1.0	1.5	2.0	2.5	3.0	3.5	4.0		
18	Cash Flows		¥57.3	¥57.3	¥57.3	¥57.3	¥57.3	¥57.3	¥57.3	¥6,156.9		
19	Present Value of Cash Flows		¥57.0	¥56.7	¥56.4	¥56.1	¥55.8	¥55.5	¥55.2	¥5,897.3		
20	Bond Price	¥6,290.1										
21												
22	**Bond Price using a Formula**											
23	Bond Price	¥6,290.1										
24												
25	**Bond Price using a Function**											
26	Bond Price	¥6,290.1										
27												
28	**Bond Price using the PRICE Function (under APR)**											
29	Bond Price	¥6,290.1										

Bond Price By Yield To Maturity

The selected exchange rate is displayed in cell **J1**, $1.00 = ¥6.0996 (rounded to ¥6.1). This exchange rate is multiplied by the $1,000 face value in cell B9 to get a ¥6,099.6 face value and this in turn spread throughout the spreadsheet. The resulting semi-annual bond price is ¥6,290.1 under APR and ¥6,290.8 under

EAR. All of the dollar amount cells have conditional formatting rule to display ¥ for Chinese Yuan, € for European Euros, and IDR for Indian Rupees (see below).

FIGURE 7.6 Bond Valuation – EAR, APR, & For. Cur. – European Euros.

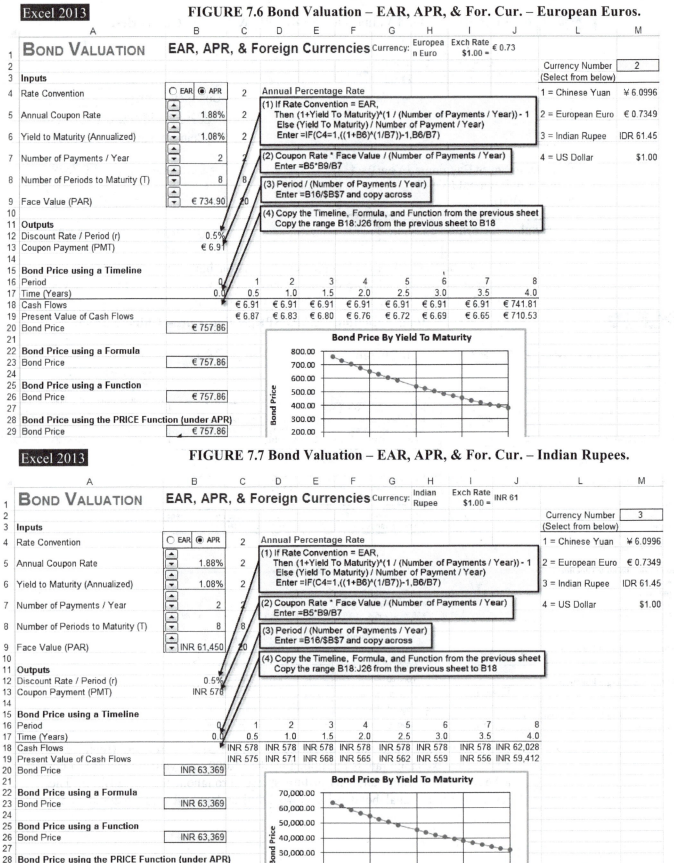

FIGURE 7.7 Bond Valuation – EAR, APR, & For. Cur. – Indian Rupees.

7.3 Duration and Convexity

Problem. On October 17, 2013, a 4 year Treasury Bond with a face value of $1,000 and an annual coupon rate of 1.88% had a yield to maturity of 1.08%. This bond makes 2 (semi-annual) coupon payments per year and thus has 8 periods until maturity. What is the duration, modified duration, and convexity of this bond based on the Annual Percentage Rate (APR) convention? What is the duration, modified duration, and convexity of this bond based on the Effective Annual Rate (EAR) convention? What is the intuitive interpretation of duration?

Solution Strategy. The choice of either the EAR or APR rate convention will determine the discount rate / period. For a given the discount rate / period, we will calculate duration and modified duration three equivalent ways. First, we will calculate duration as the weighted-average time to the bond's cash flows. This method illustrates the intuitive interpretation of duration. Second, we use a formula for duration. In both cases, modified duration is a simple adjustment of regular duration (also called Macaulay's Duration). Third, we use Excel's Analysis ToolPak Add-In **DURATION** and **MDURATION** functions, which only work under the APR convention. We will calculate convexity two equivalent ways. First, we will calculate convexity as the weighted-average (time-squared plus time) to the bond's cash flows. Second, we use a formula for convexity.

FIGURE 7.8 Bond Valuation – Duration and Convexity.

	A	B	C	D	E	F	G	H	I	J
1	**BOND VALUATION**	**Duration and Convexity**					Currency: US Dollar		Exch Rate $1.00 =	$1.00
2										
3	**Inputs**									
4	Rate Convention	○ EAR ● APR	2	Annual Percentage Rate						
5	Annual Coupon Rate	1.88%	2							
6	Yield to Maturity (Annualized)	1.08%	2							
7	Number of Payments / Year	2	2							
8	Number of Periods to Maturity (T)	8	8							
9	Face Value (PAR)	$1,000	20	(1) Copy the Outputs & Timeline from the previous sheet						
10				Copy the range B12:J20 from the previous sheet to B12						
11	**Outputs**									
12	Discount Rate / Period (r)	0.5%								
13	Coupon Payment (PMT)	$9								
14										
15	**Bond Duration using a Timeline**									
16	Period		0	1	2	3	4	5	6	7	8
17	Time (Years)		0.0	0.5	1.0	1.5	2.0	2.5	3.0	3.5	4.0
18	Cash Flows			$9.40	$9.40	$9.40	$9.40	$9.40	$9.40	$9.40	$1,009.40
19	Present Value of Cash Flows			$9.35	$9.30	$9.25	$9.20	$9.15	$9.10	$9.05	$966.83
20	Bond Price using a Timeline	$1,031.24								
21	Weight			0.9%	0.9%	0.9%	0.9%	0.9%	0.9%	0.9%	93.8%
22	Weight * Time			0.00	0.01	0.01	0.02	0.02	0.03	0.03	3.75
23	Duration using a Timeline	3.87								
24	Modified Duration using a Timeline	3.85								
25										
26	**Bond Duration using a Formula**									
27	Duration (D) using a Formula	3.87								
28	Modified Duration using a Formula	3.85								
29										
30	**Bond Duration using a Function (under APR)**									
31	Duration using a Function	3.87								
32	Modified Duration using a Function	3.85								

(2) PV of Cash Flow on Date t / Total PV of all Cash Flows
Enter =C19/$B$20 and copy across

(3) Weight * Time
Enter =C21*C17 and copy across

(4) Sum of all the Weight * Times
Enter =SUM(C22:J22)

(5) Duration / (1+(Discount Rate / Period))
Enter =B23/(1+$B$12) and copy to cell B28

(7) DURATION (Settlement Date, Maturity Date, Annual Coupon Rate, Yield to Maturity, Number of Periods)
Enter =IF($C$4=1,"",DURATION(DATE(2000,1,1), DATE(2000+B8/B7,1,1),B5,B6,B7))

(8) MDURATION (Settlement Date, Maturity Date, Annual Coupon Rate, Yield to Maturity, Number of Periods)
Enter =IF($C$4=1,"",MDURATION(DATE(2000,1,1), DATE(2000+B8/B7,1,1),B5,B6,B7))

(6) The Duration Formula is:

$$D = \frac{1+r}{r \cdot NOP} - \frac{1+r+T \cdot (CR/NOP - r)}{CR \cdot \left((1+r)^T - 1\right) + r \cdot NOP}$$

Enter =(1+B12)/(B12*B7)-(1+B12+B8*(B5/B7-B12))
/(B5*((1+B12)^B8-1)+B12*B7)

	A	B	C	D	E	F	G	H	I	J
42	**Bond Convexity**									
43	Weight * (Time^2+Time)			0.01	0.02	0.03	0.05	0.08	0.11	0.14	18.75
44	Convexity using a Timeline	18.98								
45	Convexity using a Formula	18.98								

(9) Weight * (Time^2 + Time)
Enter =C21*(C17^2+C17) and copy across

(10) (Sum of Weight * (Time ^ 2 + Time))
/ ((1 + Yield to Maturity / Number of Payments) ^ 2)
Enter =SUM(C43:J43)/((1+B6/B7)^2)

(11) The Convexity Formula is:

$$\frac{\begin{pmatrix} CR \cdot (1+r)^{1+T} \cdot (r \cdot (NOP+1)+2) \\ -CR \cdot (r^2 \cdot (NOP+T+1) \cdot (T+1) + r \cdot (NOP+2 \cdot T+3)+2) + r^3 \cdot NOP \cdot T \cdot (NOP+T) \end{pmatrix}}{r^2 \cdot NOP^2 \cdot \left(CR \cdot (1+r)^T - CR + r \cdot NOP\right)} \div \left((1+r)^2\right)$$

Enter =((B5*((1+B12)^(1+B8))*(B12*(B7+1)+2)-B5*(B12^2*(B7+B8+1)*(B8+1)+B12*(B7+2*B8+3)+2)+B12^3*B7*B8*(B7+B8))
/(B12^2*B7^2*(B5*(1+B12)^B8-B5+B12*B7)))/((1+B12)^2)

The timeline method of calculation directly illustrates the key intuition that (Macaulay's) duration is the weighted-average of the time until cash flows are received. The weights are based on the ratio of the present value of each cash flow over the present value of the total bond.

Excel's Analysis ToolPak contains several advanced bond functions, including the **DURATION** and **MDURATION** functions, which use the APR convention.

To install the Analysis ToolPak, click on 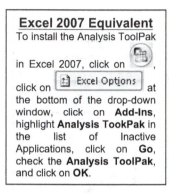 File , click on Options , click on **Add-Ins**, highlight the **Analysis ToolPak** in the list of Inactive Applications, click on **Go**, check the **Analysis ToolPak**, and click on **OK**.

The duration is 3.87 years and the modified duration is 3.85 years. Notice you get the same answer all three ways: using the cash flows, using the formula, or using the Analysis ToolPak Add-In function!

The value of bond convexity is 18.98. Again you get the same answer both ways: using the cash flows or using the formula!

Excel 2007 Equivalent
To install the Analysis ToolPak in Excel 2007, click on , click on Excel Options at the bottom of the drop-down window, click on **Add-Ins**, highlight **Analysis TookPak** in the list of Inactive Applications, click on **Go**, check the **Analysis ToolPak**, and click on **OK**.

7.4 Price Sensitivity

Bond duration is a measure of the price sensitivity of a bond to changes in interest rates. In other words, it is a measure of the bond's interest rate risk. Duration tells you approximately what percent change in bond price will result from a given change in yield to maturity.

Bond convexity complements bond duration in measuring of the price sensitivity of a bond to changes in interest rates. In other words, duration and convexity combined give you a better approximation of what percent change in bond price will result from a given change in yield to maturity than you can get from duration alone. To get the overall picture we will compare all three on a graph: the duration approximation, the duration and convexity approximation, and the actual percent change in the bond price.

Problem. On October 17, 2013, a 4 year Treasury Bond with a face value of $1,000 and an annual coupon rate of 1.88% had a yield to maturity of 1.08%. This bond makes 2 (semi-annual) coupon payments per year and thus has 8 periods until maturity. What is the price sensitivity of a bond to changes in yield and how does that compare to the duration approximation, and compare to the duration plus convexity approximation?

FIGURE 7.9 Bond Valuation – Price Sensitivity.

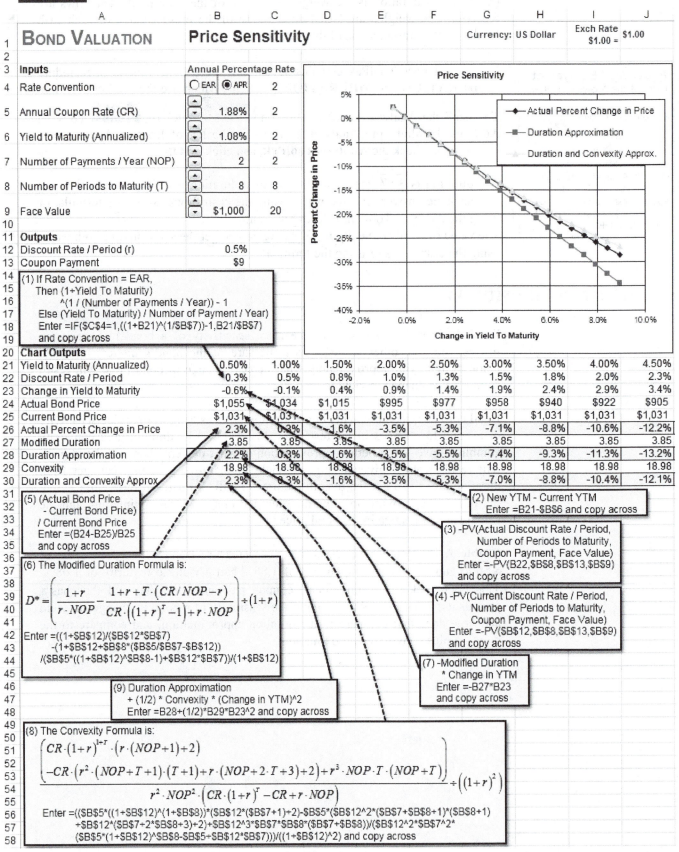

It is clear from the graph that duration does a very good job of approximating the price sensitivity of a bond. That is, the percent change in bond price from the duration approximation is very close to the actual percent change. This is especially true for relatively small changes in yield to maturity (say, plus or minus 3%). For larger changes in yield to maturity, there is a gap between the duration approximation and the actual percent change. The gap comes from the fact that the actual percent change is curved, whereas the duration approximation is a straight line.

One could do a better job of approximating the price sensitivity of a bond for larger changes in yield to maturity if one could account for the curvature. That is exactly what bond convexity does. The graph illustrates that duration and convexity approximation of the price sensitivity of a bond is better than the duration approximation alone. That is, the percent change in bond price from the duration and convexity approximation is very close to the actual percent change over a wide range of changes in yield to maturity (say, plus or minus 7%). Only for a very large change in yield to maturity is there any gap between the duration and convexity approximation and the actual percent change and the gap is pretty small.

In summary, duration alone does a good job of approximating the actual percent change using the slope only. Then convexity does a good job of adding the curvature. Together they do a great job of approximating the price sensitivity (i.e., interest rate risk) of a bond over a wide range of changes in yields.

7.5 System of Five Bond Variables

Problem. There is a system of five bond variables: (1) Number of Periods to Maturity (T), (2) Face Value (PAR), (3) Discount Rate / Period (r), (4) Coupon Payments (PMT), and (5) Bond Price (P). Given any four of these variables, show how the fifth variable can be found by using Excel functions (and in some cases by formulas).

FIGURE 7.10 Bond Valuation - System of Five Bond Variables.

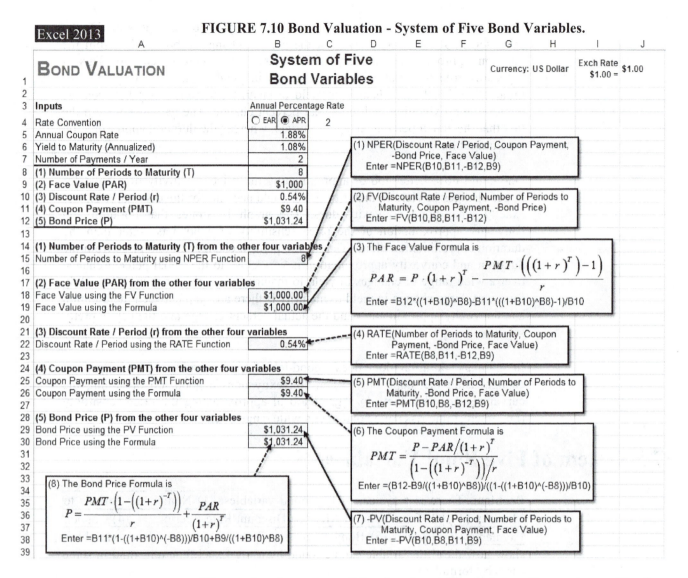

We see that the system of five bond variables is internally consistent. The five outputs in rows **15** through **30** (T = 8, PAR = $1000.00, r = 0.54%, PMT = $9.40, P = $1,031.24) are identical to the five inputs in rows **8** through **12**. Thus, any of the five bond variables can be calculated from the other four in a fully consistent manner.

Problems

1. An annual bond has a face value of $1,000.00, makes an annual coupon payment of $12.00 per year, has a discount rate per year of 4.37%, and has 8 years to maturity. What is price of this bond?

2. A 4 year Treasury Bond with a face value of $1,000 and an annual coupon rate of 6.50% had a yield to maturity of 3.15%. This bond makes 2 (semi-annual) coupon payments per year and thus has 8 periods until maturity. What is price of this bond based on the Effective Annual Rate (EAR)

convention? What is price of this bond based on the Annual Percentage Rate (APR) convention? On the same date, the following exchanges rates were observed: $1.00 = ¥9.5350, $1.00 = €0.4206, and $1 = IDR 52.75. Under both the EAR and APR conventions, what is the price of the bond in Chinese Yuan (¥), European Euros (€), and in Indian Rupees (IDR)?

3. Perform instant experiments on whether changing various inputs causes an increase or decrease in the Bond Price and by how much.

   (a.) What happens when the annual coupon rate is increased?
   (b.) What happens when the yield to maturity is increased?
   (c.) What happens when the number of payments / year is increased?
   (d.) What happens when the face value is increased?
   (e.) What is the relationship between the price of a par bond and time to maturity?
   (f.) What happens when the annual coupon rate is increased to the point that it equals the yield to maturity? What happens when it is increased further?

4. A 4 year Treasury Bond with a face value of $1,000 and an annual coupon rate of 3.20% has a yield to maturity of 2.53%. This bond makes 2 (semi-annual) coupon payments per year and thus has 8 periods until maturity. What is the duration, modified duration, and convexity of this bond based on the Annual Percentage Rate (APR) convention? What is the duration, modified duration, and convexity of this bond based on the Effective Annual Rate (EAR) convention? What is the intuitive interpretation of duration?

5. A 4 year Treasury Bond with a face value of $1,000 and an annual coupon rate of 5.80% has a yield to maturity of 4.29%. This bond makes 2 (semi-annual) coupon payments per year and thus has 8 periods until maturity. What is the price sensitivity of a bond to changes in yield and how does that compare to the duration approximation, and compare to the duration plus convexity approximation?

6. Given four of the bond variables, determine the fifth bond variable.

   (a.) Given Number of Periods to Maturity is 10, Face Value is $1,000.00, Discount Rate / Period is 3.27%, and Coupon Payment is $40.00, determine the Bond Price.
   (b.) Given Number of Periods to Maturity is 8, Face Value is $1,000.00, Discount Rate / Period is 4.54%, and the Bond Price is $880.00, determine the Coupon Payment.
   (c.) Given Number of Periods to Maturity is 6, Face Value is $1,000.00, Coupon Payment is $30.00, and the Bond Price is $865.00, determine Discount Rate / Period.
   (d.) Given Number of Periods to Maturity is 8, Discount Rate / Period is 3.81%, Coupon Payment is $45.00, and the Bond Price is $872.00, determine Face Value.

(e.) Given Face Value is $1,000.00, Discount Rate / Period is 4.38%, Coupon Payment is $37.00, and the Bond Price is $887.00, determine the Number of Periods to Maturity.

Chapter 8 Estimating the Cost of Capital

8.1 Static CAPM Using Fama-MacBeth Method

Problem. Given monthly total return data on individual stocks, US portfolios, and country portfolios, estimate the Static CAPM under three market portfolio benchmarks (SPDR "Spider" Exchange Traded Fund, CRSP Value-Weighted Market Return, and Dow Jones World Stock Index) using the standard Fama-MacBeth methodology. Next use the Static CAPM estimates from Jan 2003 – Dec 2012 data to forecast each asset's expected return over the next month (Jan 2013), or equivalently, each asset's cost of equity capital. Finally, determine how much variation of individual stocks, US portfolios, or country portfolios is explained by the Static CAPM.

Solution Strategy. First compute the monthly excess return of each asset. Next, stage one of the Fama-MacBeth method involves estimating the CAPM beta of an asset by doing a five-year, time-series regression of the asset's excess return on the excess return of a market portfolio benchmark. Repeat this time-series regression for many five-year windows and compute the average of the estimated CAPM betas. Then, stage two of the Fama-Beth method requires estimating the CAPM risk premium and intercept by doing a cross-sectional regression of the excess returns across assets in the following month on the CAPM beta from the immediately prior five-year window. Repeat this cross-sectional regression for many following months and compute the average of the estimated CAPM risk premium and intercept. Then use the estimated CAPM risk premium and intercept to forecast each asset's expected return, or equivalently, each asset's cost of equity capital. Finally, compute the R^2 ("explained variation") of both regressions.

Excel 2013

FIGURE 8.1 Static CAPM Using Fama-MacBeth Method.

	A	B	C	D	E	F	G	H	I
1	ESTIMATING THE COST OF CAPITAL				Static CAPM Using Fama-MacBeth Method				
2									
3	**Inputs**								
4	Market Portfolio Benchmark	Market Portfolio Benchmark ⦿ US S&P 500 (SPY) ○ CRSP VWMR ○ DJ World (DWG)			1				
5	Asset Type	Asset Type ○ Stock ○ US FF Port ⦿ Country ETF			3				
6									
7		Stock	Stock	Stock	Stock	Stock	Stock	US FF Port	US FF Port
8		Barrick Gold (ABX)	IBM (IBM)	Korea Electric (KEP)	Siemens (SI)	Grupo Televisa (TV)	YPF (YPF)	Small-Growth	Small-Neutral
130				(1) Monthly Return(Asset i, Month t) - Riskfree Rate(Month t) Enter =B10-$AC10 and copy to B133:V252					
131									
132	**Monthly Excess Returns**								
133	Dec 2012	1.39%	0.78%	13.85%	5.76%	12.29%	27.96%	2.55%	3.79%
134	Nov 2012	-14.26%	-1.87%	-4.82%	2.56%	4.72%	3.22%	0.74%	0.81%
135	Oct 2012	-3.03%	-6.24%	3.78%	0.75%	-3.88%	-14.09%	-3.87%	-1.29%
136	Sep 2012	8.40%	6.46%	15.96%	6.22%	2.30%	3.91%	3.23%	3.59%
137	Aug 2012	17.75%	-0.15%	-3.08%	11.32%	0.83%	9.63%	3.27%	3.36%
138	Jul 2012	-12.49%	0.20%	-1.17%	0.73%	6.09%	-7.62%	-2.98%	-1.09%
139	Jun 2012	-3.82%	1.39%	18.93%	1.78%	13.11%	-3.44%	5.88%	4.24%

FIGURE 8.2 Static CAPM Using Fama-MacBeth Method.

Excel 2013

ESTIMATING THE COST OF CAPITAL   Static CAPM Using Fama-MacBeth Method

Inputs

Market Portfolio Benchmark
- Market Portfolio Benchmark: ◉ US S&P 500 (SPY) ○ CRSP VWMR ○ DJ World (DWG)   1
- Asset Type: ○ Stock ○ US FF Port ◉ Country ETF   3

	Stock Barrick Gold (ABX)	Stock IBM (IBM)	Stock Korea Electric (KEP)	Stock Siemens (SI)	Stock Grupo Televisa (TV)	Stock YPF (YPF)	US FF Port Small-Growth	US FF Port Small-Neutral	US FF Port Small-Value	US FF Port Big-Growth

255 **CAPM Beta from the First Pass, Time-Series Regression**

(2) LINEST(Asset Excess Returns over 5 Years, Market Port Benchmark Excess Returns over 5 Yrs)
Enter =LINEST(B134:B193,OFFSET($T134,0,($E$4-1)):OFFSET($T193,0,$E$4-1))
and copy to B259:S318

257 5 Yr Estimation Per:

Beg Mon - End Mon	Barrick Gold (ABX)	IBM (IBM)	Korea Electric (KEP)	Siemens (SI)	Grupo Televisa (TV)	YPF (YPF)	Small-Growth	Small-Neutral	Small-Value	Big-Growth
259 Dec 2007 - Nov 2012	0.40	0.66	1.46	1.61	1.20	0.80	1.21	1.20	1.34	0.90
260 Nov 2007 - Oct 2012	0.42	0.68	1.46	1.57	1.19	0.81	1.22	1.20	1.35	0.90
261 Oct 2007 - Sep 2012	0.42	0.67	1.46	1.57	1.19	0.81	1.22	1.20	1.35	0.90
262 Sep 2007 - Aug 2012	0.45	0.66	1.44	1.58	1.17	0.79	1.21	1.20	1.34	0.90
263 Aug 2007 - Jul 2012	0.43	0.66	1.45	1.57	1.17	0.78	1.21	1.20	1.34	0.90
264 Jul 2007 - Jun 2012	0.41	0.65	1.42	1.58	1.18	0.78	1.22	1.20	1.35	0.90
265 Jun 2007 - May 2012	0.43	0.66	1.39	1.58	1.16	0.79	1.22	1.20	1.35	0.90

FIGURE 8.3 Static CAPM Using Fama-MacBeth Method.

Excel 2013

ESTIMATING THE COST OF CAPITAL   Static CAPM Using Fama-MacBeth Method

Inputs

Market Portfolio Benchmark
- Market Portfolio Benchmark: ◉ US S&P 500 (SPY) ○ CRSP VWMR ○ DJ World (DWG)   1
- Asset Type: ○ Stock ○ US FF Port ◉ Country ETF   3

	Stock Barrick Gold (ABX)	Stock IBM (IBM)	Stock Korea Electric (KEP)	Stock Siemens (SI)	Stock Grupo Televisa (TV)	Stock YPF (YPF)	US FF Port Small-Growth	US FF Port Small-Neutral
316 Mar 2003 - Feb 2008	0.46	0.95	1.00	1.60	1.46	1.38	1.54	1.31
317 Feb 2003 - Jan 2008	0.48	1.02	0.89	1.63	1.49	1.44	1.55	1.32
318 Jan 2003 - Dec 2007	0.86	1.09	0.92	1.47	1.57	1.21	1.56	1.35
319								
320 Average Beta	0.48	0.79	1.36	1.58	1.25	0.84	1.26	1.19

(3) Average Beta over all 5 Year Estimation Windows
Enter =AVERAGE(B259:B318) and copy across

324 **Risk Premium and Intercept from the Second Pass, Cross-Sectional Regression in the Following Month**

Following Month	Risk Prem	Intercept
327 Dec 2012	1.28%	2.44%
328 Nov 2012	6.17%	-7.09%
329 Oct 2012	-1.15%	2.70%
330 Sep 2012	5.63%	-3.91%
331 Aug 2012	1.47%	-0.17%
332 Jul 2012	4.43%	-2.63%
333 Jun 2012	6.20%	-1.37%
334 May 2012	-13.05%	6.09%
335 Apr 2012	-0.39%	0.06%

(4) LINEST(Excess Returns across Assets in Month t, Beta across Assets in Month t-1)
Enter this linear regression as an Excel matrix (Shift-Control-Enter)
Select the range B327:C327
Type =LINEST(OFFSET(B133,0,($E$5-1)*6):OFFSET(G133,0,($E$5-1)*6),
OFFSET(B259,0,($E$5-1)*6):OFFSET(G259,0,($E$5-1)*6))
Hold down the Shift and Control buttons and then press Enter
Then copy to the range B327:C327 to the range B328:C386

FIGURE 8.4 Static CAPM Using Fama-MacBeth Method.

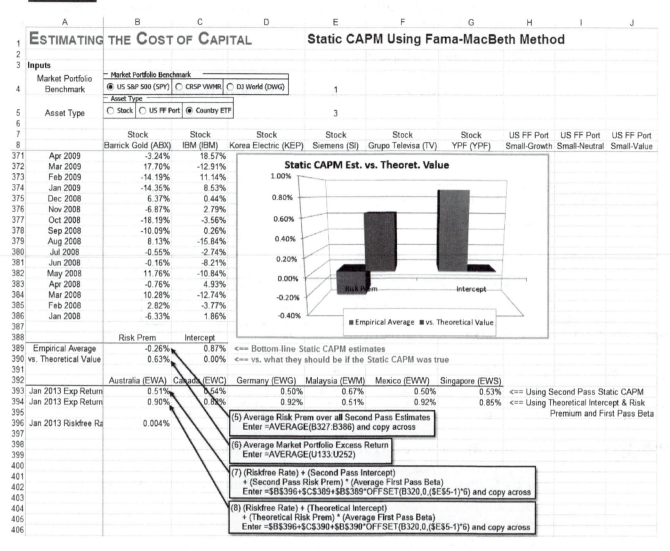

Row 389 contains the empirical average of the CAPM risk premium and intercept from the second-pass, cross-sectional regressions. Row 390 contains the theoretical value of the CAPM risk premium and intercept based on the CAPM beta from the first-pass, time-series regressions.

With a lot of extra work it would be possible to compute the statistical significance of the Static CAPM estimates. However, it is much simpler to just compare the empirical average and the theoretical value on a graph. It is clear at a glance that the empirical average and the theoretical value don't match very well.

It is interesting to make the same comparison for different market portfolio benchmarks by clicking on the option buttons in row 4 and for different asset types by clicking on the option buttons in row 5. Often the empirical average CAPM risk premium is negative, which doesn't make any economic sense. Often the empirical average of the CAPM intercept is far away from zero, which doesn't make any economic sense.

Row 393 contains the Static CAPM forecast of each asset's expected return in the next month (Jan 2013), or equivalently, each asset's cost of equity capital. This is a key output of this spreadsheet. However, given lack of economically sensible estimates for the Static CAPM, one should be very cautious about using the forecasts of each asset's expected return / cost of equity capital.

 Excel 2013

FIGURE 8.5 Static CAPM Using Fama-MacBeth Method.

	A	B	C	D	E	F	G	H	I
1	ESTIMATING THE COST OF CAPITAL				Static CAPM Using Fama-MacBeth Method				
2									
3	Inputs								
4	Market Portfolio Benchmark	Market Portfolio Benchmark ⦿ US S&P 500 (SPY) ○ CRSP VWMR ○ DJ World (DWG)			1				
5	Asset Type	Asset Type ○ Stock ○ US FF Port ⦿ Country ETF			3				
6									
7		Stock	Stock	Stock	Stock	Stock	Stock	US FF Port	US FF Port
8		Barrick Gold (ABX)	IBM (IBM)	Korea Electric (KEP)	Siemens (SI)	Grupo Televisa (TV)	YPF (YPF)	Small-Growth	Small-Neutral
408									
409		(9) LINEST(Asset Excess Returns over 5 Years, Market Port Benchmark Excess Returns over 5 Yrs)							
410		INDEX(LINEST(...), 3, 1) selects the R² of the regression above							
411		Enter =INDEX(LINEST(B134:B193,OFFSET($T134,0,($E$4-1)):OFFSET($T193,0,$E$4-1),,TRUE),3,1)							
412		and copy to B417:S476							
413	R² (Explained Variation as a Percentage of Total Variation) from the First Pass, Time-Series Regression								
414									
415	5 Yr Estimation Per:								
416	Beg Mon - End Mon	Barrick Gold (ABX)	IBM (IBM)	Korea Electric (KEP)	Siemens (SI)	Grupo Televisa (TV)	YPF (YPF)	Small-Growth	Small-Neutral
417	Dec 2007 - Nov 2012	3.0%	42.3%	45.9%	64.2%	58.7%	11.9%	87.3%	88.3%
418	Nov 2007 - Oct 2012	3.4%	42.9%	46.3%	60.5%	58.9%	12.4%	87.3%	88.3%
419	Oct 2007 - Sep 2012	3.4%	42.8%	46.6%	60.6%	58.9%	12.2%	87.3%	88.3%
420	Sep 2007 - Aug 2012	3.8%	42.3%	46.9%	60.7%	56.2%	11.8%	87.1%	87.8%

Excel 2013

FIGURE 8.6 Static CAPM Using Fama-MacBeth Method.

	A	B	C	D	E	F	G	H	I
1	ESTIMATING THE COST OF CAPITAL				Static CAPM Using Fama-MacBeth Method				
2									
3	Inputs								
4	Market Portfolio Benchmark	Market Portfolio Benchmark ⦿ US S&P 500 (SPY) ○ CRSP VWMR ○ DJ World (DWG)			1				
5	Asset Type	Asset Type ○ Stock ○ US FF Port ⦿ Country ETF			3				
6									
7		Stock	Stock	Stock	Stock	Stock	Stock	US FF Port	US FF Port
8		Barrick Gold (ABX)	IBM (IBM)	Korea Electric (KEP)	Siemens (SI)	Grupo Televisa (TV)	YPF (YPF)	Small-Growth	Small-Neutral
474	Mar 2003 - Feb 2008	1.9%	25.1%	13.5%	37.8%	31.2%	15.7%	72.8%	73.7%
475	Feb 2003 - Jan 2008	2.0%	29.2%	11.6%	38.0%	31.7%	16.6%	72.6%	73.5%
476	Jan 2003 - Dec 2007	6.4%	30.4%	11.2%	31.8%	31.5%	11.0%	70.9%	72.8%
477									
478	Average R²	3.8%	36.6%	39.5%	51.7%	49.0%	13.7%	81.7%	82.8%
479									
480		(10) Average R² over all 5 Year Estimation Windows							
481		Enter =AVERAGE(B417:B476) and copy across							
482									
483		(11) LINEST(Excess Returns across Assets in Month t, Beta across Assets in Month t)							
484		INDEX(LINEST(...), 3, 1) selects the R² of the regression above							
485		Enter =INDEX(LINEST(OFFSET(B133,0,($E$5-1)*6):OFFSET(G133,0,($E$5-1)*6),							
486		OFFSET(B259,0,($E$5-1)*6):OFFSET(G259,0,($E$5-1)*6),,TRUE),3,1)							
487		and copy down							
488									
489	R² (Explained Variation as a Percentage of Total Variation) from the Second Pass, Cross-sectional Regression in the Following Month								
490									
491	Following Month	R²							
492	Dec 2012	11.6%							
493	Nov 2012	68.8%							
494	Oct 2012	3.7%							
495	Sep 2012	31.7%							
496	Aug 2012	2.3%							
497	Jul 2012	20.0%							

The Average R^2 of the first-pass, time-series regression tells us how much of the fluctuation in an asset's excess return can be explained by market portfolio's excess return. An R^2 of 0% means the two variables are unrelated, while an R^2 of 100% means the two variables move together perfectly. With single-digit R^2s, the individual stocks are poorly explained. By contrast, the US portfolios are pretty well-explained by US benchmarks and country portfolios are pretty well-explained by a world benchmark.

FIGURE 8.7 Static CAPM Using Fama-MacBeth Method.

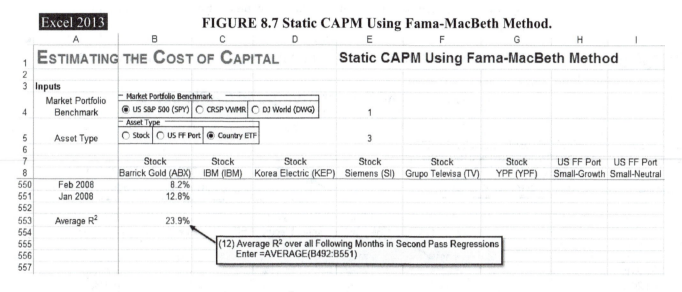

The Average R^2 of the second-pass, cross-sectional regression tells us how much of the fluctuation in the excess returns across assets in the following month can be explained by the CAPM beta from the immediately prior five-year window. With an Average R^2 of around 30%, the individual stocks and US portfolios are modestly explained by their CAPM betas. With an Average R^2 of around 25%, the country portfolios are very modestly explained by their CAPM betas.

8.2 APT or Intertemporal CAPM Using Fama-McBeth Method

Problem. Given monthly total return data on individual stocks, US portfolios, and country portfolios, estimate the APT or Intertemporal CAPM (ICAPM) under two sets of factors (Fama-French 3 factors and 3 macro factors) and using the standard Fama-MacBeth methodology. Then use the APT or ICAPM estimates from Jan 2003 – Dec 2012 data to forecast each asset's expected return in the next month (Jan 2013), or equivalently, each asset's cost of equity capital. Finally, determine how much variation of individual stocks, US portfolios, or country portfolios is explained by the APT or ICAPM.

Solution Strategy. First carry over the monthly excess return of each asset from the other sheet. Then stage one of the Fama-MacBeth method is estimating the APT or ICAPM factor betas of an asset by doing a five-year, time-series regression of the asset's excess return on sets of APT or ICAPM factors. Repeat this time-series regression for many five-year windows and compute the average of the estimated APT or ICAPM factor betas. Then stage two of the Fama-Beth method is estimating the APT or ICAPM factor risk premia and intercept by doing a cross-sectional regression of the excess returns across assets in the following month on the APT or ICAPM factor betas from the immediately prior five-year window. Repeat this cross-sectional regression for many following months and compute the average of the estimated APT or ICAPM factor risk premia and intercept. Then use the estimated APT or ICAPM factor risk premia and intercept to forecast each asset's expected return in the future (Jan 2013), or equivalently, each asset's cost of equity capital. Finally, compute the R^2 ("explained variation") of both regressions.

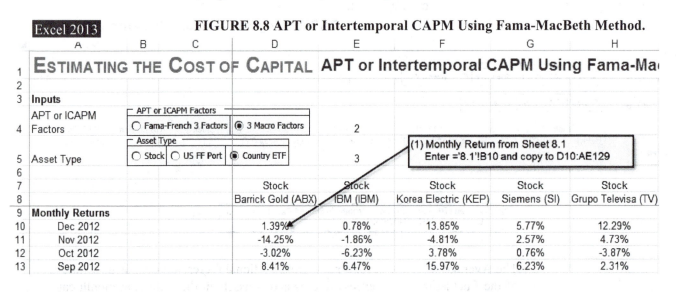

FIGURE 8.8 APT or Intertemporal CAPM Using Fama-MacBeth Method.

FIGURE 8.9 APT or Intertemporal CAPM Using Fama-MacBeth Method.

Excel 2013

(1) Monthly Return from Sheet 8.1
Enter ='8.1'!B10 and copy to D10:AE129

	A	B	C	D	E	F	G	H
7				Stock	Stock	Stock	Stock	Stock
8				Barrick Gold (ABX)	IBM (IBM)	Korea Electric (KEP)	Siemens (SI)	Grupo Televisa (TV)
9	**Monthly Returns**							
10	Dec 2012			1.39%	0.78%	13.85%	5.77%	12.29%
11	Nov 2012			-14.25%	-1.86%	-4.81%	2.57%	4.73%
12	Oct 2012			-3.02%	-6.23%	3.78%	0.76%	-3.87%
13	Sep 2012			8.41%	6.47%	15.97%	6.23%	2.31%

(2) LINEST(Asset Returns over 5 Years, 3 Factor Innovations over 5 Yrs)
Enter this linear regression as an Excel matrix (Shift-Control-Enter)
Select D143:D145
Type =TRANSPOSE(LINEST(OFFSET(D$11,$B143,0):OFFSET(D$70,$B143,0),
OFFSET($Y$11,$B143,($E$4-1)*3):OFFSET($AA$70,$B143,($E$4-1)*3)))
Hold down the Shift and Control buttons and then press Enter
Then copy to the range D143:D145 to the range E143:U145; Then copy the range D143:U145 to the range D146:U148;
Then copy the doubled range D143:U148 to the range D149:U154; Keep doubling until row 322 is reached.

	A	B	C	D	E	F	G	H
139	**Three Factor Betas from the First Pass, Time-Series Regression**							
140								
141	5 Yr Estimation Per:	Row						
142	Beg Mon - End Mon	Offset	Factors	Barrick Gold (ABX)	IBM (IBM)	Korea Electric (KEP)	Siemens (SI)	Grupo Televisa (TV)
143	Dec 2007 - Nov 2012	0	Chg Def Prem	-25.78	-31.10	-24.81	-33.76	-34.12
144			Chg Term Prem	-162.02	-32.32	-146.95	-92.67	-26.10
145			Chg Short Rate	-115.41	-23.19	-70.09	-21.70	-30.66
146	Nov 2007 - Oct 2012	1	Chg Def Prem	-26.09	-31.71	-25.10	-32.69	-34.30
147			Chg Term Prem	-160.75	-28.51	-145.42	-99.45	-24.71
148			Chg Short Rate	-108.52	-18.38	-66.56	-29.10	-30.95

Excel 2013 **FIGURE 8.10 APT or Intertemporal CAPM Using Fama-MacBeth Method.**

	A	B	C	D	E	F	G	H
1	ESTIMATING THE COST OF CAPITAL				APT or Intertemporal CAPM			
2					Using Fama-MacBeth Method			
3	Inputs							
4	APT or ICAPM Factors	APT or ICAPM Factors ○ Fama-French 3 Factors ◉ 3 Macro Factors			2			
5	Asset Type	Asset Type ○ Stock ○ US FF Port ◉ Country ETF			3			
6								
7				Stock	Stock	Stock	Stock	Stock
8				Barrick Gold (ABX)	IBM (IBM)	Korea Electric (KEP)	Siemens (SI)	Grupo Televisa (TV)
317	Feb 2003 - Jan 2008	58	Chg Def Prem	29.49	-58.06	-57.30	-101.14	-78.29
318			Chg Term Prem	-107.62	0.46	-94.52	71.86	-83.79
319			Chg Short Rate	-70.75	-20.41	-82.99	-41.48	-87.24
320	Jan 2003 - Dec 2007	59	Chg Def Prem	-4.66	-59.61	-45.57	-75.01	-53.75
321			Chg Term Prem	-106.69	3.40	-90.89	74.46	-76.18
322			Chg Short Rate	-75.10	-15.42	-74.40	-32.21	-69.26
323								
324			Average Factor Betas	Barrick Gold (ABX)	IBM (IBM)	Korea Electric (KEP)	Siemens (SI)	Grupo Televisa (TV)
325			Chg Def Prem	-21.22	-37.20	-33.92	-50.71	-42.33
326			Chg Term Prem	-218.81	-33.34	-201.74	-150.05	-86.07
327			Chg Short Rate	-162.48	-38.09	-138.65	-145.68	-88.23
328								
329								
330			(3) LINEST(Returns across Assets in Month t, Factor Betas across Assets in Month t)					
331			Enter this linear regression as an Excel matrix (Shift-Control-Enter)					
332			Select the range D340:G340					
333			Type =LINEST(OFFSET(D10,0,($E$5-1)*6):OFFSET(I10,0,($E$5-1)*6),					
334			OFFSET($D$143,B340,($E$5-1)*6):OFFSET($I$145,B340,($E$5-1)*6))					
335			Hold down the Shift and Control buttons and then press Enter					
336			Then copy to the range D340:G340 to the range D341:G399					
337	**Factor Risk Premia and Intercept from the Second Pass, Cross-Sectional Regression in the Following Month**							
338		Row						
339	Following Month	Offset		Chg Short Rate	Chg Term Prem	Chg Def Prem	Intercept	
340	Dec 2012	0		0.00%	-0.05%	0.09%	4.94%	
341	Nov 2012	3		0.03%	-0.10%	-0.02%	-4.24%	
342	Oct 2012	6		0.01%	-0.01%	0.20%	8.12%	
343	Sep 2012	9		0.02%	-0.08%	-0.06%	-2.42%	
344	Aug 2012	12		-0.03%	0.13%	0.09%	11.10%	

Excel 2013 **FIGURE 8.11 APT or Intertemporal CAPM Using Fama-MacBeth Method.**

	A	B	C	D	E	F	G	H	I
1	ESTIMATING THE COST OF CAPITAL			APT or Intertemporal CAPM					
2				Using Fama-MacBeth Method					
3	**Inputs**								
4	APT or ICAPM Factors	⌐ APT or ICAPM Factors ─ ○ Fama-French 3 Factors ⦿ 3 Macro Factors			2				
5	Asset Type	⌐ Asset Type ─ ○ Stock ○ US FF Port ⦿ Country ETF			3				
6									
7				Stock	Stock	Stock	Stock	Stock	Stock	U
8				Barrick Gold (ABX)	IBM (IBM)	Korea Electric (KEP)	Siemens (SI)	Grupo Televisa (TV)	YPF (YPF)	Sn
397	Mar 2008	171		-0.43%	0.22%	0.14%	-12.03%		
398	Feb 2008	174		0.20%	-0.17%	-0.18%	-7.83%		
399	Jan 2008	177		0.04%	-0.08%	0.16%	3.05%		
400									
401				Chg Short Rate	Chg Term Prem	Chg Def Prem			
402	Factor Premia			Premium	Premium	Premium	Intercept		
403	Average			0.00%	-0.01%	0.00%	0.48%	<= Bottom-line APT or Intertemporal	
404								CAPM estimates	
405	Expected Return using APT or ICAPM Est.			Australia (EWA)	Canada (EWC)	Germany (EWG)	Malaysia (EWM)	Mexico (EWW)	Singapore (EWS)
406	Jan 2013	3 Macro Factors		2.75%	2.10%	1.12%	0.52%	0.86%	0.82%
407									
408		Jan 2013 Riskfree Rate		0.004%					
409						(4) Average Factor Risk Prem over all Second Pass Estimates Enter =AVERAGE(D340:D399) and copy across			
410									
411									
412						(5) (Riskfree Rate) + (Second Pass Intercept)			
413						+ (Second Pass Factor 1 Risk Prem) * (First Pass Factor 1 Beta)			
414						+ (Second Pass Factor 2 Risk Prem) * (First Pass Factor 2 Beta)			
415						+ (Second Pass Factor 3 Risk Prem) * (First Pass Factor 3 Beta) Enter =$D$408+$G$403+$D$403*OFFSET(D327,0,($E$5-1)*6)			
416						+$E$403*OFFSET(D326,0,($E$5-1))			
417						+$F$403*OFFSET(D325,0,($E$5-1)*6) and copy across			
418									

Row 403 contains the empirical average of the APT or ICAPM factor risk premia and intercept from the second-pass, cross-sectional regressions. Given the wide flexibility in specifying APT or ICAPM factors in terms of either long positions or short positions, it is legitimately possible that risk premia could be either positive or negative.

Row 406 contains the APT or ICAPM forecast of each asset's expected return in the next month (Jan 2013), or equivalently, of each asset's cost of equity capital. This is a key output of this spreadsheet.

Excel 2013 **FIGURE 8.12 APT or Intertemporal CAPM Using Fama-MacBeth Method.**

	A	B	C	D	E	F	G	H
1	ESTIMATING THE COST OF CAPITAL			APT or Intertemporal CAPM				
2				Using Fama-MacBeth Method				
3	**Inputs**							
4	APT or ICAPM Factors	⌐ APT or ICAPM Factors ─ ○ Fama-French 3 Factors ⦿ 3 Macro Factors			2			
5	Asset Type	⌐ Asset Type ─ ○ Stock ○ US FF Port ⦿ Country ETF			3			
6								
7				Stock	Stock	Stock	Stock	Stock
8				Barrick Gold (ABX)	IBM (IBM)	Korea Electric (KEP)	Siemens (SI)	Grupo Televisa (TV)
419	(6) LINEST(Asset Returns over 5 Years, Three Factor Innovations over 5 Yrs)							
420	INDEX(LINEST(...), 3, 1) selects the R² of the regression above							
421	Enter =INDEX(LINEST(OFFSET(D$11,$B429,0):OFFSET(D$70,$B429,0),							
422	OFFSET($Y$11,$B429,($E$4-1)*3):OFFSET($AA$70,$B429,($E$4-1)*3),,TRUE),3,1)							
423	and copy to D429:U488							
424								
425	R² (Explained Variation as a Percentage of Total Variation) from the First Pass, Time-Series Regression							
426								
427	5 Yr Estimation Per:	Row						
428	Beg Mon - End Mon	Offset		Barrick Gold (ABX)	IBM (IBM)	Korea Electric (KEP)	Siemens (SI)	Grupo Televisa (TV)
429	Dec 2007 - Nov 2012	0		7.8%	32.1%	9.4%	12.8%	15.6%
430	Nov 2007 - Oct 2012	1		8.1%	32.7%	9.5%	12.0%	15.9%
431	Oct 2007 - Sep 2012	2		8.2%	33.5%	9.4%	12.0%	16.1%
432	Sep 2007 - Aug 2012	3		8.1%	33.7%	9.9%	11.6%	15.9%

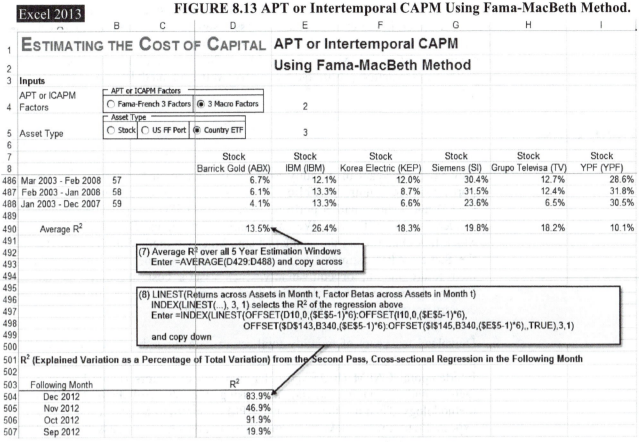

FIGURE 8.13 APT or Intertemporal CAPM Using Fama-MacBeth Method.

The Average R^2 of the first-pass, time-series regression tells us how much of the fluctuation in an asset's excess return can be explained by the APT or ICAPM factors. An R^2 of 0% means the two variables are unrelated, while an R^2 of 100% means the two variables move together perfectly. With single-digit R^2s, the individual stocks are poorly explained. With an R^2 over 90%, the US portfolios are extremely well-explained by US-based APT or ICAPM factors. With an R^2 around 50%, country portfolios are somewhat explained by US-based APT or ICAPM factors.

Excel 2013

FIGURE 8.14 APT or Intertemporal CAPM Using Fama-MacBeth Method.

	A	B	C	D	E	F	G	H
1	ESTIMATING THE COST OF CAPITAL			APT or Intertemporal CAPM				
2				Using Fama-MacBeth Method				
3	Inputs							
4	APT or ICAPM Factors	○ Fama-French 3 Factors ◉ 3 Macro Factors			2			
5	Asset Type	○ Stock ○ US FF Port ◉ Country ETF			3			
6								
7				Stock	Stock	Stock	Stock	Stock
8				Barrick Gold (ABX)	IBM (IBM)	Korea Electric (KEP)	Siemens (SI)	Grupo Televisa (TV)
561	Mar 2008			79.4%				
562	Feb 2008			59.7%				
563	Jan 2008			40.6%				
564								
565	Average R^2			58.8%				
566								
567				(9) Average R^2 over all Following Months in Second Pass Regressions				
568				Enter =AVERAGE(D504:D563)				
569								

The Average R^2 of the second-pass, cross-sectional regression tells us how much of the fluctuation in the excess returns across assets in the following month can be explained by the APT or ICAPM factor betas from the immediately prior five-year window. With an Average R^2 of 50% - 70%, the individual stocks, US portfolios, and country portfolios are pretty well-explained by their APT or ICAPM factors.[1]

Problems

1. Download ten years of monthly total return data for individual stocks, US portfolios, and country portfolios. Then use that data to estimate the Static CAPM under three market portfolio benchmarks (SPDR "Spider" Exchange Traded Fund, CRSP Value-Weighted Market Return, and Dow Jones World Stock Index) and using the standard Fama-MacBeth methodology. Then use the Static CAPM estimates to forecast each asset's expected return in the next future month, or equivalently, each asset's cost of equity capital. Finally, determine how much variation of individual stocks, US portfolios, or country portfolios is explained by the Static CAPM.

2. Download ten years of monthly total return data for individual stocks, US portfolios, and country portfolios. Then use that data to estimate the APT or Intertemporal CAPM (ICAPM) under two sets of factors (Fama-French 3 factors and 3 macro factors) and using the standard Fama-MacBeth methodology. Then use the APT or ICAPM estimates to forecast each asset's expected return in the next future month, or equivalently, each asset's cost of equity capital. Finally, determine how much variation of individual stocks, US portfolios, or country portfolios is explained by the APT or ICAPM.

---

[1] Lewellen, Nagel and Shaken (2010) suggest that apparently high cross-sectional R^2 provide quite weak support for an asset pricing model. They offer a number of suggestions for improving empirical asset pricing tests, including expanding the set of assets tested to include industry portfolios and using Generalized Least Squares (GLS) R^2, rather than regular regression (OLS) R^2. They test five popular asset pricing models, including the Static CAPM and the Fama-French 3 Factor model. They find that for an expanded set of assets which includes industry portfolios, the GLS R^2 is less than 10% for all asset pricing models. See Lewellen, J., S. Nagel, and J. Shaken, 2010, A Skeptical Appraisal of Asset-Pricing Tests, *Journal of Financial Economics* 96, 175-194.

Chapter 9 Stock Valuation

9.1 Dividend Discount Model

Problem. Currently a stock pays a dividend per share of $6.64. A security analyst projects the future dividend growth rate over the next five years to be 12.0%, 11.0%, 10.0%, 9.0%, 8.0% and then 7.0% each year thereafter to infinity. The levered cost of equity capital for the firm is 12.0% per year. What is the stock's value?

Solution Strategy. Construct a two-stage discounted dividend model. In stage one, explicitly forecast the firm's dividend over a five-year horizon. In stage two, forecast the firm's dividend from year six to infinity and calculate its continuation value as the present value of this infinitely growing annuity. Then, discount the future dividends and the date 5 continuation value back to the present to get the stock's value.

Excel 2013   **FIGURE 9.1 Excel Model for Stock Valuation – Dividend Discount Model.**

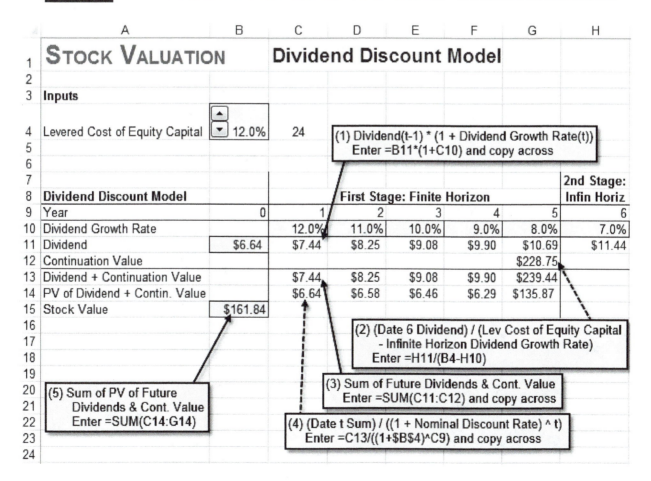

The stock value is estimated to be $161.84.

Problems

1. Currently a stock pays a dividend per share of $43.37. A security analyst projects the future dividend growth rate over the next five years to be 21.0%, 18.0%, 15.0%, 13.5%, 11.5% and then 11.0% each year thereafter to infinity. The levered cost of equity capital for the firm is 13.4% per year. What is the stock's value?

Chapter 10 Firm and Project Valuation

10.1 Cash Flows for Five Equivalent Methods

Problem. The expected future cash flows for a firm have been forecasted in two stages and correspond to two time periods. Stage one is a finite horizon from years 1 to 5. Stage two is the remaining infinite horizon from year 6 to infinity. Given these forecasted cash flows, compute the current value of the firm and the value added by the firm using five equivalent methods: (1) Adjusted Present Value, (2) Free Cash Flow to Equity, (3) Free Cash Flow to the Firm, (4) Dividend Discount Model, and (5) Residual Income. Given expected future cash flows for a project, compute the present value of future cash flows and the NPV of the project using the same five equivalent methods.

Solution Strategy. In this section, compute the cash flow streams that will be used by the five valuation methods: (1) Free Cash Flow to Equity, (2) Dividends, (3) Tax Shield Benefit, (4) Free Cash Flow to the Firm, and (5) Economic Profit. In subsequent sections, compute the current value of the firm and the value added by the firm using each of the five equivalent methods in turn. In the last section, eliminate stage two cash flows and recompute the value of the firm and the value added by the firm using the same five methods. Then, switch to evaluating a project and compute the value of future cash flows and the NPV of the project using the same five methods. Finally, restore stage two cash flows and compute the value of future cash flows and the NPV of the project using the same five methods.

FIGURE 10.1 Firm and Project Valuation–Cash Flows for 5 Equiv Methods.

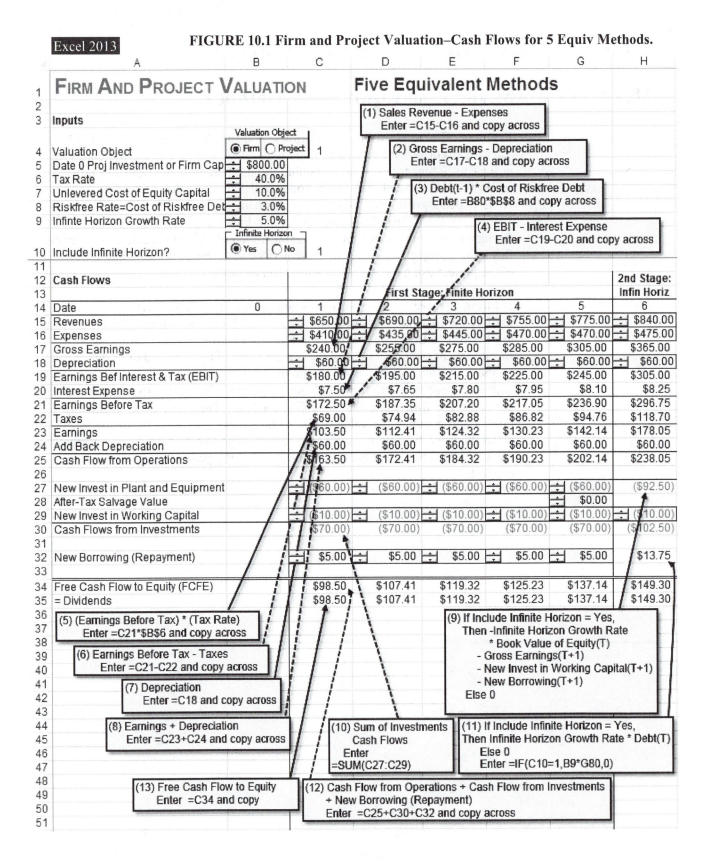

Excel 2013

FIGURE 10.2 Firm and Project Valuation–Cash Flows for 5 Equiv Methods.

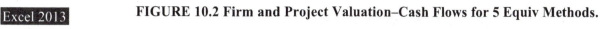

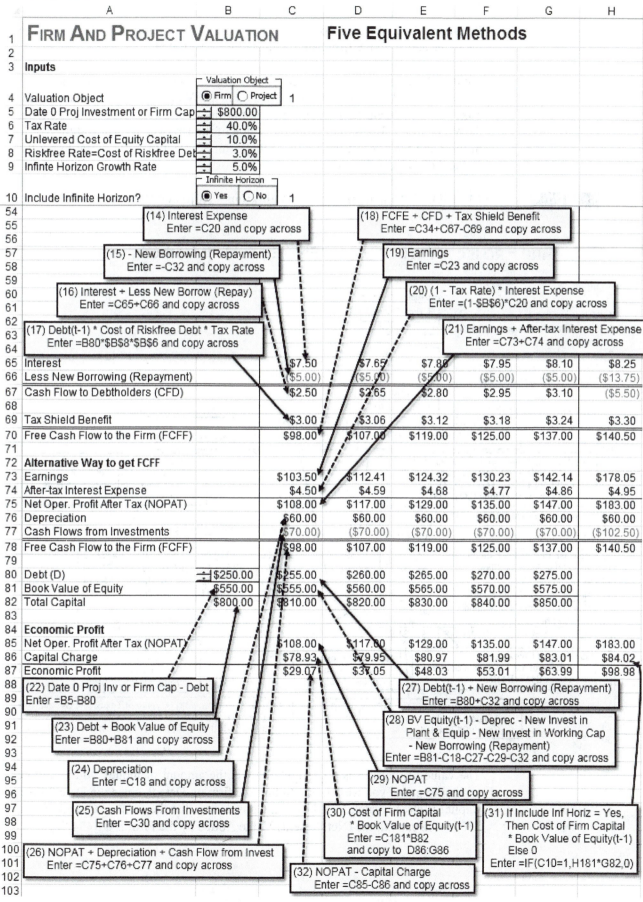

	A	B	C	D	E	F	G	H
1	**FIRM AND PROJECT VALUATION**			**Five Equivalent Methods**				
2								
3	**Inputs**							
4	Valuation Object	Valuation Object: (•) Firm ( ) Project	1					
5	Date 0 Proj Investment or Firm Cap	$800.00						
6	Tax Rate	40.0%						
7	Unlevered Cost of Equity Capital	10.0%						
8	Riskfree Rate=Cost of Riskfree Debt	3.0%						
9	Infinte Horizon Growth Rate	5.0%						
10	Include Infinite Horizon?	Infinite Horizon: (•) Yes ( ) No	1					
54–64								
65	Interest		$7.50	$7.65	$7.80	$7.95	$8.10	$8.25
66	Less New Borrowing (Repayment)		($5.00)	($5.00)	($5.00)	($5.00)	($5.00)	($13.75)
67	Cash Flow to Debtholders (CFD)		$2.50	$2.65	$2.80	$2.95	$3.10	($5.50)
68								
69	Tax Shield Benefit		$3.00	$3.06	$3.12	$3.18	$3.24	$3.30
70	Free Cash Flow to the Firm (FCFF)		$98.00	$107.00	$119.00	$125.00	$137.00	$140.50
71								
72	**Alternative Way to get FCFF**							
73	Earnings		$103.50	$112.41	$124.32	$130.23	$142.14	$178.05
74	After-tax Interest Expense		$4.50	$4.59	$4.68	$4.77	$4.86	$4.95
75	Net Oper. Profit After Tax (NOPAT)		$108.00	$117.00	$129.00	$135.00	$147.00	$183.00
76	Depreciation		$60.00	$60.00	$60.00	$60.00	$60.00	$60.00
77	Cash Flows from Investments		($70.00)	($70.00)	($70.00)	($70.00)	($70.00)	($102.50)
78	Free Cash Flow to the Firm (FCFF)		$98.00	$107.00	$119.00	$125.00	$137.00	$140.50
79								
80	Debt (D)	$250.00	$255.00	$260.00	$265.00	$270.00	$275.00	
81	Book Value of Equity	$550.00	$555.00	$560.00	$565.00	$570.00	$575.00	
82	Total Capital	$800.00	$810.00	$820.00	$830.00	$840.00	$850.00	
83								
84	**Economic Profit**							
85	Net Oper. Profit After Tax (NOPAT)		$108.00	$117.00	$129.00	$135.00	$147.00	$183.00
86	Capital Charge		$78.93	$79.95	$80.97	$81.99	$83.01	$84.02
87	Economic Profit		$29.07	$37.05	$48.03	$53.01	$63.99	$98.98
88–103								

(14) Interest Expense
Enter =C20 and copy across

(15) - New Borrowing (Repayment)
Enter =-C32 and copy across

(16) Interest + Less New Borrow (Repay)
Enter =C65+C66 and copy across

(17) Debt(t-1) * Cost of Riskfree Debt * Tax Rate
Enter =B80*$B$8*$B$6 and copy across

(18) FCFE + CFD + Tax Shield Benefit
Enter =C34+C67-C69 and copy across

(19) Earnings
Enter =C23 and copy across

(20) (1 - Tax Rate) * Interest Expense
Enter =(1-$B$6)*C20 and copy across

(21) Earnings + After-tax Interest Expense
Enter =C73+C74 and copy across

(22) Date 0 Proj Inv or Firm Cap - Debt
Enter =B5-B80

(23) Debt + Book Value of Equity
Enter =B80+B81 and copy across

(24) Depreciation
Enter =C18 and copy across

(25) Cash Flows From Investments
Enter =C30 and copy across

(26) NOPAT + Depreciation + Cash Flow from Invest
Enter =C75+C76+C77 and copy across

(27) Debt(t-1) + New Borrowing (Repayment)
Enter =B80+C32 and copy across

(28) BV Equity(t-1) - Deprec - New Invest in Plant & Equip - New Invest in Working Cap - New Borrowing (Repayment)
Enter =B81-C18-C27-C29-C32 and copy across

(29) NOPAT
Enter =C75 and copy across

(30) Cost of Firm Capital * Book Value of Equity(t-1)
Enter =C181*B82
and copy to D86:G86

(31) If Include Inf Horiz = Yes, Then Cost of Firm Capital * Book Value of Equity(t-1) Else 0
Enter =IF(C10=1,H181*G82,0)

(32) NOPAT - Capital Charge
Enter =C85-C86 and copy across

10.2 Adjusted Present Value

Problem. Given the cash flow streams, compute the current value of the firm and the value added by the firm using Adjusted Present Value.

Soluton Strategy. Take the Free Cash Flow to the Firm and discount at the Unlevered Cost of Equity Capital to obtain the Value of the Unlevered Firm. Take the Tax Shield Benefit and discount at the Cost of Riskfree Debt to obtain the Value of the Tax Shield. Sum the Value of the Unlevered Firm and the Value of the Tax Shield to get the Value of the Firm. Subtract Date 0 Capital to get the Value Added by the Firm.

`Excel 2013` **FIGURE 10.3 Firm and Project Valuation – Adjusted Present Value.**

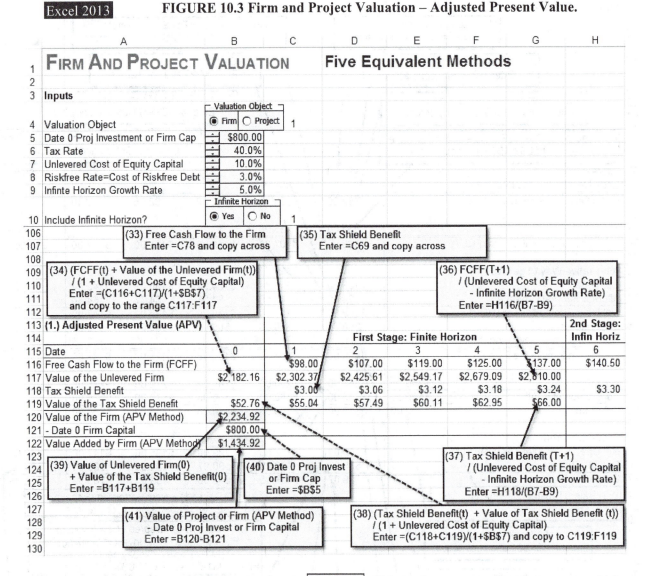

The value of the firm is $2,234.92. This is the amount of money you would be willing to pay if you were going to buy the firm on Date 0, since the Date 0 Firm Capital is already sunk into the firm. Considering that the firm is currently using $800.00 in capital, the (Net Present) Value Added by the Firm is $1,434.92.

10.3 Free Cash Flow To Equity

Problem. Given the cash flow streams, compute the current value of the firm and the value added by the firm using Free Cash Flow to Equity.

Soluton Strategy. Take the Free Cash Flow to Equity and discount at the Levered Cost of Equity Capital to obtain the Value of Equity. Take the Cash Flow to Debtholders and discount at the Cost of Riskfree Debt to obtain the Value of Debt. Sum the Value of Equity and the Value of Debt to get the Value of the Firm. Subtract Date 0 Capital to get the Value Added by the Firm.

FIGURE 10.4 Firm and Project Valuation – Free Cash Flow To Equity.

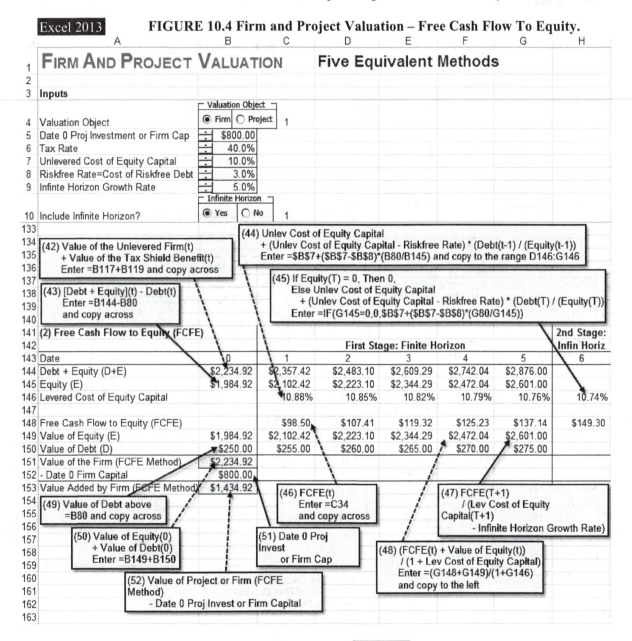

As above, the Value of the Firm is $2,234.92 and (Net Present) Value Added by the Firm is $1,434.92.

10.4 Free Cash Flow to the Firm

Problem. Given the cash flow streams, compute the current value of the firm and the value added by the firm using Free Cash Flow to the Firm.

Soluton Strategy. Take the Free Cash Flow to the Firm and discount at the Cost of Firm Capital (WACC) to obtain the Value of Firm. Subtract Date 0 Capital to get the Value Added by the Firm.

Excel 2013

FIGURE 10.5 Firm and Project Valuation – Free Cash Flow To The Firm.

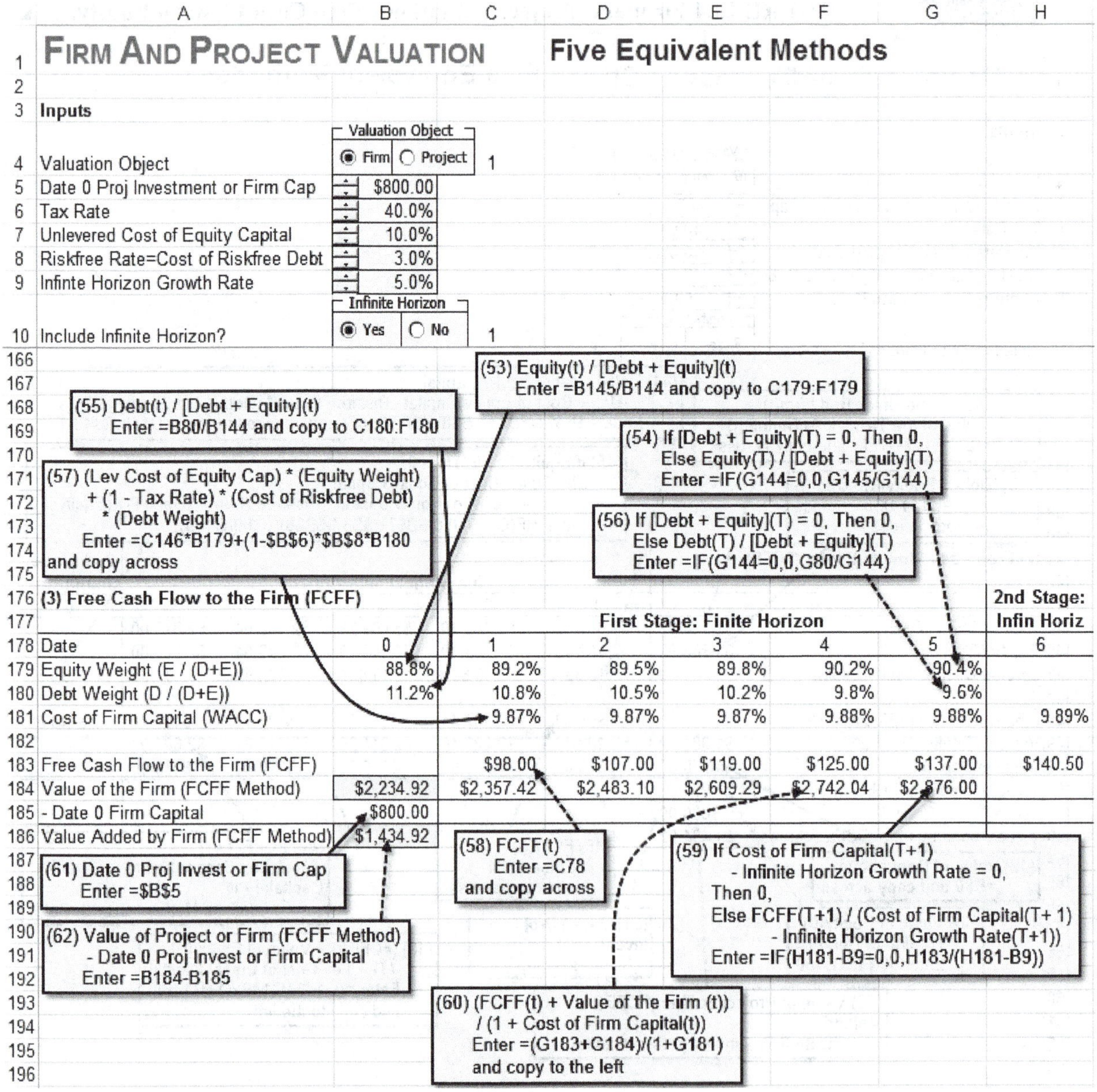

As above, the Value of the Firm is $2,234.92 and (Net Present) Value Added by the Firm is $1,434.92.

10.5 Dividend Discount Model

Problem. Given the cash flow streams, compute the current value of the firm and the value added by the firm using a Dividend Discount Model.

Solution Strategy. Take the Dividends and discount at the Levered Cost of Equity Capital to obtain the Value of Equity. Take the Cash Flow to Debtholders and discount at the Cost of Riskfree Debt to obtain the Value of Debt. Sum the Value of Equity and the Value of Debt to get the Value of the Firm. Subtract Date 0 Capital to get the Value Added by the Firm.

`Excel 2013`

FIGURE 10.6 Firm and Project Valuation – Dividend Discount Model.

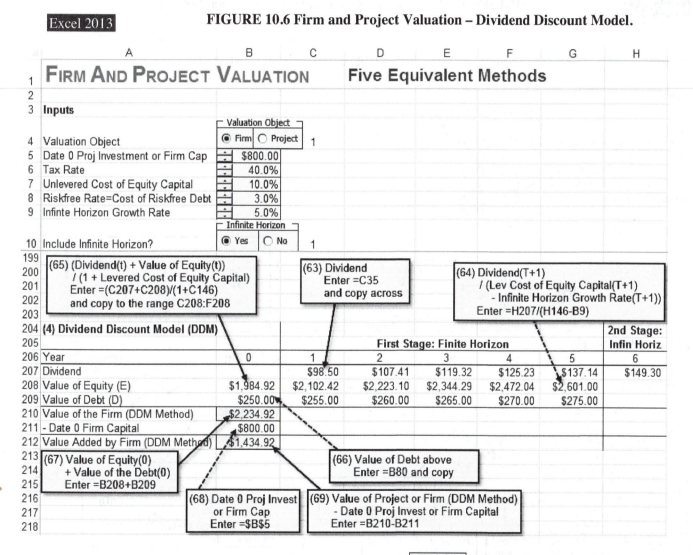

As above, the Value of the Firm is $2,234.92 and (Net Present) Value Added by the Firm is $1,434.92.

10.6 Residual Income

Problem. Given the cash flow streams, compute the current value of the firm and the value added by the firm using Residual Income.

Soluton Strategy. Take the Economic Profit and discount at the Cost of Firm Capital (WACC) to obtain the Value of Economic Profit. Add the Date 0 Book Value of the Firm to get the Value of the Firm. Subtract Date 0 Capital to get the Value Added by the Firm.

Excel 2013

FIGURE 10.7 Firm and Project Valuation – Residual Income.

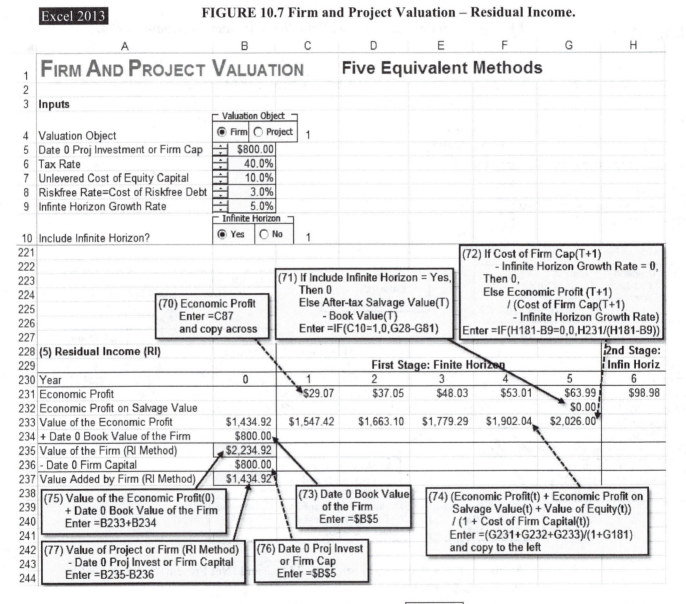

As above, the Value of the Firm is $2,234.92 and (Net Present) Value Added by the Firm is $1,434.92.

10.7 Five Equivalent Methods

Problem. Eliminate the (stage two) infinite horizon cash flows and recompute the value of the firm and the value added by the firm using the same five methods. Then, switch to evaluating a project while maintaining no infinite horizon cash flows. Compute the value of future cash flows and the NPV of the project using the same five methods. Finally, restore the infinite horizon cash flows and compute the value of future cash flows and the NPV of the project using the same five methods.

Start by considering firm valuation with no infinite. Just click on "No" option button in cell B10 (see below).

Excel 2013   **FIGURE 10.8 Five Equivalent Methods – Firm and No Infinite Horizon.**

Essentially, we are assuming that that firm lasts for 5 years and then is liquidated for an After-Tax Salvage Value of $600.

FIGURE 10.9 Five Equivalent Methods – Firm and No Infinite Horizon.

	A	B	C	D	E	F	G	H
1	**FIRM AND PROJECT VALUATION**			**Five Equivalent Methods**				
2								
3	**Inputs**							
4	Valuation Object	⊙ Firm ○ Project		1				
5	Date 0 Proj Investment or Firm Cap	$800.00						
6	Tax Rate	40.0%						
7	Unlevered Cost of Equity Capital	10.0%						
8	Riskfree Rate=Cost of Riskfree Debt	3.0%						
9	Infinte Horizon Growth Rate	5.0%						
10	Include Infinite Horizon?	○ Yes ⊙ No		2				
11								
12	**Cash Flows**							2nd Stage:
13				First Stage: Finite Horizon				Infin Horiz
14	Date	0	1	2	3	4	5	6
15	Revenues		$650.00	$690.00	$720.00	$755.00	$775.00	$0.00
16	Expenses		$410.00	$435.00	$445.00	$470.00	$470.00	$0.00
17	Gross Earnings		$240.00	$255.00	$275.00	$285.00	$305.00	$0.00
18	Depreciation		$60.00	$60.00	$60.00	$60.00	$60.00	$0.00
19	Earnings Bef Interest & Tax (EBIT)		$180.00	$195.00	$215.00	$225.00	$245.00	$0.00
20	Interest Expense		$7.50	$7.65	$7.80	$7.95	$8.10	$0.00
21	Earnings Before Tax		$172.50	$187.35	$207.20	$217.05	$236.90	$0.00
22	Taxes		$69.00	$74.94	$82.88	$86.82	$94.76	$0.00
23	Earnings		$103.50	$112.41	$124.32	$130.23	$142.14	$0.00
24	Add Back Depreciation		$60.00	$60.00	$60.00	$60.00	$60.00	$0.00
25	Cash Flow from Operations		$163.50	$172.41	$184.32	$190.23	$202.14	$0.00
26								
27	New Invest in Plant and Equipment		($60.00)	($60.00)	($60.00)	($60.00)	($60.00)	$0.00
28	After-Tax Salvage Value						$600.00	
29	New Invest in Working Capital		($10.00)	($10.00)	($10.00)	($10.00)	($10.00)	$0.00
30	Cash Flows from Investments		($70.00)	($70.00)	($70.00)	($70.00)	$530.00	$0.00
31								
32	New Borrowing (Repayment)		$5.00	$5.00	$5.00	$5.00	($270.00)	$0.00
33								
34	Free Cash Flow to Equity (FCFE)		$98.50	$107.41	$119.32	$125.23	$462.14	$0.00
35	= Dividends		$98.50	$107.41	$119.32	$125.23	$462.14	$0.00
36								
65	Interest		$7.50	$7.65	$7.80	$7.95	$8.10	$0.00
66	Less New Borrowing (Repayment)		($5.00)	($5.00)	($5.00)	($5.00)	$270.00	$0.00
67	Cash Flow to Debtholders (CFD)		$2.50	$2.65	$2.80	$2.95	$278.10	$0.00
68								
69	Tax Shield Benefit		$3.00	$3.06	$3.12	$3.18	$3.24	$0.00
70	Free Cash Flow to the Firm (FCFF)		$98.00	$107.00	$119.00	$125.00	$737.00	$0.00
71								
72	**Alternative Way to get FCFF**							
73	Earnings		$103.50	$112.41	$124.32	$130.23	$142.14	$0.00
74	After-tax Interest Expense		$4.50	$4.59	$4.68	$4.77	$4.86	$0.00
75	Net Oper. Profit After Tax (NOPAT)		$108.00	$117.00	$129.00	$135.00	$147.00	$0.00
76	Depreciation		$60.00	$60.00	$60.00	$60.00	$60.00	$0.00
77	Cash Flows from Investments		($70.00)	($70.00)	($70.00)	($70.00)	$530.00	$0.00
78	Free Cash Flow to the Firm (FCFF)		$98.00	$107.00	$119.00	$125.00	$737.00	$0.00
79								
80	Debt (D)	$250.00	$255.00	$260.00	$265.00	$270.00	$0.00	
81	Book Value of Equity	$550.00	$555.00	$560.00	$565.00	$570.00	$850.00	
82	Total Capital	$800.00	$810.00	$820.00	$830.00	$840.00	$850.00	
83								
84	**Economic Profit**							
85	Net Oper. Profit After Tax (NOPAT)		$108.00	$117.00	$129.00	$135.00	$147.00	$0.00
86	Capital Charge		$77.08	$77.91	$78.69	$79.38	$79.96	$0.00
87	Economic Profit		$30.92	$39.09	$50.31	$55.62	$67.04	$0.00

Excel 2013 **FIGURE 10.10 Five Equivalent Methods – Firm and No Infinite Horizon.**

	A	B	C	D	E	F	G	H
1	**FIRM AND PROJECT VALUATION**				**Five Equivalent Methods**			
2								
3	**Inputs**							
		┌ Valuation Object ┐						
4	Valuation Object	● Firm ○ Project	1					
5	Date 0 Proj Investment or Firm Cap	$800.00						
6	Tax Rate	40.0%						
7	Unlevered Cost of Equity Capital	10.0%						
8	Riskfree Rate=Cost of Riskfree Debt	3.0%						
9	Infinte Horizon Growth Rate	5.0%						
		┌ Infinite Horizon ┐						
10	Include Infinite Horizon?	○ Yes ● No	2					
113	**(1.) Adjusted Present Value (APV)**							2nd Stage:
114					First Stage: Finite Horizon			Infin Horiz
115	Date	0	1	2	3	4	5	6
116	Free Cash Flow to the Firm (FCFF)		$98.00	$107.00	$119.00	$125.00	$737.00	$0.00
117	Value of the Unlevered Firm	$809.92	$792.92	$765.21	$722.73	$670.00	$0.00	
118	Tax Shield Benefit		$3.00	$3.06	$3.12	$3.18	$3.24	$0.00
119	Value of the Tax Shield Benefit	$11.78	$9.96	$7.90	$5.57	$2.95	$0.00	
120	Value of the Firm (APV Method)	$821.71						
121	– Date 0 Firm Capital	$800.00						
122	Value Added by Firm (APV Method)	$21.71						
123								
141	**(2) Free Cash Flow to Equity (FCFE)**							2nd Stage:
142					First Stage: Finite Horizon			Infin Horiz
143	Date	0	1	2	3	4	5	6
144	Debt + Equity (D+E)	$821.71	$802.88	$773.11	$728.30	$672.95	$0.00	
145	Equity (E)	$571.71	$547.88	$513.11	$463.30	$402.95	$0.00	
146	Levered Cost of Equity Capital		13.06%	13.26%	13.55%	14.00%	14.69%	0.00%
147								
148	Free Cash Flow to Equity (FCFE)		$98.50	$107.41	$119.32	$125.23	$462.14	$0.00
149	Value of Equity (E)	$571.71	$547.88	$513.11	$463.30	$402.95	$0.00	
150	Value of Debt (D)	$250.00	$255.00	$260.00	$265.00	$270.00	$0.00	
151	Value of the Firm (FCFE Method)	$821.71						
152	– Date 0 Firm Capital	$800.00						
153	Value Added by Firm (FCFE Method)	$21.71						
154								
176	**(3) Free Cash Flow to the Firm (FCFF)**							2nd Stage:
177					First Stage: Finite Horizon			Infin Horiz
178	Date	0	1	2	3	4	5	6
179	Equity Weight (E / (D+E))	69.6%	68.2%	66.4%	63.6%	59.9%	0.0%	
180	Debt Weight (D / (D+E))	30.4%	31.8%	33.6%	36.4%	40.1%	0.0%	
181	Cost of Firm Capital (WACC)		9.63%	9.62%	9.60%	9.56%	9.52%	0.00%
182								
183	Free Cash Flow to the Firm (FCFF)		$98.00	$107.00	$119.00	$125.00	$737.00	$0.00
184	Value of the Firm (FCFF Method)	$821.71	$802.88	$773.11	$728.30	$672.95	$0.00	
185	– Date 0 Firm Capital	$800.00						
186	Value Added by Firm (FCFF Method)	$21.71						
187								
204	**(4) Dividend Discount Model (DDM)**							2nd Stage:
205					First Stage: Finite Horizon			Infin Horiz
206	Year	0	1	2	3	4	5	6
207	Dividend		$98.50	$107.41	$119.32	$125.23	$462.14	$0.00
208	Value of Equity (E)	$571.71	$547.88	$513.11	$463.30	$402.95	$0.00	
209	Value of Debt (D)	$250.00	$255.00	$260.00	$265.00	$270.00	$0.00	
210	Value of the Firm (DDM Method)	$821.71						
211	– Date 0 Firm Capital	$800.00						
212	Value Added by Firm (DDM Method)	$21.71						
213								
228	**(5) Residual Income (RI)**							2nd Stage:
229					First Stage: Finite Horizon			Infin Horiz
230	Year	0	1	2	3	4	5	6
231	Economic Profit		$30.92	$39.09	$50.31	$55.62	$67.04	$0.00
232	Economic Profit on Salvage Value						($250.00)	
233	Value of the Economic Profit	$21.71	($7.12)	($46.89)	($101.70)	($167.05)	$0.00	
234	+ Date 0 Book Value of the Firm	$800.00						
235	Value of the Firm (RI Method)	$821.71						
236	– Date 0 Firm Capital	$800.00						
237	Value Added by Firm (RI Method)	$21.71						

Now all five valuation methods match. The Value of the Firm is $821.71 and (Net Present) Value Added by the Firm is $21.71. It makes sense that these valuations are much lower than before because we have eliminated the (second stage) infinite horizon cash flows from period 6 to infinity.

Now switch to considering a project. The main difference between a firm and a project is how the date 0 cash flow is treated. With a firm, the date 0 capital is already invested in the firm, so the Value of the Firm is the present value of all future cash flows excluding the date 0 capital. With a project, the date 0 capital has not been invested yet and we are trying to decide whether to proceed with the project or not. So the Net Present Value of the project is the present value of all future cash flows minus the cost of the Date 0 Project Investment.

Switching to the project is done by clicking on the "**Project**" option button in cell **B4** (see below).

Excel 2013   **FIGURE 10.11 Five Equivalent Methods – Project and No Infinite Horizon.**

	A	B	C
1	**FIRM AND PROJECT VALUATION**		
2			
3	**Inputs**		
		┌ Valuation Object ┐	
4	Valuation Object	○ Firm ◉ Project	2
5	Date 0 Proj Investment or Firm Cap	$800.00	
6	Tax Rate	40.0%	
7	Unlevered Cost of Equity Capital	10.0%	
8	Riskfree Rate=Cost of Riskfree Debt	3.0%	
9	Infinte Horizon Growth Rate	5.0%	
		┌ Infinite Horizon ┐	
10	Include Infinite Horizon?	○ Yes ◉ No	2

There is no infinite horizon, so it is assumed that the project lasts for 5 years and is then liquidated for an After-Tax Salvage Value. To highlight the contrast between a project and a firm, we have assumed that the project involved a single investment on date 0 and no further investments in plant and equipment, no further investments in working capital, and no additional borrowing on future dates. However, these assumptions could be relaxed and the spreadsheet would handle it just fine.

FIGURE 10.12 Five Equivalent Methods – Project and No Infinite Horizon.

Excel 2013							
	A	B	C	D	E	F	G	H

FIRM AND PROJECT VALUATION   Five Equivalent Methods

	A	B	C	D	E	F	G	H
3	**Inputs**							
4	Valuation Object	○ Firm ● Project	2					
5	Date 0 Proj Investment or Firm Cap	$800.00						
6	Tax Rate	40.0%						
7	Unlevered Cost of Equity Capital	10.0%						
8	Riskfree Rate=Cost of Riskfree Debt	3.0%						
9	Infinte Horizon Growth Rate	5.0%						
10	Include Infinite Horizon?	○ Yes ● No	2					
11								
12	**Cash Flows**							2nd Stage:
13				First Stage: Finite Horizon				Infin Horiz
14	Date	0	1	2	3	4	5	6
15	Revenues		$650.00	$690.00	$720.00	$755.00	$775.00	$0.00
16	Expenses		$410.00	$435.00	$445.00	$470.00	$470.00	$0.00
17	Gross Earnings		$240.00	$255.00	$275.00	$285.00	$305.00	$0.00
18	Depreciation		$60.00	$60.00	$60.00	$60.00	$60.00	$0.00
19	Earnings Bef Interest & Tax (EBIT)		$180.00	$195.00	$215.00	$225.00	$245.00	$0.00
20	Interest Expense		$7.50	$7.50	$7.50	$7.50	$7.50	$0.00
21	Earnings Before Tax		$172.50	$187.50	$207.50	$217.50	$237.50	$0.00
22	Taxes		$69.00	$75.00	$83.00	$87.00	$95.00	$0.00
23	Earnings		$103.50	$112.50	$124.50	$130.50	$142.50	$0.00
24	Add Back Depreciation		$60.00	$60.00	$60.00	$60.00	$60.00	$0.00
25	Cash Flow from Operations		$163.50	$172.50	$184.50	$190.50	$202.50	$0.00
26								
27	New Invest in Plant and Equipment		$0.00	$0.00	$0.00	$0.00	$0.00	$0.00
28	After-Tax Salvage Value						$600.00	
29	New Invest in Working Capital		$0.00	$0.00	$0.00	$0.00	$0.00	$0.00
30	Cash Flows from Investments		$0.00	$0.00	$0.00	$0.00	$600.00	$0.00
31								
32	New Borrowing (Repayment)		$0.00	$0.00	$0.00	$0.00	($250.00)	$0.00
33								
34	Free Cash Flow to Equity (FCFE)		$163.50	$172.50	$184.50	$190.50	$552.50	$0.00
35	= Dividends		$163.50	$172.50	$184.50	$190.50	$552.50	$0.00
36								
65	Interest		$7.50	$7.50	$7.50	$7.50	$7.50	$0.00
66	Less New Borrowing (Repayment)		$0.00	$0.00	$0.00	$0.00	$250.00	$0.00
67	Cash Flow to Debtholders (CFD)		$7.50	$7.50	$7.50	$7.50	$257.50	$0.00
68								
69	Tax Shield Benefit		$3.00	$3.00	$3.00	$3.00	$3.00	$0.00
70	Free Cash Flow to the Firm (FCFF)		$168.00	$177.00	$189.00	$195.00	$807.00	$0.00
71								
72	**Alternative Way to get FCFF**							
73	Earnings		$103.50	$112.50	$124.50	$130.50	$142.50	$0.00
74	After-tax Interest Expense		$4.50	$4.50	$4.50	$4.50	$4.50	$0.00
75	Net Oper. Profit After Tax (NOPAT)		$108.00	$117.00	$129.00	$135.00	$147.00	$0.00
76	Depreciation		$60.00	$60.00	$60.00	$60.00	$60.00	$0.00
77	Cash Flows from Investments		$0.00	$0.00	$0.00	$0.00	$600.00	$0.00
78	Free Cash Flow to the Firm (FCFF)		$168.00	$177.00	$189.00	$195.00	$807.00	$0.00
79								
80	Debt (D)	$250.00	$250.00	$250.00	$250.00	$250.00	$0.00	
81	Book Value of Equity	$550.00	$490.00	$430.00	$370.00	$310.00	$500.00	
82	Total Capital	$800.00	$740.00	$680.00	$620.00	$560.00	$500.00	
83								
84	**Economic Profit**							
85	Net Oper. Profit After Tax (NOPAT)		$108.00	$117.00	$129.00	$135.00	$147.00	$0.00
86	Capital Charge		$77.79	$71.83	$65.85	$59.81	$53.72	$0.00
87	Economic Profit		$30.21	$45.17	$63.15	$75.19	$93.28	

Excel 2013 FIGURE 10.13 Five Equivalent Methods – Project and No Infinite Horizon.

FIRM AND PROJECT VALUATION   Five Equivalent Methods

	A	B	C	D	E	F	G	H
3	**Inputs**							
4	Valuation Object	⬭ Firm ⬤ Project 2						
5	Date 0 Proj Investment or Firm Cap	$800.00						
6	Tax Rate	40.0%						
7	Unlevered Cost of Equity Capital	10.0%						
8	Riskfree Rate=Cost of Riskfree Debt	3.0%						
9	Infinte Horizon Growth Rate	5.0%						
10	Include Infinite Horizon?	⬭ Yes ⬤ No 2						

	A	B	C	D	E	F	G	H (2nd Stage: Infin Horiz)
113	**(1.) Adjusted Present Value (APV)**							
114					First Stage: Finite Horizon			
115	Date	0	1	2	3	4	5	6
116	Free Cash Flow to the Firm (FCFF)		$168.00	$177.00	$189.00	$195.00	$807.00	$0.00
117	Value of the Unlevered Firm	$1,075.28	$1,014.81	$939.29	$844.21	$733.64	$0.00	
118	Tax Shield Benefit		$3.00	$3.00	$3.00	$3.00	$3.00	$0.00
119	Value of the Tax Shield Benefit	$11.37	$9.51	$7.46	$5.21	$2.73	$0.00	
120	Value of Fut Cash Flows (APV Met)	$1,086.65						
121	- Date 0 Project Investment	$800.00						
122	NPV of Project (APV Method)	$286.65						

	A	B	C	D	E	F	G	H (2nd Stage: Infin Horiz)
141	**(2) Free Cash Flow to Equity (FCFE)**							
142					First Stage: Finite Horizon			
143	Date	0	1	2	3	4	5	6
144	Debt + Equity (D+E)	$1,086.65	$1,024.32	$946.75	$849.42	$736.36	$0.00	
145	Equity (E)	$836.65	$774.32	$696.75	$599.42	$486.36	$0.00	
146	Levered Cost of Equity Capital		12.09%	12.26%	12.51%	12.92%	13.60%	0.00%
148	Free Cash Flow to Equity (FCFE)		$163.50	$172.50	$184.50	$190.50	$552.50	$0.00
149	Value of Equity (E)	$836.65	$774.32	$696.75	$599.42	$486.36	$0.00	
150	Value of Debt (D)	$250.00	$250.00	$250.00	$250.00	$250.00	$0.00	
151	Value of Fut Cash Flows (FCFE Met)	$1,086.65						
152	- Date 0 Project Investment	$800.00						
153	NPV of Project (FCFE Method)	$286.65						

	A	B	C	D	E	F	G	H (2nd Stage: Infin Horiz)
176	**(3) Free Cash Flow to the Firm (FCFF)**							
177					First Stage: Finite Horizon			
178	Date	0	1	2	3	4	5	6
179	Equity Weight (E / (D+E))	77.0%	75.6%	73.6%	70.6%	66.0%	0.0%	
180	Debt Weight (D / (D+E))	23.0%	24.4%	26.4%	29.4%	34.0%	0.0%	
181	Cost of Firm Capital (WACC)		9.72%	9.71%	9.68%	9.65%	9.59%	0.00%
183	Free Cash Flow to the Firm (FCFF)		$168.00	$177.00	$189.00	$195.00	$807.00	$0.00
184	Value of Fut Cash Flows (FCFF Met)	$1,086.65	$1,024.32	$946.75	$849.42	$736.36	$0.00	
185	- Date 0 Project Investment	$800.00						
186	NPV of Project (FCFF Method)	$286.65						

	A	B	C	D	E	F	G	H (2nd Stage: Infin Horiz)
204	**(4) Dividend Discount Model (DDM)**							
205					First Stage: Finite Horizon			
206	Year	0	1	2	3	4	5	6
207	Dividend		$163.50	$172.50	$184.50	$190.50	$552.50	$0.00
208	Value of Equity (E)	$836.65	$774.32	$696.75	$599.42	$486.36	$0.00	
209	Value of Debt (D)	$250.00	$250.00	$250.00	$250.00	$250.00	$0.00	
210	Value of Fut Cash Flows (DDM Met)	$1,086.65						
211	- Date 0 Project Investment	$800.00						
212	NPV of Project (DDM Method)	$286.65						

	A	B	C	D	E	F	G	H (2nd Stage: Infin Horiz)
228	**(5) Residual Income (RI)**							
229					First Stage: Finite Horizon			
230	Year	0	1	2	3	4	5	6
231	Economic Profit		$30.21	$45.17	$63.15	$75.19	$93.28	$0.00
232	Economic Profit on Salvage Value						$100.00	
233	Value of the Economic Profit	$286.65	$284.32	$266.75	$229.42	$176.36	$0.00	
234	+ Date 0 Book Value of the Firm	$800.00						
235	Value of Fut Cash Flows (RI Met)	$1,086.65						
236	- Date 0 Project Investment	$800.00						
237	NPV of Project (RI Method)	$286.65						

All five valuation methods produce the same results. The Value of Future Cash Flows is $1,086.65. After subtracting the cost of the Date 0 Project Investment, the Net Present Value of the Project is $286.65, so the project should be accepted.

Finally, restore the stage two (infinite horizon) cash flows by clicking on the "**Yes**" option button in cell **B10** (see below).

Excel 2013 **FIGURE 10.14 Five Equivalent Methods – Project and Infinite Horizon.**

	A	B	C
1	**FIRM AND PROJECT VALUATION**		
2			
3	**Inputs**		
		Valuation Object	
4	Valuation Object	○ Firm ◉ Project	2
5	Date 0 Proj Investment or Firm Cap	$800.00	
6	Tax Rate	40.0%	
7	Unlevered Cost of Equity Capital	10.0%	
8	Riskfree Rate=Cost of Riskfree Debt	3.0%	
9	Infinte Horizon Growth Rate	5.0%	
		Infinite Horizon	
10	Include Infinite Horizon?	◉ Yes ○ No	1
11			

FIGURE 10.15 Five Equivalent Methods – Project and Infinite Horizon.

Excel 2013

FIRM AND PROJECT VALUATION   Five Equivalent Methods

	A	B	C	D	E	F	G	H
3	**Inputs**							
4	Valuation Object	○ Firm ● Project	2					
5	Date 0 Proj Investment or Firm Cap	$800.00						
6	Tax Rate	40.0%						
7	Unlevered Cost of Equity Capital	10.0%						
8	Riskfree Rate=Cost of Riskfree Debt	3.0%						
9	Infinte Horizon Growth Rate	5.0%						
10	Include Infinite Horizon?	● Yes ○ No	1					
11								
12	**Cash Flows**							2nd Stage:
13				First Stage: Finite Horizon				Infin Horiz
14	Date	0	1	2	3	4	5	6
15	Revenues		$650.00	$690.00	$720.00	$755.00	$775.00	$840.00
16	Expenses		$410.00	$435.00	$445.00	$470.00	$470.00	$475.00
17	Gross Earnings		$240.00	$255.00	$275.00	$285.00	$305.00	$365.00
18	Depreciation		$60.00	$60.00	$60.00	$60.00	$60.00	$60.00
19	Earnings Bef Interest & Tax (EBIT)		$180.00	$195.00	$215.00	$225.00	$245.00	$305.00
20	Interest Expense		$7.50	$7.50	$7.50	$7.50	$7.50	$7.50
21	Earnings Before Tax		$172.50	$187.50	$207.50	$217.50	$237.50	$297.50
22	Taxes		$69.00	$75.00	$83.00	$87.00	$95.00	$119.00
23	Earnings		$103.50	$112.50	$124.50	$130.50	$142.50	$178.50
24	Add Back Depreciation		$60.00	$60.00	$60.00	$60.00	$60.00	$60.00
25	Cash Flow from Operations		$163.50	$172.50	$184.50	$190.50	$202.50	$238.50
26								
27	New Invest in Plant and Equipment		$0.00	$0.00	$0.00	$0.00	$0.00	($85.00)
28	After-Tax Salvage Value						$0.00	
29	New Invest in Working Capital		$0.00	$0.00	$0.00	$0.00	$0.00	$0.00
30	Cash Flows from Investments		$0.00	$0.00	$0.00	$0.00	$0.00	($85.00)
31								
32	New Borrowing (Repayment)		$0.00	$0.00	$0.00	$0.00	$0.00	$12.50
33								
34	Free Cash Flow to Equity (FCFE)		$163.50	$172.50	$184.50	$190.50	$202.50	$166.00
35	= Dividends		$163.50	$172.50	$184.50	$190.50	$202.50	$166.00
36								
65	Interest		$7.50	$7.50	$7.50	$7.50	$7.50	$7.50
66	Less New Borrowing (Repayment)		$0.00	$0.00	$0.00	$0.00	$0.00	($12.50)
67	Cash Flow to Debtholders (CFD)		$7.50	$7.50	$7.50	$7.50	$7.50	($5.00)
68								
69	Tax Shield Benefit		$3.00	$3.00	$3.00	$3.00	$3.00	$3.00
70	Free Cash Flow to the Firm (FCFF)		$168.00	$177.00	$189.00	$195.00	$207.00	$158.00
71								
72	**Alternative Way to get FCFF**							
73	Earnings		$103.50	$112.50	$124.50	$130.50	$142.50	$178.50
74	After-tax Interest Expense		$4.50	$4.50	$4.50	$4.50	$4.50	$4.50
75	Net Oper. Profit After Tax (NOPAT)		$108.00	$117.00	$129.00	$135.00	$147.00	$183.00
76	Depreciation		$60.00	$60.00	$60.00	$60.00	$60.00	$60.00
77	Cash Flows from Investments		$0.00	$0.00	$0.00	$0.00	$0.00	($85.00)
78	Free Cash Flow to the Firm (FCFF)		$168.00	$177.00	$189.00	$195.00	$207.00	$158.00
79								
80	Debt (D)	$250.00	$250.00	$250.00	$250.00	$250.00	$250.00	
81	Book Value of Equity	$550.00	$490.00	$430.00	$370.00	$310.00	$250.00	
82	Total Capital	$800.00	$740.00	$680.00	$620.00	$560.00	$500.00	
83								
84	**Economic Profit**							
85	Net Oper. Profit After Tax (NOPAT)		$108.00	$117.00	$129.00	$135.00	$147.00	$183.00
86	Capital Charge		$79.12	$73.21	$67.30	$61.38	$55.46	$49.53
87	Economic Profit		$28.88	$43.79	$61.70	$73.62	$91.54	$133.47

FIGURE 10.16 Five Equivalent Methods – Project and Infinite Horizon.

	A	B	C	D	E	F	G	H
	Excel 2013							
1	FIRM AND PROJECT VALUATION			Five Equivalent Methods				
2								
3	Inputs							
		Valuation Object						
4	Valuation Object	◯ Firm ◉ Project	2					
5	Date 0 Proj Investment or Firm Cap	$800.00						
6	Tax Rate	40.0%						
7	Unlevered Cost of Equity Capital	10.0%						
8	Riskfree Rate=Cost of Riskfree Debt	3.0%						
9	Infinte Horizon Growth Rate	5.0%						
		Infinite Horizon						
10	Include Infinite Horizon?	◉ Yes ◯ No	1					
113	(1.) Adjusted Present Value (APV)							2nd Stage:
114				First Stage: Finite Horizon				Infin Horiz
115	Date	0	1	2	3	4	5	6
116	Free Cash Flow to the Firm (FCFF)		$168.00	$177.00	$189.00	$195.00	$207.00	$158.00
117	Value of the Unlevered Firm	$2,664.84	$2,763.32	$2,862.65	$2,959.92	$3,060.91	$3,160.00	
118	Tax Shield Benefit		$3.00	$3.00	$3.00	$3.00	$3.00	$3.00
119	Value of the Tax Shield Benefit	$48.63	$50.49	$52.54	$54.79	$57.27	$60.00	
120	Value of Fut Cash Flows (APV Met)	$2,713.46						
121	- Date 0 Project Investment	$800.00						
122	NPV of Project (APV Method)	$1,913.46						
123								
141	(2) Free Cash Flow to Equity (FCFE)							2nd Stage:
142				First Stage: Finite Horizon				Infin Horiz
143	Date	0	1	2	3	4	5	6
144	Debt + Equity (D+E)	$2,713.46	$2,813.81	$2,915.19	$3,014.71	$3,118.18	$3,220.00	
145	Equity (E)	$2,463.46	$2,563.81	$2,665.19	$2,764.71	$2,868.18	$2,970.00	
146	Levered Cost of Equity Capital		10.71%	10.68%	10.66%	10.63%	10.61%	10.59%
147								
148	Free Cash Flow to Equity (FCFE)		$163.50	$172.50	$184.50	$190.50	$202.50	$166.00
149	Value of Equity (E)	$2,463.46	$2,563.81	$2,665.19	$2,764.71	$2,868.18	$2,970.00	
150	Value of Debt (D)	$250.00	$250.00	$250.00	$250.00	$250.00	$250.00	
151	Value of Fut Cash Flows (FCFE Met)	$2,713.46						
152	- Date 0 Project Investment	$800.00						
153	NPV of Project (FCFE Method)	$1,913.46						
154								
176	(3) Free Cash Flow to the Firm (FCFF)							2nd Stage:
177				First Stage: Finite Horizon				Infin Horiz
178	Date	0	1	2	3	4	5	6
179	Equity Weight (E / (D+E))	90.8%	91.1%	91.4%	91.7%	92.0%	92.2%	
180	Debt Weight (D / (D+E))	9.2%	8.9%	8.6%	8.3%	8.0%	7.8%	
181	Cost of Firm Capital (WACC)		9.89%	9.89%	9.90%	9.90%	9.90%	9.91%
182								
183	Free Cash Flow to the Firm (FCFF)		$168.00	$177.00	$189.00	$195.00	$207.00	$158.00
184	Value of Fut Cash Flows (FCFF Met)	$2,713.46	$2,813.81	$2,915.19	$3,014.71	$3,118.18	$3,220.00	
185	- Date 0 Project Investment	$800.00						
186	NPV of Project (FCFF Method)	$1,913.46						
187								
204	(4) Dividend Discount Model (DDM)							2nd Stage:
205				First Stage: Finite Horizon				Infin Horiz
206	Year	0	1	2	3	4	5	6
207	Dividend		$163.50	$172.50	$184.50	$190.50	$202.50	$166.00
208	Value of Equity (E)	$2,463.46	$2,563.81	$2,665.19	$2,764.71	$2,868.18	$2,970.00	
209	Value of Debt (D)	$250.00	$250.00	$250.00	$250.00	$250.00	$250.00	
210	Value of Fut Cash Flows (DDM Met)	$2,713.46						
211	- Date 0 Project Investment	$800.00						
212	NPV of Project (DDM Method)	$1,913.46						
213								
228	(5) Residual Income (RI)							2nd Stage:
229				First Stage: Finite Horizon				Infin Horiz
230	Year	0	1	2	3	4	5	6
231	Economic Profit		$28.88	$43.79	$61.70	$73.62	$91.54	$133.47
232	Economic Profit on Salvage Value						$0.00	
233	Value of the Economic Profit	$1,913.46	$2,073.81	$2,235.19	$2,394.71	$2,558.18	$2,720.00	
234	+ Date 0 Book Value of the Firm	$800.00						
235	Value of Fut Cash Flows (RI Met)	$2,713.46						
236	- Date 0 Project Investment	$800.00						
237	NPV of Project (RI Method)	$1,913.46						

All five valuation methods produce the same results. The Value of Future Cash Flows is $2,713.46. After subtracting the cost of the Date 0 Project Investment, the Net Present Value of the Project is $1,913.46, so the project should be accepted.

Problems

1. Starting from their historical financial statements, forecast the expected future cash flows for a real firm in two stages corresponding to two time periods. Stage one is a finite horizon from years 1 to 5. Stage two is the remaining infinite horizon from year 6 to infinity. Given these forecasted cash flows, compute the current value of the firm and the value added by the firm using five equivalent methods: (1) Adjusted Present Value, (2) Free Cash Flow to Equity, (3) Free Cash Flow to the Firm, (4) Dividend Discount Model, and (5) Residual Income. Given expected future cash flows for a project, compute the present value of future cash flows and the NPV of the project using the same five equivalent methods.

2. Perform instant experiments on whether changing various inputs causes an increase or decrease in the firm's value / share and by how much.

   (a.) What happens when the date 0 firm capital is increased?
   (b.) What happens when the tax rate is increased?
   (c.) What happens when the unlevered cost of equity capital is increased?
   (d.) What happens when the riskfree rate is increased?
   (e.) What happens when the infinite horizon growth rate of unlevered equity is increased?

Appendix: Reconciling the Residual Income Method with Other Approaches to Valuing Firms or Projects

By Professor Robert A. Taggart, Boston College

Craig W. Holden's book *Excel Modeling in Corporate Finance* presents five different approaches to valuation (Adjusted Present Value, Free Cash Flow to Equity, Free Cash Flow to the Firm, Dividend Discount and Residual Income). In principle, all five methods should yield consistent results when used to value either a firm or a capital investment project. However, the Residual Income method is a difficult challenge to reconcile with the other four methods.

This note analyzes the properties of the Residual Income valuation method and then uses these properties to reconcile the Residual Income method with other approaches to valuing firms or projects. This yields consistent results across all five valuation methods.

I. Properties of the Residual Income Method

The Residual Income Method is conceptually identical to what the consulting firm Stern Stewart & Co. originally trademarked as the Economic Value Added, or EVA®, approach. Ignoring accounting adjustments that may need to be made for items such as changes in "equity equivalent" reserves or "other operating income," the EVA approach measures Economic Value Added in a given year t as:

$$EVA_t = NOPAT_t - r_t^* A_{t-1} \tag{1}$$

where: $NOPAT_t$ = net operating profit after tax in year t (= revenue minus cash operating expenses minus depreciation all multiplied by one minus the corporate tax rate.

r_t^* = the company's weighted average cost of capital in year t, or

$$r_t^* = r_{Et}\left(\frac{E_{t-1}}{V_{t-1}}\right) + r_{Dt}(1-T)\left(\frac{D_{t-1}}{V_{t-1}}\right)$$

r_{Et} = the cost of equity capital in year t

r_{Dt} = the cost of debt in year t

T = the corporate tax rate

E_{t-1} = the market value of the company's equity at the beginning of year t

D_{t-1} = the market value of the company's debt at the beginning of year t

V_{t-1} = the company's total market value at the beginning of year t

A_{t-1} = the book value of the company's operating assets at the beginning of year t, net of noninterest-bearing liabilities[2]

EVA subtracts a charge for capital employed in a given year from that year's NOPAT, and it can thus be interpreted as the firm's economic profit in that year. In turn, the present value of EVA, discounted at the weighted average cost of capital over the life of a firm or project, is interpreted by Stern Stewart as MVA, or market value added:

$$MVA_0 = \sum_{t=1}^{H^*} \frac{EVA_t}{\prod_{m=1}^{t}(1+r_m^*)} = V_0 - A_0 \qquad (2)$$

where H^* is the horizon date (which could be infinite). MVA is the amount of value created by the firm or project, over and above the initial amount of capital committed.

II. The Relationship between Residual Income and Free Cash Flow

We can define the total free cash flow to the firm (FCFF) in year t as:

$$FCFF_t = (Rev_t - OpCost_t - Dep_t)(1-T) + Dep_t - CapEx_t - \Delta NWC_t \quad (3)$$

where: Rev = revenue

OpCost = cash operating cost

Dep = depreciation

CapEx = capital expenditure

ΔNWC = change in net working capital

In contrast, NOPAT in the same year t is defined as:

---

[2] See, for example, G. Bennett Stewart III, "Announcing the Stern Stewart Performance 1,000: A New Way of Viewing Corporate America, *Journal of Applied Corporate Finance* 3 (June 1990), pp. 38-59.

$$NOPAT_t = \left(\mathrm{Re}\,v_t - OpCost_t - Dep_t\right)\!\left(1 - T\right) \tag{4}$$

Together, (3) and (4) imply:

$$NOPAT_t = FCFF_t + \left(CapEx_t + \Delta NWC_t - Dep_t\right) = FCFF_t + \left(A_t - A_{t-1}\right) \tag{5}$$

We can then express the company's Market Value Added as:

$$MVA_0 = \sum_{t=1}^{H^*} \frac{\left(NOPAT_t - r_t^* A_{t-1}\right)}{\prod_{m=1}^{t}(1 + r_m^*)} = \sum_{t=1}^{H^*} \frac{FCFF_t}{\prod_{m=1}^{t}(1 + r_m^*)} + \sum_{t=1}^{H^*} \frac{A_t - (1 + r_t^*)A_{t-1}}{\prod_{m=1}^{t}(1 + r_m^*)} \tag{6}$$

The first term on the right-hand side of Equation (6) is equal to V_0, the firm's initial total market value. Consider the second term when $H^* = 1$:

$$\sum_{t=1}^{1} \frac{A_t - (1 + r_t^*)A_{t-1}}{\prod_{m=1}^{t}(1 + r_m^*)} = \frac{A_1}{(1 + r_1^*)} - A_0 \tag{7}$$

Similarly, for $H^* = 2$:

$$\sum_{t=1}^{2} \frac{A_t - (1 + r_t^*)A_{t-1}}{\prod_{m=1}^{t}(1 + r_m^*)} = \frac{A_2}{(1 + r_1^*)(1 + r_2^*)} - \frac{A_1}{(1 + r_1^*)} + \frac{A_1}{(1 + r_1^*)} - A_0$$

$$\tag{8}$$

$$= \frac{A_2}{(1 + r_1^*)(1 + r_2^*)} - A_0$$

Likewise, for any value of H^*:

$$\sum_{t=1}^{H^*} \frac{A_t - (1 + r_t^*)A_{t-1}}{\prod_{m=1}^{t}(1 + r_m^*)} = \frac{A_{H^*}}{\prod_{m=1}^{H^*}(1 + r_m^*)} - A_0 \tag{9}$$

Combining (9) with (6) then implies:

$$MVA_0 = \sum_{t=1}^{H^*} \frac{FCFF_t}{\prod_{m=1}^{t}(1 + r_m^*)} + \frac{A_{H^*}}{\prod_{m=1}^{H^*}(1 + r_m^*)} - A_0 = V_0 + \frac{A_{H^*}}{\prod_{m=1}^{H^*}(1 + r_m^*)} - A_0 \tag{10}$$

From Equation (2) we know that $MVA_0 = V_0 - A_0$, and (10) will satisfy this condition whenever the second term on the right-hand side is equal to zero. One way for this to happen is if $A_{H*} = 0$, which will occur if the firm or company's capital is liquidated at the horizon date so that $A_{H*} = 0$.

In the infinite horizon case, (2) and (10) can also hold simultaneously whenever the present value of horizon-date capital is equal to zero. This will be true if the level of capital remains constant, as in a level perpetuity model, or, in the case of constant perpetual growth (i.e., $A_t = (1+g)A_{t-1}$), as long as $g < r*$.

For a two-stage model with constant perpetual growth after H, the end of the first stage:

$$MVA_0 = \sum_{t=1}^{H} \frac{FCFF_t}{\prod_{m=1}^{t}(1+r_m^*)} + \frac{A_H}{\prod_{m=1}^{H}(1+r_m^*)} - A_0 +$$

$$\frac{1}{\prod_{m=1}^{H}(1+r_m^*)} \left[\frac{FCFF_{H+1}}{r_{H+1}^* - g} + \frac{A_H(1+g)^{H*-H}}{(1+r_{H+1}^*)^{H*-H}} - A_H \right] \qquad (11)$$

$$= V_0 + \frac{1}{\prod_{m=1}^{H}(1+r_m^*)} \left[A_H \left(\frac{1+g}{1+r_{H+1}^*} \right)^{H*-H} \right] - A_0$$

Equation (11) is equal to $V_0 - A_0$ when H* approaches infinity as long as $g < r*_{H+1}$. Thus, the two-stage model poses no special difficulties. As we shall see in Section II.D, though, it does impose some constraints on the parameter choices for periods H and H+1. Note also that, in order to make use of the growing perpetuity valuation formula, the discount rate must become constant at $r*_{H+1}$ once constant growth begins in the second stage.

III. Residual Income and Return on Invested Capital

Before moving on, let us look at an alternative representation of the residual income method. First, define Return on Invested Capital (ROIC) as[3]:

$$ROIC_t = \frac{NOPAT_t}{A_{t-1}} \qquad (12)$$

---

[3] See Robert C. Higgins, *Analysis for Financial Management*, 7th ed. (New York: McGraw-Hill/Irwin, 2004), p. 48.

Substituting (12) into (1), we can then express EVA as:

$$EVA_t = (ROIC_t - r_t^*)A_{t-1} \tag{13}$$

In the two-stage model with constant perpetual growth in the second stage, NOPAT and total net assets must grow at the same constant rate, g, in the second stage. With constant, perpetual growth in a model tied to an income statement and balance sheet, all of the individual items must grow at the same rate, g. This implies that ROIC must be constant from Year H+1 onward. Thus, we can write MVA_0 for the two-stage model as:

$$MVA_0 = \sum_{t=1}^{H} \frac{(ROIC_t - r_t^*)A_{t-1}}{\prod_{m=1}^{t}(1 + r_m^*)} + \frac{1}{\prod_{m=1}^{H}(1 + r_m^*)}\left[\frac{(ROIC_{H+1} - r_{H+1}^*)A_H}{r_{H+1}^* - g}\right] \tag{14}$$

Besides the constancy of ROIC and r*, Equation (14) emphasizes that total net assets must grow at the rate g from H to H+1, H+1 to H+2, and so on, in perpetuity.

IV. Measures of the Cost of Capital

The properties of the Residual Income, or EVA method, can now be used to identify the key issue, which is the need for a constant capital structure. A potential solution is to assume a constant debt-to-value ratio throughout the second stage and to use a set of cost of capital expressions that is predicated on this assumption. There are two available choices for the set of cost of capital expressions.

One approach is based on the analysis of Miles and Ezzell[4]. They assume that capital structure is adjusted year by year to maintain the same capital structure proportions at the end of each year. With riskfree debt, this implies that the most immediate future debt tax shield is certain, because it is based on debt already outstanding at the time of the valuation. Subsequent debt tax shields are uncertain, by contrast, because the firm will adjust its debt each year to maintain a constant debt-to-value ratio, and future firm value is uncertain. Miles and Ezzell then base their valuation on the assumption that the most immediate future debt tax shield is discounted at r_F, while all subsequent debt tax shields are discounted at the unlevered cost of capital, r_U. This in turn leads to a set of cost of capital expressions that can be used to achieve consistent valuations across all of the different valuation methods. A minor drawback of the Miles-Ezzell cost of capital expressions is their complexity.

---

[4] J. Miles and J.R. Ezzell, "The Weighted Average Cost of Capital, Perfect Capital Markets and Project Life: A Clarification," *Journal of Financial and Quantitative Analysis* 15 (September 1980), pp. 719-730.

A second approach is based on the analysis of Harris and Pringle (1985).[5] They assume that debt is adjusted continuously to maintain a constant capital structure. Even if debt remains riskfree, this assumption implies that all future debt tax shields are discounted at the unlevered cost of capital, r_U The resulting cost of capital expressions under this assumption are much simpler in form[6]:

$$r^* = r_E\left(\frac{E}{V}\right) + r_F(1-T)\left(\frac{D}{V}\right) \tag{15}$$

$$r^* = r_U - r_F T\left(\frac{D}{V}\right) \tag{16}$$

$$r_E = r_U + (r_U - r_F)\left(\frac{D}{E}\right) \tag{17}$$

Based on the Harris and Pringle (1985) approach, the five valuation methods in the Firm and Project Valuation spreadsheet of Holden's book *Excel Modeling in Corporate Finance* produce consistent results. Further, the valuations are consistent year by year working backwards to the present.

---

[5] See R.S. Harris and J.J. Pringle, "Risk-Adjusted Discount Rates – Extensions from the Average-Risk Case," *Journal of Financial Research* 8 (Fall 1985), pp. 237-244.

[6] For a comparison between the Miles-Ezzell and Harris-Pringle expressions, see R. A. Taggart, "Consistent Valuation and Cost of Capital Expressions with Corporate and Personal Taxes," *Financial Management* 20 (Autumn 1991), pp. 8-20.

Chapter 11 The Yield Curve

11.1 Obtaining It From Treasury Bills and Strips

Problem. Given bond prices and yields as published by the financial press or other information sources, obtain the U.S. Treasury Yield Curve.

Solution Strategy. Collect maturity date and yield to maturity (e.g., the "ask yield") from the *Wall Street Journal Online* (wsj.com) for Treasury Bills and Treasury Strips of a variety of maturity dates. Compute the time to maturity. Graph the yield to maturity of these bonds against their time to maturity.

FIGURE 11.1 The Yield Curve – Obtaining It From Bond Listings.

		A	B	C	D	E	F G H I J K
1	THE YIELD CURVE		Obtaining and Using It				
2			Maturity	Time To	Yield To	Forward	
3	Yield Curve Inputs		Date	Maturity	Maturity	Rates	
4	Today's Date		10/11/2013				
5	One Month Treasury Bill		11/15/2013	0.09	0.021%	0.021%	
6	Three Month Treasury Bill		1/9/2014	0.24	0.061%	0.086%	
7	Six Month Treasury Bill		4/10/2014	0.50	0.071%	0.081%	
8	One Year Treasury Strip		10/15/2014	1.01	0.180%	0.286%	
9	Two Year Treasury Strip		10/15/2015	2.01	0.350%	0.522%	
10	Three Year Treasury Strip		11/15/2016	3.09	0.730%	1.439%	
11	Four Year Treasury Strip		11/15/2017	4.09	1.130%	2.378%	
12	Five Year Treasury Strip		11/15/2018	5.09	1.480%	2.926%	
13	Ten Year Treasury Strip		11/15/2023	10.09	2.920%	4.408%	
14	Fifteen Year Treasury Bond		11/15/2028	15.09	3.550%	4.834%	
15	Twenty Year Treasury Bond		11/15/2033	20.09	3.820%	4.639%	
16	Twenty Five Year Treasury Bond		11/15/2038	25.09	3.950%	4.474%	
17	Thirty Year Treasury Bond		5/15/2043	29.59	4.010%	4.345%	
18							
19	(1) Maturity Date - Today's Date						
20	Enter =YEARFRAC($B$4,B5) and copy down						
21							

Chart: US Treasury Zero-Coupon Yield Curve — Yield To Maturity (Annual.) vs Time To Maturity (Years). Legend: Yields, Forward Rates.

For a given bond, Time To Maturity = Maturity Date - Today's Date. We can calculate the fraction of a year between two calendar dates using the **YEARFRAC** function in Excel's Analysis ToolPak Add-In. Excel's Analysis ToolPak Add-In contains several advanced date functions that are useful in finance. To access any of these functions, you need to install the Analysis ToolPak. Otherwise you will get the error message #NAME?.

To install the Analysis ToolPak, click on [File], click on [Options], click on **Add-Ins**, highlight the **Analysis ToolPak** in the list of Inactive Applications, click on **Go**, check the **Analysis ToolPak**, and click on **OK**.

Excel 2007 Equivalent

To install the Analysis ToolPak in Excel 2007, click on [icon], click on [Excel Options] at the bottom of the drop-down window, click on **Add-Ins**, highlight **Analysis TookPak** in the list of Inactive Applications, click on **Go**, check the **Analysis ToolPak**, and click on **OK**.

11.2 Using It To Price A Coupon Bond

Problem. Given the yield curve as published by the financial press, consider a coupon bond has a face value of $1,000, an annual coupon rate of 3.5%, makes 2 (semiannual) coupon payments per year, and 8 periods to maturity (or 4 years to maturity). What is price and yield to maturity of this coupon bond based on the Annual Percentage Rate (APR) convention? What is price and yield to maturity of this coupon bond based on the Effective Annual Rate (EAR) convention?

FIGURE 11.2 The Yield Curve – Using It To Price A Coupon Bond.

	A	B	C	D	E
1	THE YIELD CURVE	Using It To Price A Coupon Bond			
2		Maturity	Time To	Yield To	Forward
3	Yield Curve Inputs	Date	Maturity	Maturity	Rates
4	Today's Date	10/11/2013			
5	One Month Treasury Bill	11/15/2013	0.09	0.021%	0.021%
6	Three Month Treasury Bill	1/9/2014	0.24	0.061%	0.086%
7	Six Month Treasury Bill	4/10/2014	0.50	0.071%	0.081%
8	One Year Treasury Strip	10/15/2014	1.01	0.180%	0.286%
9	Two Year Treasury Strip	10/15/2015	2.01	0.350%	0.522%
10	Three Year Treasury Strip	11/15/2016	3.09	0.730%	1.439%
11	Four Year Treasury Strip	11/15/2017	4.09	1.130%	2.378%
12	Five Year Treasury Strip	11/15/2018	5.09	1.480%	2.926%
13	Ten Year Treasury Strip	11/15/2023	10.09	2.920%	4.408%
14	Fifteen Year Treasury Bond	11/15/2028	15.09	3.550%	4.834%
15	Twenty Year Treasury Bond	11/15/2033	20.09	3.820%	4.639%
16	Twenty Five Year Treasury Bond	11/15/2038	25.09	3.950%	4.474%
17	Thirty Year Treasury Bond	5/15/2043	29.59	4.010%	4.345%

	A	B	C
25	Bond Inputs	Effective Annual Rate	
26	Rate Convention	● EAR ○ APR	1
27	Annual Coupon Rate	3.5%	
28	Number of Payments / Year	2	
29	Number of Periods to Maturity	8	
30	Face Value	$1,000	
32	Outputs		
33	Coupon Payment	$18	

(3) Coupon Rate * Face Value / (Number of Payments/Year)
Enter =B27*B30/B28

(4) Periods 1 - 7 = Coupon Payment
Enter =$B$33 and copy across

(5) Period 8 = Coupon Payment + Face Value
Enter =B33+B30

(6) Corresponding yield on the yield curve
Enter =D7 in C39, =D8 in D39, =D9 in F39, =D10 in H39, =D11 in J39
Enter =(D39+F39)/2 in E39, =(F39+H39)/2 in G39, =(H39+J39)/2 in I39

Bond Price and Yield To Maturity using a Timeline

	A	C	D	E	F	G	H	I	J
36	Period	0	1	2	3	4	5	6	7	8
37	Time (Years)	0.0	0.5	1.0	1.5	2.0	2.5	3.0	3.5	4.0
38	Cash Flows		$17.50	$17.50	$17.50	$17.50	$17.50	$17.50	$17.50	$1,017.50
39	Yield to Maturity (Annualized)		0.07%	0.18%	0.27%	0.35%	0.54%	0.73%	0.93%	1.13%
40	Discount Rate / Period		0.04%	0.09%	0.13%	0.17%	0.27%	0.36%	0.46%	0.56%
41	Present Value of Cash Flow		$17.49	$17.47	$17.43	$17.38	$17.27	$17.12	$16.94	$972.78

	A	B
42	Coupon Bond Price	$1,093.88
43	Coupon Bond Discount Rate / Period	0.55%
44	Coupon Bond Yield to Maturity	1.10%

(7) If Rate Convention = EAR,
Then (1+Yield To Maturity)^(1 / (Number of Payments / Year)) - 1
Else (Yield To Maturity) / (Number of Payment / Year)
Enter =IF($C$26=1,((1+C39)^(1/$B$28))-1,C39/$B$28)
and copy across

(8) (Cash Flow) / ((1+Discount Rate / Period) ^ Period)
Enter =C38/((1+C40)^C36) and copy across

(9) Sum of all the Present Value of Cash Flows
Enter =SUM(C41:J41)

(10) RATE(Number of Periods to Maturity, Coupon Bond,
-Bond Price, Par Value)
Enter =RATE(B29,B33,-B42,B30)

(11) If Rate Convention = EAR,
Then (1+Discount Rate / Period)^(Number of Payments / Year) - 1
Else (Discount Rate / Period) * (Number of Payment / Year)
Enter =IF($C$26=1,((1+B43)^(B28))-1,B43*B28)

Solution Strategy. We will use the yield curve you entered in **The Yield Curve - Obtaining It From Bond Listings**. We will calculate the bond price as the present value of the bond's cash flows, where each cash flow is discounted based on the corresponding yield on the yield curve (e.g., a cash flow in year three will be discounted based on the yield curve's yield at year three). We will use Excel's **RATE** function to determine the yield to maturity of this coupon bond.

Results. The Coupon Bond's price is $1,093.88 and its Yield To Maturity is 1.10%. Note that this yield is not the same as four year yield or any other point on the yield curve. The yield of the coupon bond is a weighted average of the yields for each of the eight periods. Since the bond's biggest cash flow is on the maturity date, the biggest weight in the weighted average is on the maturity date. Thus the coupon bond's yield is closest to the yield of the maturity date, but it is not the same.

11.3 Using It To Determine Forward Rates

Problem. Given the yield curve as published by the financial press, calculate the implied forward rates at all maturities.

Solution Strategy. We will use the yield curve that you entered in an Excel model for **The Yield Curve - Obtaining It From Bond Listings**. We will calculate the forward rates implied by the yield curve and then graph our results.

FIGURE 11.3 The Yield Curve – Using It To Determine Forward Rates.

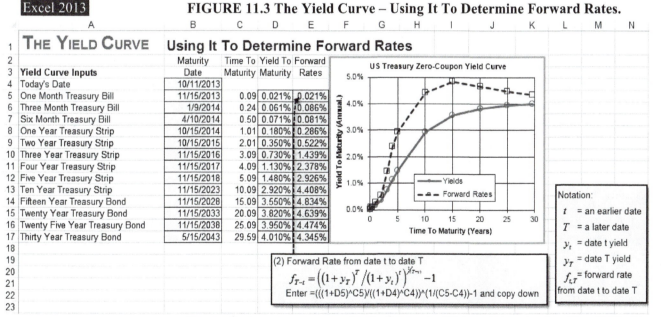

Forward rates are an approximate forecast of future interest rates. One difficulty with taking this interpretation literally has to do with market segmentation in the demand for treasury securities. There is significantly more demand for short-term bonds than bonds of other maturities, for their use in short-term cash management. There is also extra demand by institutional bond funds for the newly-issued, longest maturity treasury bond (the so-called, "on-the-run" bond).

High demand means high prices, which means low yields. Thus, the yield curve often has lower yields at the short end and the long end due to this segmentation.

Problems

1. Given bond prices and yields as published by the financial press or other information sources, obtain the U.S. Treasury Yield Curve.

2. Given the yield curve as published by the financial press, consider a coupon bond has a face value of $2,000, an annual coupon rate of 4.2%, makes 2 (semiannual) coupon payments per year, and 8 periods to maturity (or 4 years to maturity). Determine the price and yield to maturity of this coupon bond based on the Effective Annual Rate (EAR) convention. Then use it to determine the price and yield to maturity of this coupon bond based on the Annual Percentage Rate (APR) convention.

3. Given the yield curve as published by the financial press, calculate the implied forward rates at all maturities.

Chapter 12 US Yield Curve Dynamics

12.1 Dynamic Chart

How does the US yield curve change over time? What determines the volatility of changes in the yield curve? Are there differences in the volatility of short rates, medium rates, long rates, etc.? All of these questions and more can be answered using a *Dynamic Chart* of the yield curve, which is based on more than 43 years of monthly US zero-coupon, yield curve data. I update this Excel model each year with the latest yield curve data and make it available for free in the "Free Samples" section of www.excelmodeling.com.

FIGURE 12.1 Excel Model of US Yield Curve Dynamics – Dynamic Chart.

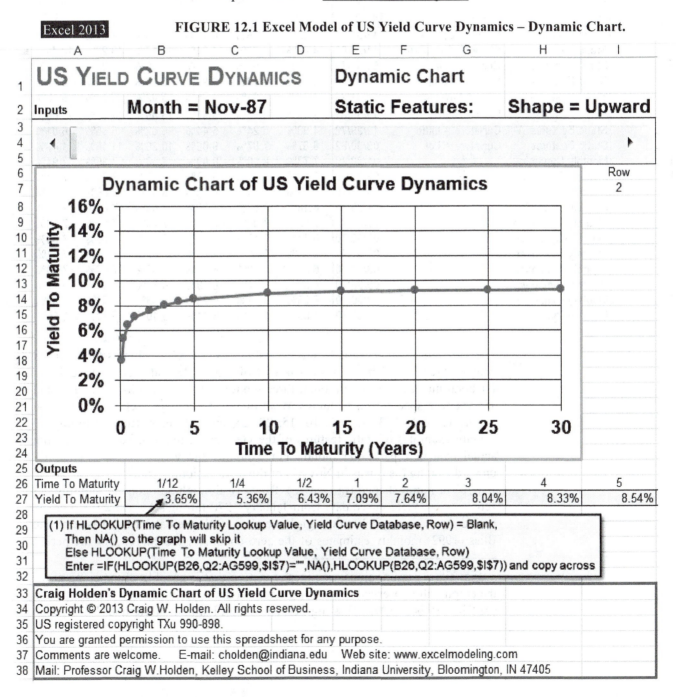

Time To Maturity	1/12	1/4	1/2	1	2	3	4	5
Yield To Maturity	3.65%	5.36%	6.43%	7.09%	7.64%	8.04%	8.33%	8.54%

(1) If HLOOKUP(Time To Maturity Lookup Value, Yield Curve Database, Row) = Blank,
Then NA() so the graph will skip it
Else HLOOKUP(Time To Maturity Lookup Value, Yield Curve Database, Row)
Enter =IF(HLOOKUP(B26,Q2:AG599,$I$7)="",NA(),HLOOKUP(B26,Q2:AG599,$I$7)) and copy across

Craig Holden's Dynamic Chart of US Yield Curve Dynamics
Copyright © 2013 Craig W. Holden. All rights reserved.
US registered copyright TXu 990-898.
You are granted permission to use this spreadsheet for any purpose.
Comments are welcome.   E-mail: cholden@indiana.edu   Web site: www.excelmodeling.com
Mail: Professor Craig W.Holden, Kelley School of Business, Indiana University, Bloomington, IN 47405

The dynamic chart uses a vertical scroll bar in rows **3** to **5**. Clicking on the right arrow of the scroll bar moves the yield curve forward by one month. Clicking on the left arrow moves back by one month. Clicking right of the position bar, moves the yield curve forward by one *year*. Clicking left of the position bar moves back by one *year*. This allows you to see a dynamic "movie" or animation of the yield curve over time. Thus, you can directly observe the volatility of the yield curve and other dynamic properties. For details of what to look for, see the discussion below on "using the Excel model."

Excel 2013

FIGURE 12.2 Excel Model of the Yield Curve Database.

	P	Q	R	S	T	U	V	W	X	Y
					Time To Maturity	Time To Maturity	Time To Maturity	Time To Maturity	Time To Maturity	Time To Maturity
1										
2		Title 1	Title 2	Title 3	1/12	1/4	1/2	1	2	3
3		Static Features:	Shape = Upward	11/30/87	3.65%	5.36%	6.43%	7.09%	7.64%	8.04%
4		Static Features:	Shape = Downward	11/28/80	14.83%	14.60%	14.64%	14.17%	13.22%	12.75%
5		Static Features:	Shape = Flat	01/30/70	7.73%	8.00%	8.03%	7.98%	7.95%	7.94%
6		Static Features:	Shape = Hump	12/29/78	8.82%	9.48%	9.99%	10.18%	9.76%	9.40%
7		Static Features:	Level = Low	12/31/70	4.62%	4.91%	4.95%	5.02%	5.40%	5.69%
8		Static Features:	Level = High	10/30/81	12.65%	13.13%	13.53%	13.85%	14.01%	14.06%
9		Static Features:	Curvature = Little	12/29/72	4.93%	5.24%	5.44%	5.62%	5.86%	6.01%
10		Static Features:	Curvature = Lot	09/30/82	6.67%	7.87%	9.05%	10.29%	11.16%	11.43%
11		Monthly Dynamics		01/30/70	7.73%	8.00%	8.03%	7.98%	7.95%	7.94%
12		Monthly Dynamics		02/27/70	6.23%	6.99%	6.97%	6.96%	7.02%	7.04%
13		Monthly Dynamics		03/31/70	6.33%	6.44%	6.53%	6.67%	6.85%	6.95%
14		Monthly Dynamics		04/30/70	6.48%	7.03%	7.35%	7.50%	7.60%	7.67%
15		Monthly Dynamics		05/29/70	6.22%	7.03%	7.28%	7.45%	7.58%	7.63%
16		Monthly Dynamics		06/30/70	6.14%	6.47%	6.81%	7.17%	7.43%	7.53%
17		Monthly Dynamics		07/31/70	6.32%	6.38%	6.55%	6.87%	7.19%	7.31%
18		Monthly Dynamics		08/31/70	6.22%	6.38%	6.57%	6.83%	7.07%	7.18%
19		Monthly Dynamics		09/30/70	5.32%	6.04%	6.49%	6.63%	6.64%	6.77%
20		Monthly Dynamics		10/30/70	5.23%	5.91%	6.23%	6.33%	6.50%	6.69%
21		Monthly Dynamics		11/30/70	4.86%	5.05%	5.11%	5.10%	5.29%	5.59%

The yield curve database is located in columns **Q** to **AG**. Columns **Q**, **R**, and **S** contain three sets of titles for the dataset. Columns **T**, **U**, and **V** contain yield data for bond maturities of one month, three months, and six months (1/12, 1/4, and 1/2 years, respectively). Columns **W** through **AG** contain yield data for bond maturities of 1, 2, 3, 4, 5, 7, 10, 15, 20, 25, and 30 years. Rows **2** through **9** contain examples of static features of the yield curve that can be observed from actual data in a particular month. For example, the yield curve is sometimes upward sloping (as it was in Nov 87) or downward sloping (in Nov 80) or flat (in Jan 70) or hump shaped (in Dec 78). Rows **10** through **533** contain monthly US zero-coupon, yield curve data from January 1970 through August 2013. For the period from January 1970 through December 1991, the database is based on the Bliss (1992) monthly estimates of the zero-coupon, yield curve.[7] For the period

---

[7] Bliss fits a parsimonious, nonlinear function that is capable of matching all of the empirically observed shapes of the zero-coupon, yield curve. For more details see Bliss, Robert, 1992, "Testing Term Structure Estimation Methods."

from January 1992 to July 2001, the yield curve is directly observed from Treasury Bills and Strips in the *Wall Street Journal*. For the period from August 2001 to August 2013, the data is from the St Louis Fed's free online "FRED Economic Data" at research.stlouisfed.org.

Using The US Yield Curve Dynamic Chart.

To run the Dynamic Chart, click on the right arrow of the scroll bar. The movie / animation begins with some background on the yield curve's static features. In the 40-year database we observe:

- four different **shapes**: upward-sloping, downward-sloping, flat, and hump-shaped,
- the overall **level** of the yield curve ranges from low to high, and
- the amount of **curvature** at the short end ranges from a little to a lot.

Keep clicking on the right arrow of the scroll bar and you will get to the section of the Dynamic Chart covering 43 years of US yield curve history. This section shows the yield curve on a month by month basis. For example, the figure below shows the US yield curve in January 1970.

Excel 2013   **FIGURE 12.3 The Yield Curve in January 1970.**

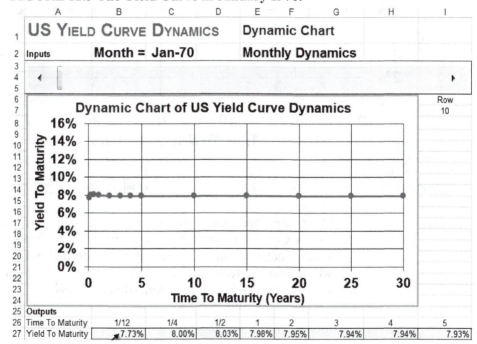

Keep clicking on the right arrow and you will see the yield curve fluctuate over time. By observing this movie / animation, you should be able to recognize the following key **dynamic** properties of the yield curve:

- short rates (the 0 to 5 year piece of the yield curve) are more volatile than long rates (the 15 to 30 year piece),

- the overall volatility of the yield curve is higher when the level is higher (especially in the early 80's), and
- sometimes there are sharp reactions to government intervention.

As an example of the latter, consider what happened in 1980. The figure below shows the yield curve in January 1980.

FIGURE 12.4 The Yield Curve in January 1980.

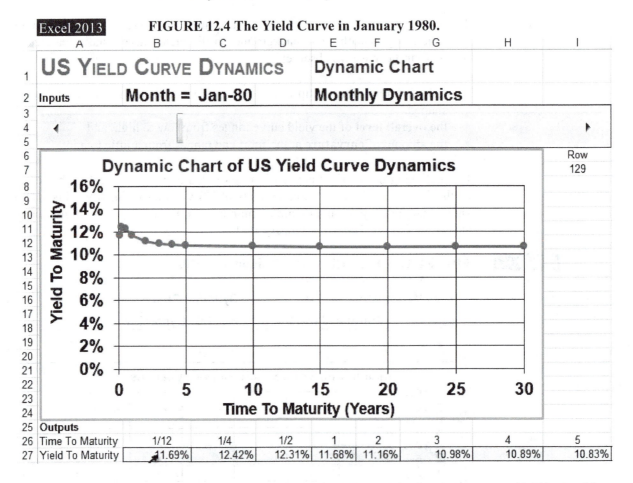

	Time To Maturity	1/12	1/4	1/2	1	2	3	4	5
27	Yield To Maturity	11.69%	12.42%	12.31%	11.68%	11.16%	10.98%	10.89%	10.83%

Short rates were approximately 12% and long rates were at 10.7%. President Jimmy Carter was running for re-election. He wished to manipulate the election year economy to make it better for his re-election bid. His strategy for doing this was to impose credit controls on the banking system. Click on the right arrow to see what the reaction of the financial market was.

FIGURE 12.5 The Yield Curve in March 1980.

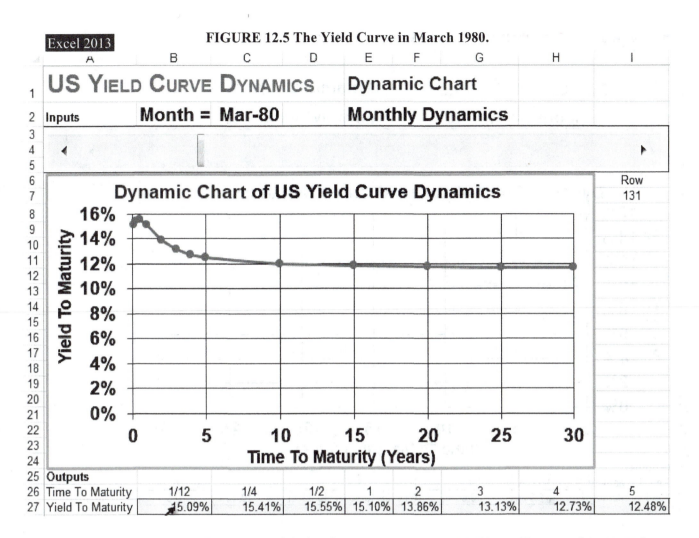

	A	B	C	D	E	F	G	H	I
1	US Yield Curve Dynamics				Dynamic Chart				
2	Inputs	Month = Mar-80			Monthly Dynamics				
6									Row
7									131
25	Outputs								
26	Time To Maturity	1/12	1/4	1/2	1	2	3	4	5
27	Yield To Maturity	15.09%	15.41%	15.55%	15.10%	13.86%	13.13%	12.73%	12.48%

In two months, the short rate went up to 15.5%, an increase of 3.5%! What a disaster! This was the opposite of what Carter intended. Notice that long rates went up to 11.7%, an increase of only 1%. Apparently, the market expected that this intervention would only be a short-lived phenomenon. Carter quickly realized what a big political mistake he had made and announced that the credit controls were being dropped. Click on the right arrow to see what the reaction of the financial market was.

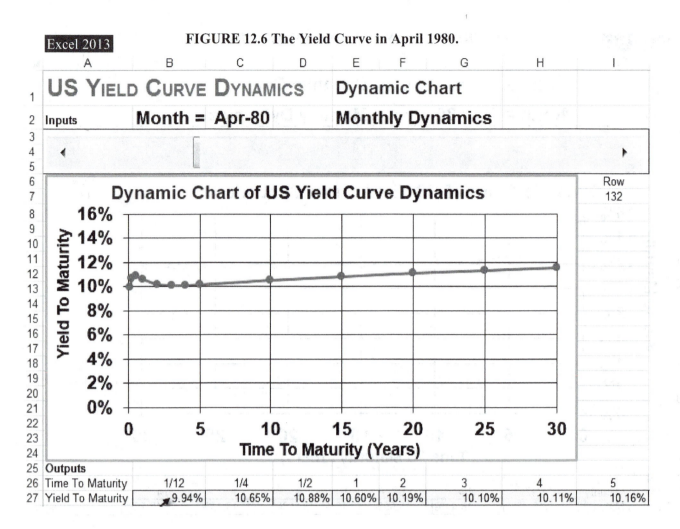

FIGURE 12.6 The Yield Curve in April 1980.

Outputs

Time To Maturity	1/12	1/4	1/2	1	2	3	4	5
Yield To Maturity	9.94%	10.65%	10.88%	10.60%	10.19%	10.10%	10.11%	10.16%

Short rates dropped to 10.9%! A drop of 4.6% in one month! The high interest rates went away, but the political damage was done. This is the single biggest one month change in the yield curve in 43 years.

Problems

1. How volatile are short rates versus medium rates versus long rates?

   (a.) Get a visual sense of the answer to this question by clicking on the right arrow of the scroll bar to run through all of the years of US Yield Curve history in the database.

   (b.) Calculate the variance of the time series of: (i) one-month yields, (ii) five-year yields, (iii) fifteen-year yields, and (iv) thirty-year yields. Use Excel's VAR function to calculate the variance of the yields in columns **T, AA, AD,** and **AG.**

2. Determine the relationship between the volatility of the yield curve and the level of the yield curve. Specifically, for each five year time period (70-74, 75-79, 80-84, etc.) calculate the variance and the average level of the time

series of: (i) one-month yields, (ii) five-year yields, (iii) fifteen-year yields, and (iv) thirty-year yields. Use Excel's VAR and AVERAGE functions to calculate the variance and the average of five-year ranges of the yields in columns **T**, **AA**, **AD**, and **AG**. For example:

o   The 70-74 time series of one-month yields is in the range **T11-T69**.
o   The 75-79 time series of one-month yields is in the range **T70-T129**.
o   The 80-84 time series of one-month yields is in the range **T130-T189**.
o   And so on.

Summarize what you have learned from this analysis.

PART 3 CAPITAL STRUCTURE

Chapter 13 Capital Structure

13.1 Modigliani-Miller With No Taxes

Problem. For a particular firm, the value of its debt is $1,300 and the value of its equity is $1,800. Given the firm's risk exposure, the unlevered cost of equity capital is 11.00%. The cost of debt is 7.00%. Plot the cost of equity, the weighted average cost of capital (WACC), and the cost of debt against the debt / equity ratio.

Solution Strategy. Create a data table with various input values for debt and compute the variables to be plotted.

Results. As the Debt/Equity ratio increases, the Cost of Equity rises, but equity is a smaller fraction of all capital. The net effect is that the weighted average cost of capital (WACC) stays constant. WACC is independent of the Debt/Equity ratio and so is the value of the firm. Thus, in a world without taxes or other frictions, capital structure is irrelevant.

FIGURE 13.1 Capital Structure – Modigliani-Miller With No Taxes.

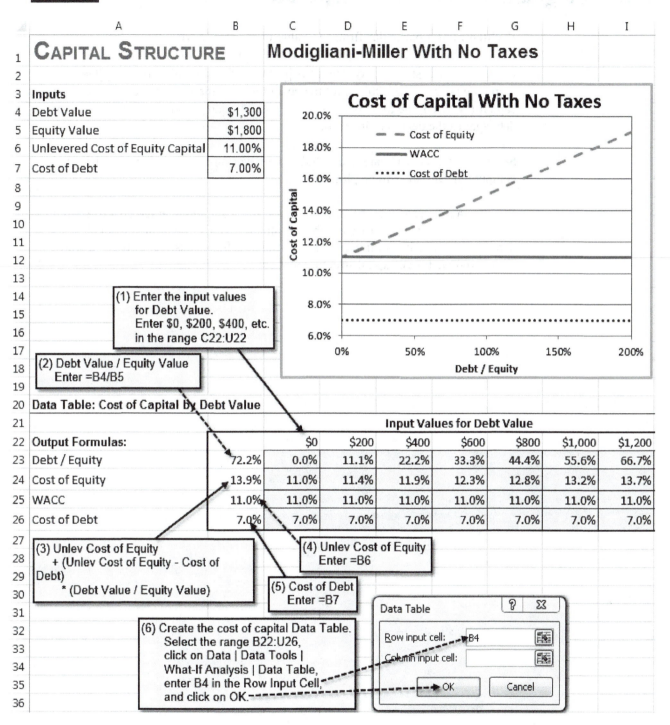

13.2 Modigliani-Miller With Corporate Taxes

Problem. For a particular firm, the value of its debt is $1,300 and the expected free cash flow on all future dates forever is $500. Given the firm's risk exposure, the unlevered cost of equity capital is 11.00%. The cost of debt is 7.00%. The corporate tax rate is 33.00%. Plot the cost of equity, the weighted average cost of capital (WACC), the after-tax unlevered cost of equity, and the after-tax cost of debt against the debt / equity ratio.

Solution Strategy. Create a data table with various input values for debt and compute the variables to be plotted.

Results. As the Debt/Equity ratio increases, the weighted average cost of capital (WACC) decreases due to the debt tax shield. WACC continues to decline as debt increases, so it is optimal to have as much debt as possible. Thus, in a world with corporate taxes, capital structure matters.

Excel 2013

FIGURE 13.2 Capital Structure – Modigliani-Miller With Corporate Taxes.

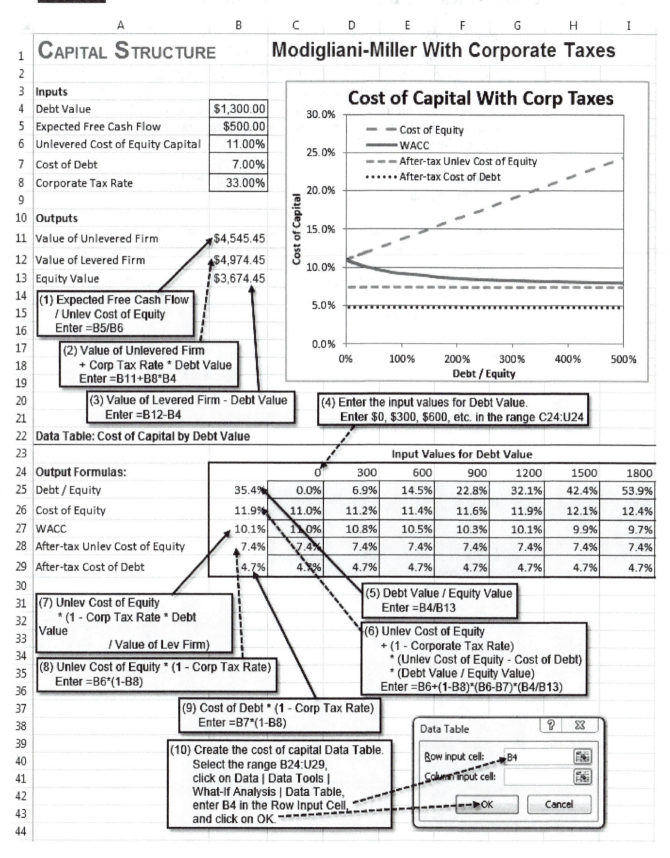

13.3 Trade-off Model: Tax Shield vs. Distress Cost

Problem. For a particular firm, the value of its debt is $\boxed{\$1,300}$ and the expected free cash flow on all future dates forever is $\boxed{\$500}$. Given the firm's risk exposure, the unlevered cost of equity capital is $\boxed{11.00\%}$. The corporate tax rate is $\boxed{33.00\%}$. Distress cost is modeled as a quadratic function – specifically, as $\boxed{0.00008}$ times debt squared. Plot the value of an unlevered firm, the value of a levered firm with a tax shield, and the value of a levered firm with a tax shield and distress cost against the amount of debt.

Solution Strategy. Create a data table with various input values for debt and compute the variables to be plotted.

Results. As the amount of debt increases, the value of a levered firm with a tax shield increases as a linear function of debt. As the amount of debt increases, the value of a levered firm with a tax shield and distress cost is a quadratic function that increases for a while, reaches a peak, and then decreases. Thus, in a world with corporate taxes and distress cost, there is an optimal amount of debt that maximizes firm value.

Excel 2013

FIGURE 13.3 Capital Structure – Trade-Off Model: Tax Shield vs. Distress Cost.

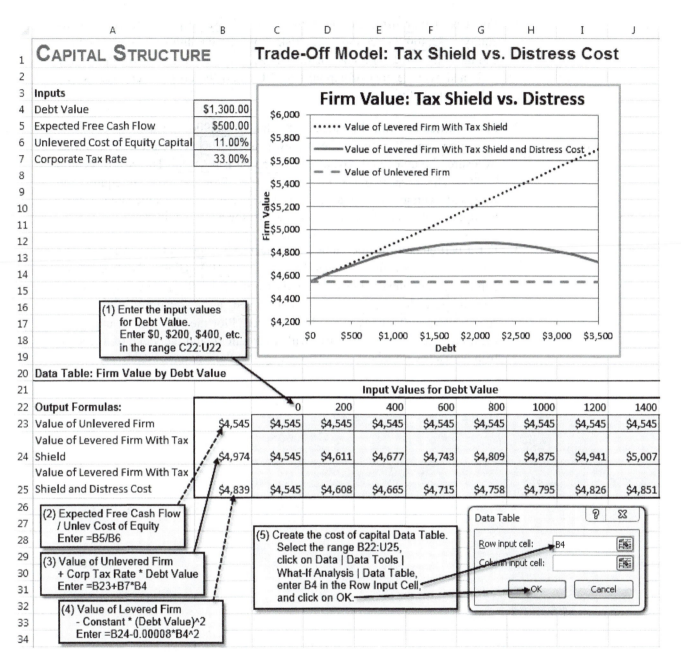

Problems

1. For a particular firm, the value of its debt is $2,900 and the value of its equity is $3,400. Given the firm's risk exposure, the unlevered cost of equity capital is 14.50%. The cost of debt is 8.30%. Plot the cost of equity, the weighted average cost of capital (WACC), and the cost of debt against the debt / equity ratio.

2. For a particular firm, the value of its debt is $2,900 and the expected free cash flow on all future dates forever is $1,100. Given the firm's risk exposure, the unlevered cost of equity capital is 12.80%. The cost of debt is 7.50%. The corporate tax rate is 33.00%. Plot the cost of equity, the weighted average cost of capital (WACC), the after-tax unlevered cost of equity, and the after-tax cost of debt against the debt / equity ratio.

3. For a particular firm, the value of its debt is $2,900 and the expected free cash flow on all future dates forever is $1,100. Given the firm's risk exposure, the unlevered cost of equity capital is 13.90%. The corporate tax rate is 33.00%. Distress cost is modeled as a quadratic function – specifically, as 0.00009 times debt squared. Plot the value of an unlevered firm, the value of a levered firm with a tax shield, and the value of a levered firm with a tax shield and distress cost against the amount of debt.

PART 4 CAPITAL BUDGETING

Chapter 14 Project NPV

14.1 Basics

Problem. Suppose a firm is considering the following project, where all of the dollar figures are in thousands of dollars. In year 0, the project requires an $11,350 investment in plant and equipment, is depreciated using the straight-line method over seven years, and has a salvage value of $1,400 in year 7. The project is forecast to generate sales of 2,000 units in year 1, rising to 7,400 units in year 5, declining to 1,800 units in year 7, and dropping to zero in year 8. The inflation rate is forecast to be 2.0% in year 1, rising to 4.0% in year 5, and then leveling off. The real cost of capital is forecast to be 11.0% in year 1, rising to 12.2% in year 7. The tax rate is forecast to be a constant 35.0%. Sales revenue per unit is forecast to be $9.70 in year 1 and then grow with inflation. Variable cost per unit is forecast to be $7.40 in year 1 and then grow with inflation. Cash fixed costs are forecast to be $5,280 in year 1 and then grow with inflation. What is the project's NPV?

Solution Strategy. Forecast key assumptions, discounting, sales revenue per unit, variable costs per unit, and fixed costs over the seven year horizon. Then, forecast the project income and expense items. Calculate the net cash flows. Discount each cash flow back to the present and sum to get the NPV.

Modeling Issue. The inflation rate is forecast separately and explicitly enters into the calculation of: (1) the discount rate (= cost of capital) and (2) price or cost / unit items. This guarantees that we are *consistent* in the way we are treating the inflation component of cash flows in the numerator of the NPV calculation and the inflation component of the discount rate in the denominator of the NPV calculation. This avoids a common error in practice: people often treat cash flows and discount rates *as if* they were unrelated to each other and thus they are *inconsistent* in the way that they implicitly treat the inflation component of each.

Excel 2013

FIGURE 14.1 Excel Model for Project NPV - Basics.

	A	B	C	D	E	F	G	H	I
1	**PROJECT NPV**	**Basics**							
2	(in thousands of $)								
3		Year 0	Year 1	Year 2	Year 3	Year 4	Year 5	Year 6	Year 7
4	**Key Assumptions**								
5	Unit Sales		2000	4000	5600	6800	7400	3700	1800
6	Inflation Rate		2.0%	2.5%	3.0%	3.5%	4.0%	4.0%	4.0%
7	Real Cost of Capital		11.0%	11.2%	11.4%	11.6%	11.8%	12.0%	12.2%
8	Tax Rate		35.0%	35.0%	35.0%	35.0%	35.0%	35.0%	35.0%
9									
10	**Discounting**								
11	Discount Rate = Cost of Capital		13.2%	14.0%	14.7%	15.5%	16.3%	16.5%	16.7%
12	Cumulative Discount Factor	0.0%	13.2%	29.0%	48.1%	71.0%	98.9%	131.6%	170.3%
13									
14	**Price or Cost / Unit**								
15	Sales Revenue / Unit		$9.70	$9.94	$10.24	$10.60	$11.02	$11.46	$11.92
16	Variable Cost / Unit		$7.40	$7.59	$7.81	$8.09	$8.41	$8.75	$9.10
17	Cash Fixed Costs		$5,280	$5,412	$5,574	$5,769	$6,000	$6,240	$6,490

(1) (1 + Inflation Rate) * (1 + Real Discount Rate) - 1
  Enter =(1+C6)*(1+C7)-1 and copy across

(2) (1 + Last Year's Cumulative Discount Factor)
  * (1 + This Year's Discount Rate) - 1
  Enter =(1+B12)*(1+C11)-1 and copy across

(3) (Last Year's Price/Cost) * (1 + This Year's Inflation Rate)
  Enter =C15*(1+D$6) and copy to the range D15:I17

FIGURE 14.2 Excel Model for Project NPV – Basics (Continued).

	A	B	C	D	E	F	G	H	I
	Excel 2013								
1	**PROJECT NPV**	**Basics**							
2	(in thousands of $)								
3			Year 0	Year 1	Year 2	Year 3	Year 4	Year 5	Year 6	Year 7

(4) (Sales Revenue / Unit) * (Units Sold)
Enter =C15*C5 and copy across

(5) (Variable Costs / Unit) * (Units Sold)
Enter =C16*C5 and copy across

(6) Sales Revenue - Variable Costs
Enter =C43-C44 and copy across

(7) Cash Fixed Costs from above.
Enter =C17 and copy across

(8) (-Investment in Plant & Equipment - Salvage Value)
/ (Number of years to fully depreciate)
Enter =(-$B$58-$I$58)/7 and copy across

(9) Cash Fixed Costs + Depreciation
Enter =C47+C48 and copy across

	A	B	C	D	E	F	G	H	I
42	**Cash Flow Forecasts**								
43	Sales Revenue		$19,400	$39,770	$57,348	$72,075	$81,571	$42,417	$21,461
44	Variable Costs		$14,800	$30,340	$43,750	$54,985	$62,230	$32,359	$16,372
45	Gross Margin		$4,600	$9,430	$13,598	$17,090	$19,342	$10,058	$5,089
46									
47	Cash Fixed Costs		$5,280	$5,412	$5,574	$5,769	$6,000	$6,240	$6,490
48	Depreciation		$1,421	$1,421	$1,421	$1,421	$1,421	$1,421	$1,421
49	Total Fixed Costs		$6,701	$6,833	$6,996	$7,191	$7,422	$7,662	$7,911
50									
51	Operating Profit		($2,101)	$2,597	$6,602	$9,899	$11,920	$2,396	($2,823)
52	Taxes		($736)	$909	$2,311	$3,465	$4,172	$839	($988)
53	Net Profit		($1,366)	$1,688	$4,291	$6,434	$7,748	$1,557	($1,835)
54									
55	Add Back Depreciation		$1,421	$1,421	$1,421	$1,421	$1,421	$1,421	$1,421
56	Operating Cash Flow		$55	$3,109	$5,713	$7,856	$9,169	$2,979	($413)
57									
58	Investment in Plant & Equip	($11,350)							$1,400
59	Cash Flows	($11,350)	$55	$3,109	$5,713	$7,856	$9,169	$2,979	$987
60	Present Value of Each Cash Flow	($11,350)	$49	$2,409	$3,858	$4,593	$4,611	$1,286	$365
61	Net Present Value	$5,822							

(10) Gross Margin - Total Fixed Costs
Enter =C45-C49 and copy across

(15) (Operating Cash Flow)
+ (Investment in Plant & Equip)
Enter =B56+B58 and copy

(11) Operating Profit * Tax Rate
Enter =C51*C8 and copy across

(16) (Cash Flow) / (1 + Cumulative Discount Factor)
Enter =B59/(1+B12) and copy across

(12) Operating Profit - Taxes
Enter =C51-C52 and copy across

(17) Sum of Present Value of Each Cash Flow
Enter =SUM(B60:I60)

(13) Depreciation from above
Enter =C48 and copy across

(14) Net Profit + Add Back Depreciation
Enter =C53+C55 and copy across

The Net Present Value of the project is $5,822. The project should be accepted.

14.2 Forecasting Cash Flows

Problem. Consider the same project as Project NPV - Basics. Let's examine the details of how you forecast the project cash flows. Suppose that Direct Labor, Materials, Selling Expenses, and Other Variable Costs are forecast to be $3.50, $2.00, $1.20, and $0.70, respectively, in year 1 and then grow with inflation. Lease Payment, Property Taxes, Administration, Advertising, and Other cash fixed costs are forecast to be $2,800, $580, $450, $930, and $520, respectively, in year 1 and then grow with inflation. What is the Total Variable Cost / Unit and the Total Cash Fixed Costs?

Solution Strategy. Forecast the variable cost / unit and cash fixed costs in more detail. Then sum up all of the items in each category to get the total.

FIGURE 14.3 Excel Model for Project NPV – Forecasting Cash Flows.

`Excel 2013`

	A	B	C	D	E	F	G	H	I	J
1	PROJECT NPV		Sensitivity Analysis							
2	(in thousands of $)									
3			Year 0	Year 1	Year 2	Year 3	Year 4	Year 5	Year 6	Year 7
4	**Key Assumptions**									
5	Base Case Unit Sales			2000	4000	5600	6800	7400	3700	1800
6	Unit Sales Scale Factor			100.0%						
7	Unit Sales			2000	4000	5600	6800	7400	3700	1800
8	Inflation Rate			2.0%	2.5%	3.0%	3.5%	4.0%	4.0%	4.0%
9	Real Cost of Capital Increment				0.2%	0.4%	0.6%	0.8%	1.0%	1.2%
10	Real Cost of Capital			11.0%	11.2%	11.4%	11.6%	11.8%	12.0%	12.2%
11	Tax Rate			35.0%	35.0%	35.0%	35.0%	35.0%	35.0%	35.0%
12										
13	**Discounting**									
14	Discount Rate = Cost of Capital			13.2%	14.0%	14.7%	15.5%	16.3%	16.5%	16.7%
15	Cumulative Discount Factor		0.0%	13.2%	29.0%	48.1%	71.0%	98.9%	131.6%	170.3%
16										
17	**Price or Cost / Unit**									
18	Sales Revenue / Unit			$9.70	$9.94	$10.24	$10.60	$11.02	$11.46	$11.92
19										
20	Variable Costs / Unit:									
21	Direct Labor			$3.50	$3.59	$3.70	$3.82	$3.98	$4.14	$4.30
22	Materials			$2.00	$2.05	$2.11	$2.19	$2.27	$2.36	$2.46
23	Selling Expenses			$1.20	$1.23	$1.27	$1.31	$1.36	$1.42	$1.47
24	Other			$0.70	$0.72	$0.74	$0.76	$0.80	$0.83	$0.86
25	Total Variable Cost / Unit			$7.40	$7.59	$7.81	$8.09	$8.41	$8.75	$9.10
26										
27	Cash Fixed Costs:									
28	Lease Payment			$2,800	$2,870	$2,956	$3,060	$3,182	$3,309	$3,442
29	Property Taxes			$580	$595	$612	$634	$659	$685	$713
30	Administration			$450	$461	$475	$492	$511	$532	$553
31	Advertising			$930	$953	$982	$1,016	$1,057	$1,099	$1,143
32	Other			$520	$533	$549	$568	$591	$615	$639
33	Total Cash Fixed Costs			$5,280	$5,412	$5,574	$5,769	$6,000	$6,240	$6,490
34										

(3) (Last Year's Cost / Unit) * (1 + This Year's Inflation Rate)
Enter =C21*(1+D$8) and copy to the ranges D21:I24 and D28:I32

(4) Sum the components of Variable Cost / Unit
Enter =SUM(C21:C24) and copy across

(5) Sum the components of Cash Fixed Costs
Enter =SUM(C28:C32) and copy across

14.3 Working Capital

Problem. Consider the same project as above. Suppose we add that the project will require working capital in the amount of $0.87 in year 0 for every unit of next year's forecasted sales and this amount will grow with inflation going forward. What is the project NPV?

Excel 2013

FIGURE 14.4 Excel Model for Project NPV – Working Capital.

	A	B	C	D	E	F	G	H	I
1	**PROJECT NPV**	**Sensitivity Analysis**							
2	(in thousands of $)								
3		Year 0	Year 1	Year 2	Year 3	Year 4	Year 5	Year 6	Year 7
43									
44	(7) (This Year's Work Cap / Next Yr Unit Sales)			(6) (Last Year's Work Cap / Next Yr Unit Sales)					
45	* (Next Yr Unit Sales) Enter =B48*C7 and copy across			* (1 + This Year's Inflation Rate) Enter =B48*(1+C$8) and copy across					
46									
47	**Working Capital**								
48	Work Cap / Next Yr Unit Sales	$0.87	$0.89	$0.91	$0.94	$0.97	$1.01	$1.05	$1.09
49	Working Capital	$1,740	$3,550	$5,094	$6,371	$7,176	$3,731	$1,888	$0
50									
51	**Cash Flow Forecasts**								
52	Sales Revenue		$19,400	$39,770	$57,348	$72,075	$81,571	$42,417	$21,461
53	Variable Costs		$14,800	$30,340	$43,750	$54,985	$62,230	$32,359	$16,372
54	Gross Margin		$4,600	$9,430	$13,598	$17,090	$19,342	$10,058	$5,089
55									
56	Cash Fixed Costs		$5,280	$5,412	$5,574	$5,769	$6,000	$6,240	$6,490
57	Depreciation		$1,421	$1,421	$1,421	$1,421	$1,421	$1,421	$1,421
58	Total Fixed Costs		$6,701	$6,833	$6,996	$7,191	$7,422	$7,662	$7,911
59									
60	Operating Profit		($2,101)	$2,597	$6,602	$9,899	$11,920	$2,396	($2,823)
61	Taxes		($736)	$909	$2,311	$3,465	$4,172	$839	($988)
62	Net Profit		($1,366)	$1,688	$4,291	$6,434	$7,748	$1,557	($1,835)
63									
64	Add Back Depreciation		$1,421	$1,421	$1,421	$1,421	$1,421	$1,421	$1,421
65	Operating Cash Flow		$55	$3,109	$5,713	$7,856	$9,169	$2,979	($413)
66									
67	Investment in Working Capital	($1,740)	($1,810)	($1,544)	($1,277)	($805)	$3,444	$1,843	$1,888
68	Investment in Plant & Equip	($11,350)							$1,400
69	Investment Cash Flow	($13,090)	($1,810)	($1,544)	($1,277)	($805)	$3,444	$1,843	$3,288
70									
71	Cash Flows	($13,090)	($1,754)	$1,565	$4,436	$7,051	$12,614	$4,822	$2,875
72	Present Value of Each Cash Flow	($13,090)	($1,549)	$1,213	$2,996	$4,123	$6,343	$2,082	$1,063
73	Net Present Value	$3,180							
74				(8) (Last Year's Working Capital) - (This Year's Working Capital)					
75				Enter =-B49 in cell B67 and					
76				enter =B49-C49 in cell C67 and copy across					
77			(9) (Investment in Working Capital) + (Investment in Plant & Equipment)						
78			Enter =SUM(B67:B68) and copy across						
79									
80	(10) (Operating Cash Flow) + (Investment Cash Flow) Enter =B65+B69 and copy across								
81									

Solution Strategy. Forecast the working capital amount per next year's unit sales. Then multiply by the forecasted unit sales to determine the required working capital each year. Include the investment in working capital to the total investment cash flows and calculate the project NPV.

The Net Present Value of the project drops to $3,180, because of the additional investment in working capital.

14.4 Sensitivity Analysis

Problem. Consider the same project as above. Assume that the product life-cycle of seven years is viewed as a safe bet, but that the scale of demand for the product is highly uncertain. Analyze the sensitivity of the project NPV to the unit sales scale factor and to the cost of capital.

Solution Strategy. Copy the pattern of unit sales in the base case to a new location and multiply this pattern by a scale factor to get the new unit sales scenario. Assume that the real cost of capital is constant. Thus, forecast the future cost of capital by taking the year 1 cost of capital and adding the change in the inflation rate. Create a two-way data table using a range of input values for unit sales scale factor and a range of input values for the year 1 cost of capital. Using the data table results, create a 3-D surface chart.

Excel 2013   **FIGURE 14.5 Excel Model for Sensitivity Analysis.**

	A	B	C	D	E	F	G	H	I
1	**PROJECT NPV**	**Sensitivity Analysis**							
2	(in thousands of $)								
3		Year 0	Year 1	Year 2	Year 3	Year 4	Year 5	Year 6	Year 7
4	**Key Assumptions**								
5	Base Case Unit Sales		2000	4000	5600	6800	7400	3700	1800
6	Unit Sales Scale Factor		100.0%						
7	Unit Sales		2000	4000	5600	6800	7400	3700	1800
8	Inflation Rate		2.0%	2.5%	3.0%	3.5%	4.0%	4.0%	4.0%
9	Real Cost of Capital Increment			0.2%	0.4%	0.6%	0.8%	1.0%	1.2%
10	Real Cost of Capital		11.0%	11.2%	11.4%	11.6%	11.8%	12.0%	12.2%
11	Tax Rate		35.0%	35.0%	35.0%	35.0%	35.0%	35.0%	35.0%
12									
13	**Discounting**								
14	Discount Rate = Cost of Capital		13.2%	14.0%	14.7%	15.5%	16.3%	16.5%	16.7%
15	Cumulative Discount Factor	0.0%	13.2%	29.0%	48.1%	71.0%	98.9%	131.6%	170.3%
16									
17	**Price or Cost / Unit**								
18	Sales Revenue / Unit		$9.70	$9.94	$10.24	$10.60	$11.02	$11.46	$11.92
19									
20	Variable Costs / Unit:								
21	Direct Labor		$3.50	$3.59	$3.70	$3.82	$3.98	$4.14	$4.30
22	Materials		$2.00	$2.05	$2.11	$2.19	$2.27	$2.36	$2.46
23	Selling Expenses		$1.20	$1.23	$1.27	$1.31	$1.36	$1.42	$1.47
24	Other		$0.70	$0.72	$0.74	$0.76	$0.80	$0.83	$0.86
25	Total Variable Cost / Unit		$7.40	$7.59	$7.81	$8.09	$8.41	$8.75	$9.10
26									
27	Cash Fixed Costs:								
28	Lease Payment		$2,800	$2,870	$2,956	$3,060	$3,182	$3,309	$3,442
29	Property Taxes		$580	$595	$612	$634	$659	$685	$713
30	Administration		$450	$461	$475	$492	$511	$532	$553
31	Advertising		$930	$953	$982	$1,016	$1,057	$1,099	$1,143
32	Other		$520	$533	$549	$568	$591	$615	$639
33	Total Cash Fixed Costs		$5,280	$5,412	$5,574	$5,769	$6,000	$6,240	$6,490

34	(1) (Base Case Unit Sales)
35	* (Unit Sales Scale Factor)
36	Enter =C5*$C$6 and copy across
37	
38	(2) (Date 0 Real Cost of Capital) + (Increment on date t)
39	Enter =$C$10+D9 and copy across

FIGURE 14.6 Excel Model for Two-Way Data Table and 3-D Surface Chart.

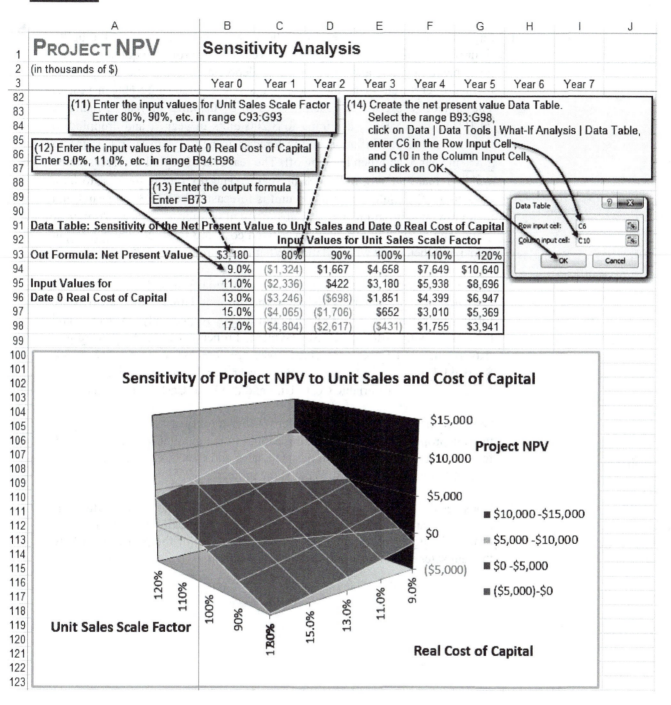

The sensitivity analysis shows that the Project NPV is highly sensitive to the Unit Sales Scale Factor and the Cost of Capital. If the sales forecast is overly optimistic and/or cost of capital estimate is too low, then the project might actually have a negative NPV. Hence, it is worth spending extra resources to verify the accuracy of the sales forecast and the cost of capital estimate.

Problems

1. Suppose a firm is considering the following project, where all of the dollar figures are in thousands of dollars. In year 0, the project requires $37,500 investment in plant and equipment, is depreciated using the straight-line method over seven years, and there is a salvage value of $5,600 in year 7. The project is forecast to generate sales of 5,700 units in year 1, rising to 24,100 units in year 5, declining to 8,200 units in year 7, and dropping to zero in year 8. The inflation rate is forecast to be 1.5% in year 1, rising to 2.8% in year 5, and then leveling off. The real cost of capital is forecast to be 9.3% in year 1, rising to 10.6% in year 7. The tax rate is forecast to be a constant 42.0%. Sales revenue per unit is forecast to be $15.30 in year 1 and then grow with inflation. Variable cost per unit is forecast to be $9.20 in year 1 and then grow with inflation. Cash fixed costs are forecast to be $7,940 in year 1 and then grow with inflation. What is the project's NPV?

2. Consider the same project as problem 1, but modify it as follows. Suppose that Direct Labor, Materials, Selling Expenses, and Other Variable Costs are forecast to be $5.20, $3.70, $2.30, and $0.80, respectively, in year 1 and then grow with inflation. Lease Payment, Property Taxes, Administration, Advertising, and Other cash fixed costs are forecast to be $4,100, $730, $680, $1,120, and $730, respectively, in year 1 and then grow with inflation. What are the Total Variable Cost / Unit and the Total Cash Fixed Costs?

3. Consider the same project as problem 2, but modify it as follows: suppose that the project will require working capital in the amount of $1.23 in year 0 for every unit of next year's forecasted sales and that this amount will grow with inflation going forward. What is the project's NPV?

4. Consider the same project as problem 3. Assume that the product life-cycle of seven years is viewed as a safe bet, but that the scale of demand for the product is highly uncertain. Analyze the sensitivity of the project's NPV to the unit sales scale factor and to the cost of capital.

Chapter 15 Cost-Reducing Project

15.1 Basics

Problem. Suppose a firm is considering a labor-saving investment. In year 0, the project requires a $6,300 investment in equipment (all figures are in thousands of dollars). This investment is depreciated using the straight-line method over five years and has a salvage value in year 5 of $1,200. With or without the cost-reducing investment, all cash flows start in year 1 and end in year 5. The inflation rate is 3.0% in year 2 and declines to 2.0% in year 5. The real growth rate is 16.0% in year 2 and declines to 7.0% in year 5. The tax rate is 38.0% in all years. The real cost of capital is 9.5% in year 1 and declines to 8.9% in year 5. Without the cost-reducing investment, the firm's existing investments will generate year 1 revenue, labor costs, other cash expenses, and depreciation of $11,500, $3,200, $4,500, and $1,800, respectively. With the cost-reducing investment, the firm's year 1 labor costs will be $1,300 and revenues and other cash expenses will remain the same. What is the cost-reducing project's NPV?

Solution Strategy. Forecast revenues and expenses both with and without the cost-reducing investment. Calculate the Net Cash Flow both with and without the cost-reducing investment. Subtract one from the other to obtain the incremental Difference Due to Investment. Discount the project net cash flows back to the present and determine the NPV.

Excel 2013

FIGURE 15.1 Excel Model for Cost-Reducing Project - Basics.

	A	B	C	D	E	F	G	H	I	J
1	**COST-REDUCING PROJECT**			**Basics**						
2	**(in thousands of $)**									
3		Year 0	Year 1	Year 2	Year 3	Year 4	Year 5			
4	**Key Assumptions**									
5	Inflation Rate		3.0%	2.8%	2.5%	2.2%	2.0%			
6	Real Cost of Capital		9.5%	9.3%	9.1%	9.0%	8.9%			
7	Real Growth Rate			16.0%	13.0%	9.0%	7.0%			
8	Tax Rate		38.0%	38.0%	38.0%	38.0%	38.0%			
9										
10	**Discounting**									
11	Discount Rate = Cost of Capital		12.8%	12.4%	11.8%	11.4%	11.1%			
12	Cumulative Discount Factor	0.0%	12.8%	26.7%	41.7%	57.9%	75.4%			
13										
14	**Without Investment**									
15	Revenue		$11,500	$13,714	$15,884	$17,694	$19,311			
16	Labor Costs		$3,200	$3,816	$4,420	$4,924	$5,374			
17	Other Cash Expenses		$4,500	$5,366	$6,215	$6,924	$7,557			
18	Gross Margin		$3,800	$4,531	$5,249	$5,847	$6,381			
19										
20	Depreciation		$1,800	$1,800	$1,800	$1,800	$1,800			
21	Pretax Profit		$2,000	$2,731	$3,449	$4,047	$4,581			
22										
23	Income Taxes		$760	$1,038	$1,310	$1,538	$1,741			
24	After-tax Profit		$1,240	$1,693	$2,138	$2,509	$2,840			
25										
26	Add Back Depreciation		$1,800	$1,800	$1,800	$1,800	$1,800			
27	Cash Flows		$3,040	$3,493	$3,938	$4,309	$4,640			

(1) (1 + Inflation Rate) *
(1 + Real Discount Rate) - 1
Enter =(1+C5)*(1+C6)-1
and copy across

(2) (1 + Last Year's Cumulative
Discount Factor) *
(1 + This Year's Discount Rate)
- 1
Enter =(1+B12)*(1+C11)-1
and copy across

(3) (Last Year's Revenue/Exp)
* (1 + Inflation Rate)
* (1 + Real Growth Rate)
Enter =C15*(1+D$5)*(1+D$7)
and copy to the range D15:G17

(7) Operating Income * Tax Rate
Enter =C21*C$8 and copy across

(8) Pretax Profit - Income Taxes
Enter =C21-C23 and copy across

(9) Depreciation from above
Enter =C20 and copy across

(10) After-tax Profit + Add Back Depreciation
Enter =C24+C26 and copy across

(4) Revenue - (Labor Costs) - (Other Cash Expenses)
Enter =C15-C16-C17 and copy across

(5) Depreciation is constant due to the
use of the straight line method
Enter =C20 and copy across

(6) (Gross Margin) - Depreciation
Enter =C18-C20 and copy across

FIGURE 15.2 Excel Model for Cost-Reducing Project – Basics (Continued).

`Excel 2013`

	A	B	C	D	E	F	G
1	**COST-REDUCING PROJECT**			**Basics**			
2	**(in thousands of $)**						
3			Year 0	Year 1	Year 2	Year 3	Year 4	Year 5

(11) Set "With Investment" formulas = "Without Investment" formulas
Copy the range C15:G27 to the cell C45

(12) Change "With Investment" Labor Costs Enter 1300

(13) "Without Investment" Depreciation +(-New Investment - Salvage Value) / (Number of Years to Depreciate) Enter =C20+(-$B$61-$G$61)/5

	A	B	C	D	E	F	G
44	**With Investment**						
45	Revenue		$11,500	$13,714	$15,884	$17,694	$19,311
46	Labor Costs		$1,300	$1,550	$1,796	$2,000	$2,183
47	Other Cash Expenses		$4,500	$5,366	$6,215	$6,924	$7,557
48	Gross Margin		$5,700	$6,797	$7,873	$8,770	$9,572
49							
50	Depreciation		$2,820	$2,820	$2,820	$2,820	$2,820
51	Pretax Profit		$2,880	$3,977	$5,053	$5,950	$6,752
52							
53	Income Taxes		$1,094	$1,511	$1,920	$2,261	$2,566
54	After-tax Profit		$1,786	$2,466	$3,133	$3,689	$4,186
55							
56	Add Back Depreciation		$2,820	$2,820	$2,820	$2,820	$2,820
57	Cash Flows		$4,606	$5,286	$5,953	$6,509	$7,006
58							
59	**Project Difference**						
60	Difference Due to Investment		$1,566	$1,792	$2,015	$2,200	$2,366
61	Investment and Salvage Value	($6,300)					$1,200
62	Project Cash Flows	($6,300)	$1,566	$1,792	$2,015	$2,200	$3,566
63	Present Value of Each Cash Flow	($6,300)	$1,388	$1,414	$1,422	$1,394	$2,033
64	Project Net Present Value	$1,351					

(14) With Investment Cash Flows
- Without Investment Cash Flows
Enter =C57-C27 and copy across

(15) (Difference Due to Investment) + (Investment and Salvage Value) Enter =B60+B61 and copy across

(16) (Cash Flow) / (1 + Cumulative Discount Factor) Enter =B62/(1+B12) and copy across

(17) Sum of Present Value of Cash Flows Enter =SUM(B63:G63)

The Net Present Value of this Cost-reducing Project is $1,351. The project should be accepted.

15.2 Sensitivity Analysis

Problem. For the same cost-reducing project as the previous section, analyze the sensitivity of the Project's NPV to the assumed With Investment Labor Costs.

Solution Strategy. Create a Data Table using With Investment Labor Costs as the input variable and Project NPV as the output variable. Then graph the relationship.

FIGURE 15.3 Excel Model for Cost-Reducing Project - Sensitivity Analysis.

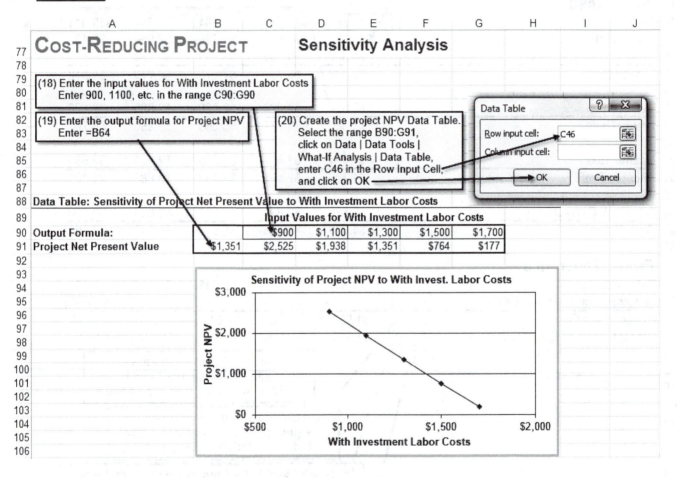

The sensitivity analysis indicates that the Project NPV is not very sensitive to a wide range of values of With Investment Labor Costs. In all cases the project has a positive NPV. This provides confidence that the project's positive NPV is robust to any reasonable error in estimating the labor cost savings.

Problems

1. Suppose a firm is considering a labor-saving investment. In year 0, the project requires a $11,700 investment in equipment (all figures are in thousands of dollars). This investment is depreciated using the straight-line method over five years and there is salvage value in year 5 of $4,500. With or without the cost-reducing investment, all cash flows start in year 1 and end in year 5. The inflation rate is 2.6% in year 2 and declines to 1.4% in year 5. The real growth rate is 21.3% in year 2 and declines to 9.5% in year 5. The tax rate is 41.0% in all years. The real cost of capital is 8.7% in year 1 and declines to 7.5% in year 5. Without the cost-reducing investment, the firm's existing investments will generate year 1 revenue, labor costs, other cash expenses, and depreciation of $15,200, $4,100, $5,300, and $3,300, respectively. With the cost-reducing investment, the firm's year 1 labor costs will be $1,600 and revenues and other cash expenses will remain the same. What is the cost-reducing project's NPV?

2. For the same cost-reducing project as problem 1, analyze the sensitivity of the Project NPV to the assumed With Investment Labor Costs.

Chapter 16 Break-Even Analysis

16.1 Based On Accounting Profit

Problem. A project has a fixed cost of $30,000, variable costs of $4.00 per unit, and generates sales revenue of $6.00 per unit. What is the break-even point in unit sales, where accounting profit exactly equals zero, and what is the intuition for it?

Solution Strategy. First, we solve for the break-even point in unit sales using the formula. Second, we use Excel's Solver to back solve for the break-even point using the income statement. Lastly, we will determine the sensitivity of costs, revenues, and accounting profits to unit sales. This will allow us to graphically illustrate the intuition of the break-even point.

FIGURE 16.1 Excel Model for Break-Even Analysis - Based On Acct Profit.

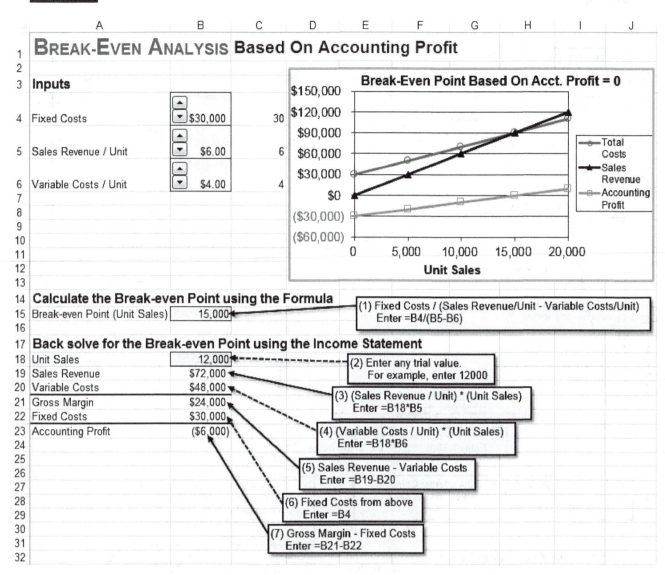

The formula and the graph show that the Break-Even Point is 15,000 units. The graph illustrates two equivalent intuitions for this result. First, the Break-Even Point is where the Sales Revenue line (in blue) crosses Total Costs line (in red). Second, the Break-Even Point is where Accounting Profit (in orange) hits zero and thus decisively switches from negative to positive.

Excel 2013

FIGURE 16.2 Excel Model for Break-Even Analysis - Based On Acct Profit.

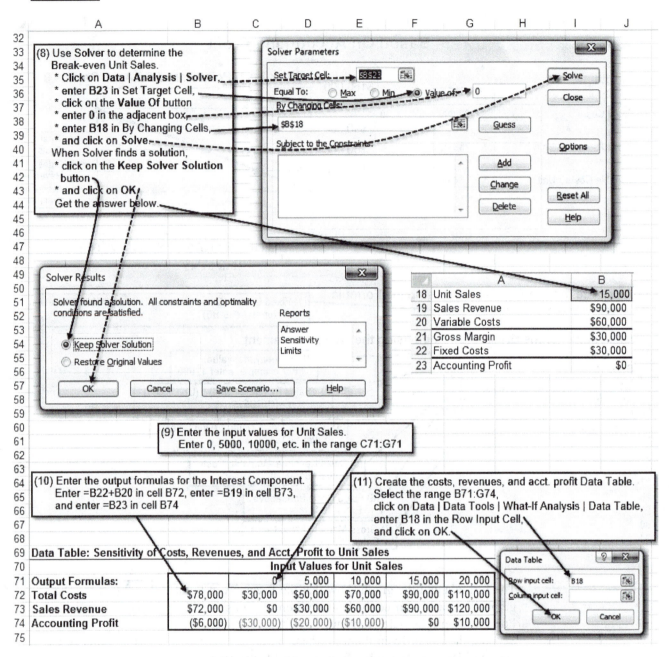

Excel 2007 Equivalent

To install Solver in Excel 2007, click on ⬤, click on 📄 Excel Options at the bottom of the drop-down window, click on **Add-Ins**, highlight **Solver** in the list of Inactive Applications, click on **Go**, check **Solver**, and click on **OK**.

If you don't see **Solver** on the **Data** Tab in the **Analysis** Group, then you need to install the Solver. To install Solver, click on **File**, click on **Options**, click on **Add-Ins**, highlight **Solver** in the list of Inactive Applications, click on **Go** near the bottom of the dialog box, check **Solver**, and click on **OK**.

By trial and error, the Solver adjusts the value of Unit Sales in cell **B18** until the Accounting Profit in cell **B23** equals zero (within a very small error tolerance). This results in a Break-even Point of 15,000, where Accounting Profit equals zero. Your results may differ by a slight amount depending on the level of precision specified for Solver's error tolerance.

16.2 Based On NPV

Problem. Suppose a firm is considering the following project, where all of the dollar figures are in thousands of dollars. In year 0, the project requires $11,350 investment in plant and equipment, is depreciated using the straight-line method over seven years, and has a salvage value of $1,400 in year 7. The project is forecast to generate sales of 2,100 units in year 1 and grow at a sales growth rate of 55.0% in year 2. The sales growth rate is forecast to decline by 15.0% in years 3 and 4, to decline by 20.0% in year 5, to decline by 25.0% in year 6, and to decline by 30.0% in year 7. Unit sales will drop to zero in year 8. The inflation rate is forecast to be 2.0% in year 1, rising to 4.0% in year 5, and then leveling off. The real cost of capital is forecast to be 11.0% in year 1, rising to 12.2% in year 5, and then leveling off. The tax rate is forecast to be a constant 35.0%. Sales revenue per unit is forecast to be $9.70 in year 1 and then to grow with inflation. Variable cost per unit is forecast to be $7.40 in year 1 and then to grow with inflation. Cash fixed costs are forecast to be $5,280 in year 1 and then to grow with inflation. What is the project NPV? What is the NPV Break-Even Point in Year 1 Unit Sales, where NPV equals zero? What is the NPV Break-Even Point in the Year 2 Sales Growth Rate, where NPV equals zero? What is the NPV Break-Even Contour in the two-dimensional space of Year 1 Unit Sales and Year 2 Sales Growth Rate?

Solution Strategy. Start with the Project NPV - Basics Excel model. Move the Unit Sales line out of the Key Assumptions area, since that is what we are going to solve for. Restructure the Unit Sales forecast to depend on the Sales Growth Rate, which will be a key variable. Structure the Sales Growth Rate forecast over the entire period to depend on how fast the growth rate is initially. This will make it easy to use Solver and to create a Data Table later on. Project the cash flows of the project and calculate the NPV. Use Solver to determine the amount of year 1 unit sales that will cause the NPV to equal zero when the sales growth rate is at the base case level of 5% per year. Use Solver to determine the sales growth rate that will cause the NPV to equal zero when the year 1 unit sales is at the base case level of 39,000. Create a two-variable data table using two input variables (year 1 unit sales and sales growth rate) and the output variable: NPV. Use the data table to create a three-dimensional graph showing the NPV Break-Even Contour.

Excel 2013		FIGURE 16.3 Excel Model for Break-Even Analysis Based On NPV.

	A	B	C	D	E	F	G	H	I
1	**BREAK-EVEN ANALYSIS**		**Based On NPV**						
2	(in thousands of $)								
3		Year 0	Year 1	Year 2	Year 3	Year 4	Year 5	Year 6	Year 7
4	**Key Assumptions**								
5	Sales Growth Rate			55.0%	40.0%	25.0%	5.0%	-20.0%	-50.0%
6	Change in Sales Growth Rate				-15.0%	-15.0%	-20.0%	-25.0%	-30.0%
7	Inflation Rate		2.0%	2.5%	3.0%	3.5%	4.0%	4.0%	4.0%
8	Real Cost of Capital		11.0%	11.2%	11.4%	11.6%	11.8%	12.0%	12.2%
9	Tax Rate		35.0%	35.0%	35.0%	35.0%	35.0%	35.0%	35.0%
10									
11	**Discounting**								
12	Discount Rate = Cost of Capital		13.2%	14.0%	14.7%	15.5%	16.3%	16.5%	16.7%
13	Cumulative Discount Factor	0.0%	13.2%	29.0%	48.1%	71.0%	98.9%	131.6%	170.3%
14									
15	**Price or Cost / Unit**								
16	Unit Sales		2,100	3255	4557	5696	5981	4785	2392
17	Sales Revenue / Unit		$9.70	$9.94	$10.24	$10.60	$11.02	$11.46	$11.92
18	Variable Cost / Unit		$7.40	$7.59	$7.81	$8.09	$8.41	$8.75	$9.10
19	Cash Fixed Costs		$5,280	$5,412	$5,574	$5,769	$6,000	$6,240	$6,490
20									
21-23		(2) (Unit Sales on date t-1) * (1 + Unit Sales Growth Rate) Enter =C16*(1+D5) and copy across				(1) (Sales Growth Rate on date t-1) + (Change in Sales Growth Rate on date t) Enter =D5+E6 and copy across			
24	**Cash Flow Forecasts**								
25	Sales Revenue		$20,370	$32,363	$46,667	$60,376	$65,930	$54,854	$28,524
26	Variable Costs		$15,540	$24,689	$35,602	$46,060	$50,297	$41,847	$21,761
27	Gross Margin		$4,830	$7,674	$11,065	$14,316	$15,633	$13,007	$6,763
28									
29	Cash Fixed Costs		$5,280	$5,412	$5,574	$5,769	$6,000	$6,240	$6,490
30	Depreciation		$1,421	$1,421	$1,421	$1,421	$1,421	$1,421	$1,421
31	Total Fixed Costs		$6,701	$6,833	$6,996	$7,191	$7,422	$7,662	$7,911
32									
33	Operating Profit		($1,871)	$840	$4,070	$7,125	$8,211	$5,345	($1,148)
34	Taxes		($655)	$294	$1,424	$2,494	$2,874	$1,871	($402)
35	Net Profit		($1,216)	$546	$2,645	$4,631	$5,337	$3,474	($746)
36									
37	Add Back Depreciation		$1,421	$1,421	$1,421	$1,421	$1,421	$1,421	$1,421
38	Operating Cash Flow		$205	$1,968	$4,067	$6,053	$6,759	$4,896	$675
39									
40	Investment in Plant & Equip	($11,350)							$1,400
41	Cash Flows	($11,350)	$205	$1,968	$4,067	$6,053	$6,759	$4,896	$2,075
42	Present Value of Each Cash Flow	($11,350)	$181	$1,525	$2,746	$3,539	$3,399	$2,114	$768
43	Net Present Value	$2,921							

The project NPV is $2,921 and should be accepted. But how sure are you of this result? How sensitive is this result to small changes in the assumptions? The Break-Even Point gives you an idea of the robustness of this result.

FIGURE 16.4 Excel Model for Break-Even Analysis Based On NPV (Cont.).

	A		B	C	D	E	F	G	H	I	J
1	**BREAK-EVEN ANALYSIS**			**Based On NPV**							
2	(in thousands of $)										
3			Year 0	Year 1	Year 2	Year 3	Year 4	Year 5	Year 6	Year 7	

(3) Use Solver to determine the NPV Break-even in Year 1 Unit Sales.
* Click on Data | Analysis | Solver,
* enter B43 in Set Target Cell,
* click on the **Value Of** button
* enter 0 in the adjacent box,
* enter C16 in By Changing Cells,
* and click on Solve.
When Solver finds a solution,
* click on the **Keep Solver Solution** button
* and click on OK.

Solver Parameters

Set Target Cell: `$B$43`
Equal To: ○ Max ○ Min ● Value of: `0`
By Changing Cells:
`$C$16`
Subject to the Constraints:

[Solve] [Close] [Guess] [Options] [Add] [Change] [Delete] [Reset All] [Help]

(4) Use Solver to determine the NPV Break-even in Sales Growth Rate.
* Reset cell C16 by entering 2100
* Click on Data | Analysis | Solver,
* enter B43 in Set Target Cell,
* click on the **Value Of** button
* enter 0 in the adjacent box,
* enter D5 in By Changing Cells,
* and click on Solve.
When Solver finds a solution,
* click on the **Keep Solver Solution** button
* and click on OK.

Solver Results

Solver found a solution. All constraints and optimality conditions are satisfied.

Reports
Answer
Sensitivity
Limits

● Keep Solver Solution
○ Restore Original Values

[OK] [Cancel] [Save Scenario...] [Help]

By trial and error, the Solver adjusts the value of the Year 1 Unit Sales in cell **C16** until the Net Present Value in cell **B40** equals zero (within a very small error tolerance). This results in a NPV Break-Even Point in Year 1 Unit Sales (shown in cell **C16**) of 1,875.

By trial and error, the Solver adjusts the value of the Sales Growth Rate in cell **D5** until the Net Present Value in cell **B40** equals zero. This results in a NPV Break-Even Point in Sales Growth Rate (shown in cell **D5**) of 50.1%.

FIGURE 16.5 Two Way Data Table and 3D Graph.

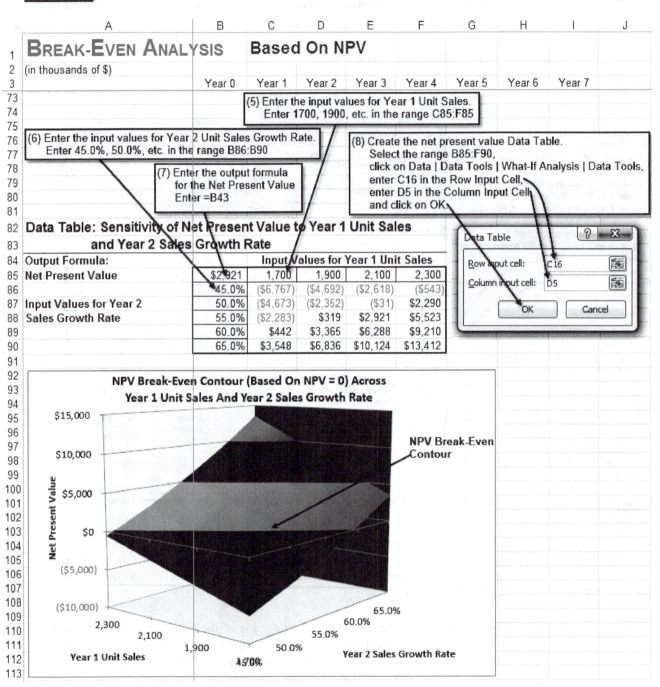

The 3-D Graph shows the Net Present Value of the project for combinations of Year 1 Unit Sales and Year 2 Sales Growth Rate. The multi-color surface illustrates various ranges of NPV. In the top corner, the blue color is for NPV > $10,000. Below it, a dark purple section is for a NPV of $5,000 to $10,000. And so on. At the intersection of the light green section ($0 to $5,000) and the red section (-$5,000 to $0) is a contour highlighted by the arrow. This is the NPV Break-Even Contour, where NPV = 0. Every point on this contour represents a combination of Year 1 Unit Sales and Year 2 Sales Growth Rate for which the

NPV = 0. The 3-D Graph shows that the project's positive NPV is *very sensitive*. If the Year 1 Unit Sales are a little bit lower than assumed or if the year 2 Sales Growth Rate is a little bit lower than assumed, then the whole project could have a negative NPV.

Problems

1. A project has a fixed cost of $73,000, variable costs of $9.20 per unit, and generates sales revenue of $15.40 per unit. What is the break-even point in unit sales, where accounting profit exactly equals zero, and what is the intuition for it?

2. Suppose a firm is considering the following project, where all of the dollar figures are in thousands of dollars. In year 0, the project requires $24,490 investment in plant and equipment, is depreciated using the straight-line method over seven years, and has a salvage value of $5,800 in year 7. The project is forecast to generate sales of 4,800 units in year 1 and grow at a sales growth rate of 72.0% in year 2. The sales growth rate is forecast to decline by 12.0% in years 3, to decline by 15.0% in year 4, to decline by 18.0% in year 5, to decline by 23.0% in year 6, to decline by 29.0% in year 7. Unit sales will drop to zero in year 8. The inflation rate is forecast to be 2.7% in year 1 and rising to 3.5% in year 7. The real cost of capital is forecast to be 10.2% in year 1, rising to 11.9% in year 7. The tax rate is forecast to be a constant 38.0%. Sales revenue per unit is forecast to be $12.20 in year 1 and then to grow with inflation. Variable cost per unit is forecast to be $7.30 in year 1 and then to grow with inflation. Cash fixed costs are forecast to be $6,740 in year 1 and then to grow with inflation. What is the project's NPV? What is the NPV Break-Even Point in Year 1 Unit Sales, where NPV equals zero? What is the NPV Break-Even Point in the Year 2 Sales Growth Rate, where NPV equals zero? What is the NPV Break-Even Contour in the two-dimensional space of Year 1 Unit Sales and Year 2 Sales Growth Rate?

PART 5 FINANCIAL PLANNING

Chapter 17 Corporate Financial Planning

17.1 Actual

Problem. Construct actual (historical) financial statements for **Cutting Edge B2B Inc.** in preparation for forecasting their financial statements.

Solution Strategy. Enter actual values in the yellow input sections. Enter appropriate additions and subtractions to complete the Income Statement and Balance sheet. Then calculate the Key Assumptions over the actual years.

Excel 2013

FIGURE 17.1 Actual Income Statement for Cutting Edge B2B Inc.

	A	B	C	D	E	F	G	H	I
1	CORPORATE FINANCIAL PLANNING				Actual				
2	Cutting Edge B2B Inc.	2010	2011	2012	2013	2014	2015	2016	Ave Hist.
3	Financial Plan	Actual	Actual	Actual	Actual	Forecast	Forecast	Forecast	% of Sales
24									
25	(1) Sales - Cost of Goods Sold								
26	Enter =B34-B35 and copy across								
27									
28	(2) Gross Margin								
29	- SG&A Expense								
30	- Depreciation								
31	Enter =B36-B38-B39								
32	and copy across								
33	Income Statement (Mil.$)								
34	Sales	$73.84	$93.28	$115.93	$138.84				
35	Cost of Goods Sold	$41.83	$58.39	$75.49	$89.83				
36	Gross Margin	$32.01	$34.89	$40.44	$49.01				
37									
38	Selling, Gen & Adm Expenses	$6.58	$7.28	$8.56	$10.21				
39	Depreciation	$5.91	$6.37	$7.31	$9.86				
40	EBIT	$19.52	$21.24	$24.57	$28.94				
41									
42	Interest Expense	$4.76	$5.23	$6.69	$8.88				
43	Taxes	$6.21	$6.96	$7.52	$7.60				
44	Net Income	$8.55	$9.05	$10.36	$12.46				
45	Shares Outstanding (Millions)	39.60	40.36	44.93	53.91				
46	Earnings Per Share	$0.22	$0.22	$0.23	$0.23				
47									
48	Allocation of Net Income:								
49	Dividends	$2.90	$3.17	$3.63	$4.36				
50	Change in Equity	$5.65	$5.88	$6.73	$8.10				
51									
52	(3) EBIT - Interest Expense		(4) Net Income						
53	- Taxes		/ Shares Outstanding						
54	Enter =B40-B42-B43		Enter =B44/B45						
55	and copy across		and copy across						
56	(5) Net Income - Dividends								
57	Enter =B44-B49 and copy across								

FIGURE 17.2 Actual Balance Sheet for Cutting Edge B2B Inc.

	A	B	C	D	E	F	G	H	I	J
1	**CORPORATE FINANCIAL PLANNING**				**Actual**					
2	**Cutting Edge B2B Inc.**	2010	2011	2012	2013	2014	2015	2016	Ave Hist.	
3	**Financial Plan**	Actual	Actual	Actual	Actual	Forecast	Forecast	Forecast	% of Sales	
60										
61	(6) Sum of all Current Assets									
62	Enter =SUM(B71:B73)									
63	and copy across									
64										
65	(7) Property, Plant & Equipment		(8) Total Current Assets							
66	- Accumulated Depreciation		+ Net PPE							
67	Enter =B76-B77 and copy across		Enter =B74+B78							
68	**Balance Sheet (Mil.$)**		and copy across							
69	**Assets**									
70	Current Assets									
71	Cash & Equivalents	$4.27	$6.38	$7.62	$8.83					
72	Receivables	$20.58	$24.39	$28.77	$34.11					
73	Inventories	$26.73	$30.45	$36.75	$43.27					
74	Total Current Assets	$51.58	$61.22	$73.14	$86.21					
75										
76	Property, Plant & Equip. (PP	$331.64	$423.92	$503.87	$613.28					
77	Accumulated Depreciation	$98.72	$105.09	$112.40	$122.26					
78	Net PPE	$232.92	$318.83	$391.47	$491.02					
79										
80	Total Assets	$284.50	$380.05	$464.61	$577.23					
81	(12) Total Liabilities and		(13) Accounts Payable + Short-term Debt							
82	Shareholders' Equity		Enter =B88+B89 and copy across							
83	- Total Shareholders' Equity									
84	Enter =B100-B98		(14) Total Liabilities							
85	and copy across		- Total Current Liabilities							
86	**Liabilities and Shareholders' Equity**		Enter =B93-B90							
87	Current Liabilities		and copy across							
88	Accounts Payable	$31.83	$62.43	$83.84	$94.41					
89	Short-term Debt	$30.86	$43.03	$64.85	$79.49					
90	Total Current Liabilities	$62.69	$106.46	$148.69	$173.90					
91										
92	Long-term Debt	$40.00	$45.90	$51.50	$70.81					
93	Total Liabilities	$102.69	$152.36	$200.19	$244.71					
94										
95	Shareholders' Equity									
96	Paid-in Capital	$90.00	$130.00	$160.00	$220.00					
97	Retained Earnings	$91.81	$97.69	$104.42	$112.52					
98	Total Shareholders' Equity	$181.81	$227.69	$264.42	$332.52					
99										
100	Total Liab. & Share. Equity	$284.50	$380.05	$464.61	$577.23					
101										
102	Debt / (Debt + Equity)	28.0%	28.1%	30.6%	31.1%					
103	Market Price / Share	$6.21	$6.57	$6.68	$6.71					
104	External Funds Needed		$58.07	$57.42	$93.95					
105		(9) Total Assets				(15) (Short-term Debt + Long-term Debt)				
106		Enter =B80				/ (Short-term Debt + Long-term Debt				
107		and copy across				+ Total Shareholders' Equity)				
108						Enter =(B89+B92)/(B89+B92+B98) and copy across				
109	(10) (Retained Earnings on date t-1)		(11) Paid-in Capital							
110	+ (Change in Equity)		+ Retained Earnings		(16) (Increase in Total Assets)					
111	Enter =B97+C50		Enter =B96+B97		- (Increase in Retained Earnings)					
112	and copy across		and copy across		- (Increase in Accounts Payable)					
113					Enter =(C80-B80)-(C97-B97)-(C88-B88)					
114					and copy across					

FIGURE 17.3 Actual Key Assumptions for Cutting Edge B2B Inc.

	A	B	C	D	E	F	G	H	I	J
1	CORPORATE FINANCIAL PLANNING				Actual					
2	Cutting Edge B2B Inc.	2010	2011	2012	2013	2014	2015	2016	Ave Hist.	
3	Financial Plan	Actual	Actual	Actual	Actual	Forecast	Forecast	Forecast	% of Sales	
4	Key Assumptions									
5	Sales Growth Rate		26.3%	24.3%	19.8%					
6	Tax Rate	42.1%	43.5%	42.1%	37.9%					
7	Int Rate on Short-Term Debt	6.5%	6.7%	6.9%	7.1%					
8	Int Rate on Long-Term Debt	7.7%	7.9%	8.1%	8.3%					
9	Dividend Payout Rate	33.9%	35.0%	35.0%	35.0%					
10	Price / Earnings	28.8	29.3	29.0	29.0					
11										
12										
13										
14										
15										
16										
17										
18										
19										
20										
21										

(17) (Sales (date t) - Sales (date t-1)) / Sales (date t-1)
Enter =(C34-B34)/B34 and copy across

(18) Taxes / (Before-tax Income) = Taxes / (EBIT - Interest Expense)
Enter =B43/(B40-B42) and copy across

(19) Dividend Payout Rate = Dividends / Net Income
Enter =B49/B44 and copy across

(20) Price / Earnings = (Market Price per Share) / (Earnings per Share)
Enter =B103/B46 and copy across

Now you are ready to forecast the financial statements.

17.2 Forecast

Problem. Given actual financial statements for **Cutting Edge B2B Inc.**, forecast their financial statements for the next three years. Explore the impact of the financing *choice variables*: debt or equity.

Solution Strategy. Analyze the historical financial statements to determine which income statement and balance sheet items are close to being a constant percentage of sales and which items are not. Then, forecast sales as accurately as possible. Then, apply the average historical percentage of sales to generate most of the income statement and balance sheet items. Forecast other key assumptions to generate most of the rest and work out the implications for additional financing. Make the Balance Sheet balance by calculating long-term debt as the plug item. Raise (or lower) the portion of equity relative to the portion of debt by raising (or lowering) paid-in capital.

FIGURE 17.4 Forecast % of Sales for Cutting Edge B2B Inc.

	A	B	C	D	E	F	G	H	I	J
1	**CORPORATE FINANCIAL PLANNING**				**Forecast**					
2	**Cutting Edge B2B Inc.**	2010	2011	2012	2013	2014	2015	2016	Ave Hist.	
3	**Financial Plan**	Actual	Actual	Actual	Actual	Forecast	Forecast	Forecast	% of Sales	
116	(21) (Each Income Statement item) / Sales					(24) Average of historical (actual) Percent of Sales				
117	Enter =B34/B$34 and copy to the range B121:H137					Enter =AVERAGE(B121:E121) and copy to range I121:I167				
118	Delete ranges that should be blank (B124:H124, etc.)					Delete cells that should be blank (I124, I128, etc.)				
119										
120	**Income Statement (% of Sales)**									
121	Sales	100.0%	100.0%	100.0%	100.0%	100.0%	100.0%	100.0%	100.0%	
122	Cost of Goods Sold	56.6%	62.6%	65.1%	64.7%	62.3%	62.3%	62.3%	62.3%	
123	Gross Margin	43.4%	37.4%	34.9%	35.3%	37.7%	37.7%	37.7%	37.7%	
124										
125	Selling, Gen & Adm Expenses	8.9%	7.8%	7.4%	7.4%	7.9%	7.9%	7.9%	7.9%	
126	Depreciation	8.0%	6.8%	6.3%	7.1%	7.1%	7.1%	7.1%	7.1%	
127	EBIT	26.4%	22.8%	21.2%	20.8%	22.8%	22.8%	22.8%	22.8%	
128										
129	Interest Expense	6.4%	5.6%	5.8%	6.4%	7.1%	6.8%	6.7%	6.1%	
130	Taxes	8.4%	7.5%	6.5%	5.5%	6.3%	6.4%	6.4%	7.0%	
131	Net Income	11.6%	9.7%	8.9%	9.0%	9.5%	9.6%	9.6%	9.8%	
132	Shares Outstanding (Millions)	53.6%	43.3%	38.8%	38.8%	37.2%	35.8%	34.2%	43.6%	
133	Earnings Per Share	0.3%	0.2%	0.2%	0.2%	0.2%	0.1%	0.1%	0.2%	
134										
135	Allocation of Net Income:									
136	Dividends	3.9%	3.4%	3.1%	3.1%	3.3%	3.4%	3.4%	3.4%	
137	Change in Equity	7.7%	6.3%	5.8%	5.8%	6.1%	6.3%	6.3%	6.4%	
138										
139	**Balance Sheet (% of Sales)**			(22) (Each Balance Sheet Asset item) / Sales						
140	**Assets**			Enter =B71/B$34 and copy to range B142:H151						
141	Current Assets			Delete ranges that should be blank (B146:H146, etc.)						
142	Cash & Equivalents	5.8%	6.8%	6.6%	6.4%	6.4%	6.4%	6.4%	6.4%	
143	Receivables	27.9%	26.1%	24.8%	24.6%	25.9%	25.9%	25.9%	25.9%	
144	Inventories	36.2%	32.6%	31.7%	31.2%	32.9%	32.9%	32.9%	32.9%	
145	Total Current Assets	69.9%	65.6%	63.1%	62.1%	65.2%	65.2%	65.2%	65.2%	
146										
147	Property, Plant & Equip. (PPE)	449.1%	454.5%	434.6%	441.7%	420.1%	417.6%	416.7%	445.0%	
148	Accum Depreciation	133.7%	112.7%	97.0%	88.1%	83.0%	80.5%	79.6%	107.8%	
149	Net PPE	315.4%	341.8%	337.7%	353.7%	337.1%	337.1%	337.1%	337.1%	
150										
151	Total Assets	385.3%	407.4%	400.8%	415.8%	402.3%	402.3%	402.3%	402.3%	
152				(23) (Each Balance Sheet Liab. & Equity item) / Sales						
153	**Liabilities and Shareholders' Equity**			Enter =B88/B$34 and copy to range B155:H167						
154	Current Liabilities			Delete ranges that should be blank (B158:H158, etc.)						
155	Accounts Payable	43.1%	68.0%	72.3%	68.0%	62.9%	62.9%	62.9%	62.9%	
156	Short-term Debt	41.8%	46.1%	55.9%	57.3%	50.3%	50.3%	50.3%	50.3%	
157	Total Current Liabilities	84.9%	114.1%	128.3%	125.3%	113.1%	113.1%	113.1%	113.1%	
158										
159	Long-term Debt	54.2%	49.2%	44.4%	51.0%	51.7%	50.8%	53.3%	49.7%	
160	Total Liabilities	139.1%	163.3%	172.7%	176.3%	164.9%	164.0%	166.5%	162.8%	
161										
162	Shareholders' Equity									
163	Paid-in Capital	121.9%	139.4%	138.0%	158.5%	161.4%	164.8%	163.4%	139.4%	
164	Retained Earnings	124.3%	104.7%	90.1%	81.0%	76.0%	73.5%	72.5%	100.0%	
165	Total Shareholders' Equity	246.2%	244.1%	228.1%	239.5%	237.4%	238.4%	235.9%	239.5%	
166										
167	Total Liabilities and Equity	385.3%	407.4%	400.8%	415.8%	402.3%	402.3%	402.3%	402.3%	

Excel 2013

Excel 2013 **FIGURE 17.5 Forecast Key Assumptions for Cutting Edge B2B Inc.**

	A	B	C	D	E	F	G	H	I	J
1	CORPORATE FINANCIAL PLANNING					Forecast				
2	**Cutting Edge B2B Inc.**	2010	2011	2012	2013	2014	2015	2016	Ave Hist.	
3	**Financial Plan**	Actual	Actual	Actual	Actual	Forecast	Forecast	Forecast	% of Sales	
4	**Key Assumptions**									
5	Sales Growth Rate		26.3%	24.3%	19.8%	16.0%	13.0%	11.0%		
6	Tax Rate	42.1%	43.5%	42.1%	37.9%	40.0%	40.0%	40.0%		
7	Int Rate on Short-Term Debt	6.5%	6.7%	6.9%	7.1%	7.0%	6.9%	6.8%		
8	Int Rate on Long-Term Debt	7.7%	7.9%	8.1%	8.3%	8.2%	8.1%	8.0%		
9	Dividend Payout Rate	33.9%	35.0%	35.0%	35.0%	35.0%	35.0%	35.0%		
10	Price / Earnings	28.8	29.3	29.0	29.0	29.4	29.4	29.4		

(25) Forecast key assumptions Enter forecast values in the range F5:H10 (done for you)

Excel 2013 **FIGURE 17.6 Forecast Income Statement for Cutting Edge B2B Inc.**

	A	B	C	D	E	F	G	H	I	J
1	CORPORATE FINANCIAL PLANNING					Forecast				
2	**Cutting Edge B2B Inc.**	2010	2011	2012	2013	2014	2015	2016	Ave Hist.	
3	**Financial Plan**	Actual	Actual	Actual	Actual	Forecast	Forecast	Forecast	% of Sales	
22										
23										
24										
25										
26										
27										
28										
29										
30										
31										
32										
33	**Income Statement (Mil.$)**									
34	Sales	$73.84	$93.28	$115.93	$138.84	$161.05	$181.99	$202.01		
35	Cost of Goods Sold	$41.83	$58.39	$75.49	$89.83	$100.28	$113.32	$125.78		
36	Gross Margin	$32.01	$34.89	$40.44	$49.01	$60.77	$68.67	$76.23		
37										
38	Selling, Gen & Adm Expenses	$6.58	$7.28	$8.56	$10.21	$12.66	$14.31	$15.88		
39	Depreciation	$5.91	$6.37	$7.31	$9.86	$11.37	$12.85	$14.26		
40	EBIT	$19.52	$21.24	$24.57	$28.94	$36.74	$41.51	$46.08		
41										
42	Interest Expense	$4.76	$5.23	$6.69	$8.88	$11.37	$12.34	$13.62		
43	Taxes	$6.21	$6.96	$7.52	$7.60	$10.15	$11.67	$12.98		
44	Net Income	$8.55	$9.05	$10.36	$12.46	$15.22	$17.51	$19.48		
45	Shares Outstanding (Millions)	39.60	40.36	44.93	53.91	59.87	65.22	69.02		
46	Earnings Per Share	$0.22	$0.22	$0.23	$0.23	$0.25	$0.27	$0.28		
47										
48	Allocation of Net Income:									
49	Dividends	$2.90	$3.17	$3.63	$4.36	$5.33	$6.13	$6.82		
50	Change in Equity	$5.65	$5.88	$6.73	$8.10	$9.89	$11.38	$12.66		
51										
52										
53										
54										
55										
56										
57										
58										

(26) (Sales on date t-1) * (1 + Sales Growth Rate) Enter =E34*(1+F5) and copy across

(27) (Ave. Hist. Goods Sold / Sales) * Sales Enter =$I122*F$34 and copy across

(28) (Ave. Hist. SG&A / Sales) * Sales Copy cell F35 to the range F38:H39

(29) (Interest Rate on Short-term Debt) * (Prior Year Short-term Debt Amount) + (Interest Rate on Long-term Debt) * (Prior Year Long-term Debt Amount) Enter =F7*E89+F8*E92 and copy across

(30) (EBIT - Interest Expense) * (Tax Rate) Enter =(F40-F42)*F6 and copy across

(31) (Shares Outstanding on date t-1) + (Paid in Capital on date t - Paid in Capital on date t-1) / (Market Price / Share on date t-1) Enter =E45+(F96-E96)/E103 and copy across

(32) (Net Income) * (Dividend Payout Rate) Enter =F44*F9

(33) Net Income - Dividends Enter =F44-F49 and copy across

FIGURE 17.7 Forecast Balance Sheet for Cutting Edge B2B Inc.

Excel 2013									
	A	B	C	D	E	F	G	H	I	J

	A	B	C	D	E	F	G	H	I	J
1	CORPORATE FINANCIAL PLANNING					Forecast				
2	Cutting Edge B2B Inc.	2010	2011	2012	2013	2014	2015	2016	Ave Hist.	
3	Financial Plan	Actual	Actual	Actual	Actual	Forecast	Forecast	Forecast	% of Sales	
60										
61										
62										
63										
64										
65										
66										
67										
68	Balance Sheet (Mil.$)									
69	Assets									
70	Current Assets									
71	Cash & Equivalents	$4.27	$6.38	$7.62	$8.83	$10.29	$11.63	$12.91		
72	Receivables	$20.58	$24.39	$28.77	$34.11	$41.63	$47.05	$52.22		
73	Inventories	$26.73	$30.45	$36.75	$43.27	$53.03	$59.92	$66.52		
74	Total Current Assets	$51.58	$61.22	$73.14	$86.21	$104.95	$118.60	$131.64		
75										
76	Property, Plant & Equip. (PP	$331.64	$423.92	$503.87	$613.28	$676.62	$760.05	$841.81		
77	Accumulated Depreciation	$98.72	$105.09	$112.40	$122.26	$133.63	$146.48	$160.74		
78	Net PPE	$232.92	$318.83	$391.47	$491.02	$542.98	$613.57	$681.07		
79										
80	Total Assets	$284.50	$380.05	$464.61	$577.23	$647.94	$732.17	$812.71		
81										
82										
83										
84										
85										
86	Liabilities and Shareholders' Equity									
87	Current Liabilities									
88	Accounts Payable	$31.83	$63.43	$83.84	$94.41	$101.23	$114.39	$126.98		
89	Short-term Debt	$30.86	$43.03	$64.85	$79.49	$80.98	$91.50	$101.57		
90	Total Current Liabilities	$62.69	$106.46	$148.69	$173.90	$182.21	$205.90	$228.54		
91										
92	Long-term Debt	$40.00	$45.90	$51.50	$70.81	$83.32	$92.48	$107.71		
93	Total Liabilities	$102.69	$152.36	$200.19	$244.71	$265.53	$298.38	$336.26		
94										
95	Shareholders' Equity									
96	Paid-in Capital	$90.00	$130.00	$160.00	$220.00	$260.00	$300.00	$330.00		
97	Retained Earnings	$91.81	$97.69	$104.42	$112.52	$122.41	$133.79	$146.45		
98	Total Shareholders' Equity	$181.81	$227.69	$264.42	$332.52	$382.41	$433.79	$476.45		
99										
100	Total Liab. & Share. Equity	$284.50	$380.05	$464.61	$577.23	$647.94	$732.17	$812.71		
101										
102	Debt / (Debt + Equity)	28.0%	28.1%	30.6%	31.1%	30.1%	29.8%	30.5%		
103	Market Price / Share	$6.21	$6.57	$6.68	$6.71	$7.47	$7.89	$8.30		
104	External Funds Needed		$58.07	$57.42	$93.95	$53.99	$59.69	$55.30		

Annotations:

(34) (Ave. Hist. Current Asset Item / Sales) * Sales
Enter =$I142*F$34 and copy to the range F71:H73

(35) Accumulated Depreciation + Net PPE
Enter =F77+F78 and copy across

(36) Accumulated Depreciation (t-1) + Depreciation
Enter =E77+F39 and copy across

(37) (Ave. Hist. PPE / Sales) * Sales
Copy F71 to the range F78:H78

(38) (Ave. Hist. Liab. & Equity Item / Sales) * Sales
Enter =$I155*F$34 and copy to the range F88:H89

(39) Adjust Paid-in Capital to keep Debt / (Debt + Equity) in row 102 near the target level, which is 30% in this case (done for you)

(40) (Price / Earnings) * (Earnings / Share)
Enter =F10*F46

After all of the forecasting is done, it is important to check Long-term Debt to make sure that it isn't growing explosively or dropping rapidly (perhaps going negative!). If it is going wild, then backtrack to identify the source of sharp up or down movements and check for errors.

The forecast for the next three years is a steady increase in Earnings Per Share from $0.25 to $0.27 to $0.28.

17.3 Cash Flow

Problem. Given historical and forecasted Income Statements and Balance Sheets for **Cutting Edge B2B Inc.**, create the historical and forecasted Cash Flow Statement.

Solution Strategy. Construct the Cash Flow Statement by starting with Net Income from the Income Statement and then picking up the year to year changes from the Balance Sheets.

Excel 2013

FIGURE 17.8 Cash Flows for Cutting Edge B2B Inc.

	A	B	C	D	E	F	G	H	I
1	**CORPORATE FINANCIAL PLANNING**				**Cash Flow**				
2	**Cutting Edge B2B Inc.**	2010	2011	2012	2013	2014	2015	2016	Ave Hist.
3	**Financial Plan**	Actual	Actual	Actual	Actual	Forecast	Forecast	Forecast	% of Sales
170									
171									
172									
173									
174									
175									
176									
177									
178									
179									
180									
181	**Cash Flow Statement (Mil.$)**								
182	Cash Flow From Operating Activities								
183	Net Income		$9.05	$10.36	$12.46	$15.22	$17.51	$19.48	
184	+ Depreciation		$6.37	$7.31	$9.86	$11.37	$12.85	$14.26	
185	- Inc in Accts Receivable		($3.81)	($4.38)	($5.34)	($7.52)	($5.41)	($5.18)	
186	- Inc in Inventories		($3.72)	($6.30)	($6.52)	($9.76)	($6.89)	($6.59)	
187	+ Inc in Accounts Payable		$31.60	$20.41	$10.57	$6.82	$13.16	$12.58	
188	Cash Flow From Operat Act		$39.49	$27.40	$21.03	$16.13	$31.21	$34.55	
189									
190	Cash Flow From Investing Activities								
191	- Invest in Plant and Equip		($92.28)	($79.95)	($109.41)	($63.34)	($83.44)	($81.75)	
192	Cash Flow From Invest Act		($92.28)	($79.95)	($109.41)	($63.34)	($83.44)	($81.75)	
193									
194	Cash Flow From Financing Activities								
195	+ Inc in Long-term Debt		$5.90	$5.60	$19.31	$12.51	$9.17	$15.23	
196	+ Inc in Short-term Debt		$12.17	$21.82	$14.64	$1.49	$10.53	$10.07	
197	+ Inc in Paid in Capital		$40.00	$30.00	$60.00	$40.00	$40.00	$30.00	
198	- Dividends Paid		($3.17)	($3.63)	($4.36)	($5.33)	($6.13)	($6.82)	
199	Cash Flow From Financ Act		$54.90	$53.79	$89.59	$48.67	$53.56	$48.48	
200									
201	Change in Cash and Equiv		$2.11	$1.24	$1.21	$1.46	$1.34	$1.28	
202	Cash and Equiv, Begin of Yr		$4.27	$6.38	$7.62	$8.83	$10.29	$11.63	
203	Cash and Equiv, End of Yr		$6.38	$7.62	$8.83	$10.29	$11.63	$12.91	
204									

Callout boxes:

(41) Net Income from above
Enter =C44 and copy across

(42) Accumulated Depreciation (t) - Accumulated Depreciation (t-1)
Enter =C77-B77 and copy across

(43) - [Receivables (t) - Receivables (t-1)]
Enter =-(C72-B72) and copy across

(44) - [Inventories (t) - Inventories (t-1)]
Enter =-(C73-B73) and copy across

(45) Accounts Payable (t) - Accounts Payable (t-1)
Enter =C88-B88 and copy across

(46) Sum of Cash Flow from Operating Activities
Enter =SUM(C183:C187) and copy across

(47) - [PPE (t) - PPE (t-1)]
Enter =-(C76-B76) and copy across

(48) - Invest in Plant and Equip
Enter =C191 and copy across

(49) Long-term Debt (t) - Long-term Debt (t-1)
Enter =C92-B92 and copy across

(50) Short-term Debt (t) - Short-term Debt (t-1)
Enter =C89-B89 and copy across

(51) Paid in Capital (t) - Paid in Capital (t-1)
Enter =C96-B96 and copy across

(52) - Dividends Paid from Income Statement
Enter =-C49 and copy across

(53) Sum of Cash Flow from Financing Activities
Enter =SUM(C195:C198) and copy across

(54) Cash Flow from Operating Activity
+ Cash Flow from Investing Activity
+ Cash Flow from Financing Activity
Enter =C188+C192+C199
and copy across

(55) Cash & Equivalents (t-1)
Enter =B71 and copy across

(56) Change in Cash and Equiv
+ Cash & Equivalents
Enter =C201+C202 and copy across

Notice that the $6.38 Cash and Equivalents at the End of Year 2004, which was obtained by summing all of the cash flows from operations, investments, and financing together with the Beginning of the Year balance for 2004, does indeed equal the $6.38 Cash and Equivalents at the Beginning of Year 2005. Thus, the sum of the cash flows from operations, investments, and financing does equal the Change in Cash and Equivalents. This balancing of the Cash Flow Statement is a direct consequence of the balancing of the Balance Sheet. It is also a good way to check for possible errors in your Excel model.

17.4 Ratios

Problem. Given historical and forecasted financial statements for **Cutting Edge B2B Inc.**, create the historical and forecasted financial ratios.

Solution Strategy. Calculate the financial ratios by referencing the appropriate items on the Income Statement or Balance Sheet.

FIGURE 17.9 Ratios for Cutting Edge B2B Inc.

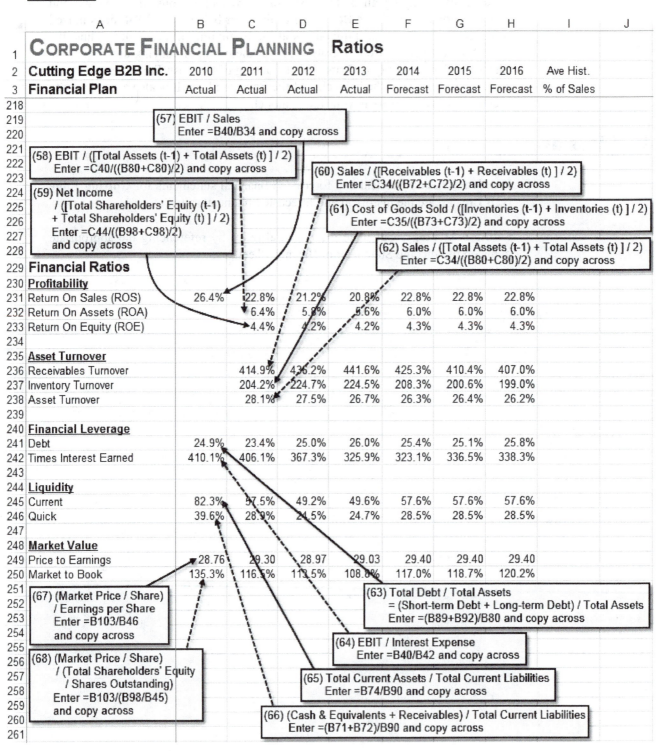

The financial ratios are very useful in interpreting the financial condition of the firm.

17.5 Sensitivity

Problem. Given historical and forecasted financial statements for **Cutting Edge B2B Inc.**, analyze the sensitivity of the 2007 External Funds Needed to the assumed 2007 Sales Growth Rate.

Solution Strategy. Create a Data Table using Sales Growth Rate as the input variable and External Funds Needed as the output variable. Then graph the relationship.

Excel 2013 **FIGURE 17.10 Sensitivity Analysis for Cutting Edge B2B Inc.**

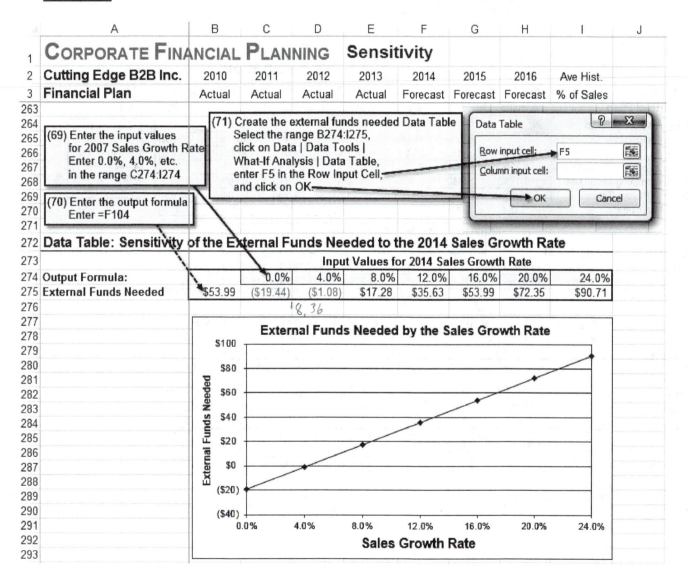

The sensitivity analysis indicates that 2007 External Funds Needed is very sensitive to the assumption about 2007 Sales Growth Rate. Further, there is a linear relationship between 2007 Sales Growth Rate and 2007 External Funds Needed.

17.6 Full-Scale Estimation

Problem. Given historical 10K financial statements for **Nike, Inc.**, forecast their financial statements over the next three years.

Solution Strategy. Modify the financial statement Excel model developed for the fictional firm **Cutting Edge B2B Inc.** by adding an additional level of detail found in the actual 10K financial statements of **Nike, Inc.** Then forecast the financial statements in the same way as before.

Excel 2013

FIGURE 17.11 Historical and Forecasted Assumptions and Income Statement for Nike, Inc.

	A	B	C	D	E	F	G	H	I	J
1	**CORPORATE FINANCIAL PLANNING**					**Full-Scale Estimation**				
2	**Nike, Inc.**	5/31/2010	5/31/2011	5/31/2012	5/31/2013	5/31/2014	5/31/2015	5/31/2016	Ave. %	
3	**Financial Plan**	Actual	Actual	Actual	Actual	Forecast	Forecast	Forecast	of Sales	
4	**Key Assumptions**								(1) Forecast key	
5	Sales Growth Rate		5.8%	16.0%	8.5%	9.0%	10.0%	11.0%	assumptions	
6	Tax Rate	24.2%	24.1%	25.0%	24.7%	24.0%	24.0%	24.0%	Enter forecast	
7	Int Rate on Short-Term Debt	0.12%	0.04%	0.09%	0.05%	0.10%	0.15%	0.20%	values in the	
8	Int Rate on Long-Term Debt	1.17%	0.71%	0.39%	0.58%	0.70%	0.80%	0.90%	range F5:H10	
9	Dividend Payout Rate	26.9%	26.3%	28.8%	29.1%	28.0%	29.0%	30.0%	(done for you)	
10	Price / Earnings	18.4	18.6	21.6	22.2	21.0	21.0	21.0		
11										
12				(2) Gross Margin - SG&AE + Non-Op Inc - Depreciation						
13	**Income Statement (Mil.$)**			Enter =B16-B18+B19-B20 and copy across						
14	Sales	$19,014.0	$20,117.0	$23,331.0	$25,313.0	$27,591.2	$30,350.3	$33,688.8		
15	Cost of Goods Sold	$10,213.6	$10,915.0	$13,183.0	$14,279.0	$15,236.4	$16,760.0	$18,603.6		
16	Gross Margin	$8,800.4	$9,202.0	$10,148.0	$11,034.0	$12,354.8	$13,590.3	$15,085.2		
17										
18	Selling, Gen & Adm Expenses	$6,326.4	$6,361.0	$7,051.0	$7,766.0	$8,677.0	$9,544.7	$10,594.6		
19	Non-Operating Income	$42.9	$21.0	($58.0)	$18.0	$10.5	$11.6	$12.8		
20	Depreciation	$0.0	$0.0	$14.0	$14.0	$8.0	$8.7	$9.7		
21	EBIT	$2,516.9	$2,862.0	$3,025.0	$3,272.0	$3,680.4	$4,048.4	$4,493.7		
22										
23	Interest Expense	$0.0	$0.0	$0.0	$0.0	$8.53	$2.93	$3.51		
24	Taxes	$610.2	$690.0	$756.0	$808.0	$881.2	$970.9	$1,077.7		
25	Extraordinary Items	$0.0	$39.0	$46.0	($21.0)	$21.2	$23.4	$25.9		
26	Net Income	$1,906.7	$2,133.0	$2,223.0	$2,485.0	$2,769.3	$3,051.2	$3,386.6		
27	Shares Outstanding (Millions)	968.0	936.0	916.0	894.0	894.0	894.0	894.0		
28	Earnings Per Share	$1.97	$2.28	$2.43	$2.78	$3.10	$3.41	$3.79		
29										
30	Allocation of Net Income:									
31	Dividends	$513.0	$561.6	$641.2	$724.1	$775.4	$884.8	$1,016.0		
32	Change in Equity	$1,393.7	$1,571.4	$1,581.8	$1,760.9	$1,993.9	$2,166.3	$2,370.6		

Excel 2013

FIGURE 17.12 Historical and Forecasted Balance Sheet for Nike, Inc.

	A	B	C	D	E	F	G	H	I	J
1	**CORPORATE FINANCIAL PLANNING**				**Full-Scale Estimation**					
2	**Nike, Inc.**	5/31/2010	5/31/2011	5/31/2012	5/31/2013	5/31/2014	5/31/2015	5/31/2016	Ave. %	
3	**Financial Plan**	Actual	Actual	Actual	Actual	Forecast	Forecast	Forecast	of Sales	
34	**Balance Sheet (Mil.$)**									
35	**Assets**									
36	Current Assets									
37	Cash & Equivalents	$3,079.1	$1,955.0	$2,317.0	$3,337.0	$3,603.5	$3,901.5	$4,232.1		
38	Marketable Securities	$2,066.8	$2,583.0	$1,440.0	$2,628.0	$2,777.3	$3,055.0	$3,391.1		
39	Receivables	$2,649.8	$3,138.0	$3,132.0	$3,117.0	$3,812.6	$4,193.9	$4,655.2		
40	Inventories	$2,040.8	$2,715.0	$3,222.0	$3,434.0	$3,559.6	$3,915.6	$4,346.3		
41	Other Current Assets	$1,122.7	$906.0	$1,734.0	$1,110.0	$1,533.1	$1,686.4	$1,871.9		
42	Total Current Assets	$10,959.2	$11,297.0	$11,845.0	$13,626.0	$15,286.1	$16,752.3	$18,496.5		
43										
44	Property, Plant & Equip Gross	$4,389.8	$4,906.0	$5,057.0	$5,500.0	$6,268.5	$6,895.4	$7,653.9		
45	Accumulated Depreciation	($2,457.9)	($2,791.0)	($2,848.0)	($3,048.0)	($3,521.2)	($3,873.4)	($4,299.4)		
46	Goodwill, Net	$187.6	$205.0	$131.0	$131.0	$212.8	$234.1	$259.8		
47	Intangibles, Net	$467.0	$487.0	$370.0	$382.0	$549.9	$604.9	$671.4		
48	Other Long Term Assets	$873.6	$894.0	$910.0	$993.0	$1,163.1	$1,279.4	$1,420.1		
49	Total Assets	$14,419.3	$14,998.0	$15,465.0	$17,584.0	$19,959.1	$21,892.7	$24,202.3		
50										
51	**Liabilities and Shareholders' Equity**									
52	Current Liabilities									
53	Notes Payable	$138.6	$187.0	$108.0	$121.0	$179.3	$197.2	$218.9		
54	Accounts Payable	$1,254.5	$1,469.0	$1,549.0	$1,646.0	$1,865.3	$2,051.8	$2,277.5		
55	Current Portion of L.T. Debt	$7.4	$200.0	$49.0	$57.0	$101.3	$111.4	$123.7		
56	Accrued Expenses	$1,610.1	$1,654.0	$1,552.0	$1,572.0	$2,038.5	$2,242.3	$2,488.9		
57	Other Current Liabilities	$353.6	$448.0	$624.0	$530.0	$610.8	$671.9	$745.8		
58	Total Current Liabilities	$3,364.2	$3,958.0	$3,882.0	$3,926.0	$4,795.1	$5,274.6	$5,854.8		
59										
60	Long-term Debt	$445.8	$276.0	$228.0	$1,210.0	$346.8	$364.9	$392.8		
61	Deferred Income Tax	$855.3	$921.0	$974.0	$1,292.0	$1,266.1	$1,392.7	$1,545.9		
62	Total Liabilities	$4,665.3	$5,155.0	$5,084.0	$6,428.0	$6,408.0	$7,032.3	$7,793.6		
63										
64										
65	Shareholders' Equity									
66	Preferred Stock	$0.3	$0.0	$0.0	$0.0	$0.0	$0.0	$0.0		
67	Common Stock Net	$2.8	$3.0	$3.0	$3.0	$3.0	$3.0	$3.0		
68	Additional Paid-In Capital	$3,440.6	$3,944.0	$4,641.0	$5,184.0	$5,630.0	$4,750.0	$3,900.0		
69	Other Equities	$214.8	$95.0	$149.0	$274.0	$229.2	$252.1	$279.9		
70	Retained Earnings	$6,095.5	$5,801.0	$5,588.0	$5,695.0	$7,688.9	$9,855.3	$12,225.9		
71	Total Shareholders' Equity	$9,754.0	$9,843.0	$10,381.0	$11,156.0	$13,551.1	$14,860.4	$16,408.8		
72										
73	Total Liab. & Share. Equity	$14,419.3	$14,998.0	$15,465.0	$17,584.0	$19,959.1	$21,892.7	$24,202.3		
74										
75	Debt / (Debt + Equity)	15.9%	16.4%	15.4%	21.1%	15.0%	15.0%	15.0%		
76	Market Price / Share	$36.19	$42.31	$52.30	$61.66	$65.05	$71.67	$79.55		
77	External Funds Needed		$658.7	$600.0	$1,915.0	$161.9	($419.3)	($286.7)		

Annotation callouts:

(3) Sum of Current Assets items
Enter =SUM(B37:B41) and copy across

(4) Total Current Assets + Sum of Rest of Assets
Enter =B42+SUM(B44:B48) and copy across

(5) Sum of Current Liabilities items
Enter =SUM(B53:B57) and copy across

(6) Total Liab -Total Cur Liab - Long-term Debt
Enter =F62-F58-F61 and copy across

(7) Sum of Shareholders' Equity Items
Enter =SUM(B66:B70) and copy across

(8) Adjust Additional Paid-In Capital to keep Debt / (Debt + Equity) in row 75 near the target level, which is 15% in this case

Excel 2013

FIGURE 17.13 Historical and Forecasted Income Statement Percent of Sales for Nike, Inc.

	A	B	C	D	E	F	G	H	I	J
1	CORPORATE FINANCIAL PLANNING				Full-Scale Estimation					
2	Nike, Inc.	5/31/2010	5/31/2011	5/31/2012	5/31/2013	5/31/2014	5/31/2015	5/31/2016	Ave. %	
3	Financial Plan	Actual	Actual	Actual	Actual	Forecast	Forecast	Forecast	of Sales	
78										
79	(9) (Each Income Statement item) / Sales				(11) Average of historical (actual) Percent of Sales					
80	Enter =B14/B$14 and copy to the range B84:H102				Enter =AVERAGE(B84:E84) and copy to range I84:I143					
81	Delete ranges that should be blank (B87:H87, etc.)				Delete cells that should be blank (I87, I92, etc.)					
82	(done for you)				(done for you)					
83	**Income Statement (% of Sales)**									
84	Sales	100.0%	100.0%	100.0%	100.0%	100.0%	100.0%	100.0%	100.0%	
85	Cost of Goods Sold	53.7%	54.3%	56.5%	56.4%	55.2%	55.2%	55.2%	55.2%	
86	Gross Margin	46.3%	45.7%	43.5%	43.6%	44.8%	44.8%	44.8%	44.8%	
87										
88	Selling, Gen & Adm Expenses	33.3%	31.6%	30.2%	30.7%	31.4%	31.4%	31.4%	31.4%	
89	Non-Operating Income	0.2%	0.1%	-0.2%	0.1%	0.0%	0.0%	0.0%	0.0%	
90	Depreciation	0.0%	0.0%	0.1%	0.1%	0.0%	0.0%	0.0%	0.0%	
91	EBIT	13.2%	14.2%	13.0%	12.9%	13.3%	13.3%	13.3%	13.3%	
92										
93	Interest Expense	0.0%	0.0%	0.0%	0.0%	0.0%	0.0%	0.0%	0.0%	
94	Taxes	3.2%	3.4%	3.2%	3.2%	3.2%	3.2%	3.2%	3.3%	
95	Extraordinary Items	0.0%	0.2%	0.2%	-0.1%	0.1%	0.1%	0.1%	0.1%	
96	Net Income	10.0%	10.6%	9.5%	9.8%	10.0%	10.1%	10.1%	10.0%	
97	Shares Outstanding (Millions)	5.1%	4.7%	3.9%	3.5%	3.2%	2.9%	2.7%	4.3%	
98	Earnings Per Share	0.0%	0.0%	0.0%	0.0%	0.0%	0.0%	0.0%	0.0%	
99										
100	Allocation of Net Income:	0.0%	0.0%	0.0%	0.0%	0.0%	0.0%	0.0%	0.0%	
101	Dividends	2.7%	2.8%	2.7%	2.9%	2.8%	2.9%	3.0%	2.8%	
102	Change in Equity	7.3%	7.8%	6.8%	7.0%	7.2%	7.1%	7.0%	7.2%	

FIGURE 17.14 Historical and Forecasted Balance Sheet Percent of Sales for Nike, Inc.

Excel 2013

	A	B	C	D	E	F	G	H	I
1	**CORPORATE FINANCIAL PLANNING**				**Full-Scale Estimation**				
2	**Nike, Inc.**	5/31/2010	5/31/2011	5/31/2012	5/31/2013	5/31/2014	5/31/2015	5/31/2016	Ave. %
3	**Financial Plan**	Actual	Actual	Actual	Actual	Forecast	Forecast	Forecast	of Sales
103									
104			(10) (Each Balance Sheet Asset item) / Sales						
105	**Balance Sheet (% of Sales)**		Enter =B37/B$14 and copy to range B108:H143						
106	Assets		Delete ranges that should be blank (B114:H114, etc.)						
107	Current Assets		(done for you)						
108	Cash & Equivalents	16.2%	9.7%	9.9%	13.2%	13.1%	12.9%	12.6%	12.3%
109	Short-term Investments	10.9%	12.8%	6.2%	10.4%	10.1%	10.1%	10.1%	10.1%
110	Receivables	13.9%	15.6%	13.4%	12.3%	13.8%	13.8%	13.8%	13.8%
111	Inventories	10.7%	13.5%	13.8%	13.6%	12.9%	12.9%	12.9%	12.9%
112	Other Current Assets	5.9%	4.5%	7.4%	4.4%	5.6%	5.6%	5.6%	5.6%
113	Total Current Assets	57.6%	56.2%	50.8%	53.8%	55.4%	55.2%	54.9%	54.6%
114									
115	Property, Plant & Equip Gross	23.1%	24.4%	21.7%	21.7%	22.7%	22.7%	22.7%	22.7%
116	Accumulated Depreciation	-12.9%	-13.9%	-12.2%	-12.0%	-12.8%	-12.8%	-12.8%	-12.8%
117	Goodwill, Net	1.0%	1.0%	0.6%	0.5%	0.8%	0.8%	0.8%	0.8%
118	Intangibles, Net	2.5%	2.4%	1.6%	1.5%	2.0%	2.0%	2.0%	2.0%
119	Other Long Term Assets	4.6%	4.4%	3.9%	3.9%	4.2%	4.2%	4.2%	4.2%
120	Total Assets	75.8%	74.6%	66.3%	69.5%	72.3%	72.1%	71.8%	71.5%
121									
122	Liabilities and Shareholders' Equity								
123	Current Liabilities								
124	Notes Payable	0.7%	0.9%	0.5%	0.5%	0.6%	0.6%	0.6%	0.6%
125	Accounts Payable	6.6%	7.3%	6.6%	6.5%	6.8%	6.8%	6.8%	6.8%
126	Current Portion of L.T. Debt	0.0%	1.0%	0.2%	0.2%	0.4%	0.4%	0.4%	0.4%
127	Accrued Expenses	8.5%	8.2%	6.7%	6.2%	7.4%	7.4%	7.4%	7.4%
128	Other Current Liabilities	1.9%	2.2%	2.7%	2.1%	2.2%	2.2%	2.2%	2.2%
129	Total Current Liabilities	17.7%	19.7%	16.6%	15.5%	17.4%	17.4%	17.4%	17.4%
130									
131	Long-term Debt	2.3%	1.4%	1.0%	4.8%	1.3%	1.2%	1.2%	2.4%
132	Deferred Income Tax	4.5%	4.6%	4.2%	5.1%	4.6%	4.6%	4.6%	4.6%
133	Total Liabilities	24.5%	25.6%	21.8%	25.4%	23.2%	23.2%	23.1%	24.3%
134									
135	Shareholders' Equity								
136	Preferred Stock	0.0%	0.0%	0.0%	0.0%	0.0%	0.0%	0.0%	0.0%
137	Common Stock Net	0.0%	0.0%	0.0%	0.0%	0.0%	0.0%	0.0%	0.0%
138	Additional Paid-In Capital	18.1%	19.6%	19.9%	20.5%	20.4%	15.7%	11.6%	19.5%
139	Other Equities	1.1%	0.5%	0.6%	1.1%	0.8%	0.8%	0.8%	0.8%
140	Retained Earnings	32.1%	28.8%	24.0%	22.5%	27.9%	32.5%	36.3%	26.8%
141	Total Shareholders' Equity	51.3%	48.9%	44.5%	44.1%	49.1%	49.0%	48.7%	47.2%
142									
143	Total Liab. & Share. Equity	75.8%	74.6%	66.3%	69.5%	72.3%	72.1%	71.8%	71.5%

Excel 2013

FIGURE 17.15 Historical and Forecasted Cash Flow Statement for Nike, Inc.

	A	B	C	D	E	F	G	H	I	J
1	**CORPORATE FINANCIAL PLANNING**				**Full-Scale Estimation**					
2	**Nike, Inc.**	5/31/2010	5/31/2011	5/31/2012	5/31/2013	5/31/2014	5/31/2015	5/31/2016	Ave. %	
3	**Financial Plan**	Actual	Actual	Actual	Actual	Forecast	Forecast	Forecast	of Sales	
145	**Cash Flow Statement (Mil.$)**									
146	**Cash from Operating Activities**									
147	Net Income	$1,906.7	$2,133.0	$2,223.0	$2,485.0	$2,769.3	$3,051.2	$3,386.6		
148	Depreciation	$323.7	$335.0	$373.0	$438.0	$461.9	$508.1	$564.0		
149	Amortization	$71.8	$23.0	$32.0	$75.0	$63.8	$70.2	$77.9		
150	Deferred Taxes	$8.3	($76.0)	($60.0)	$21.0	($35.1)	($38.6)	($42.8)		
151	Non-Cash Items	$159.0	$105.0	$130.0	$50.0	$145.7	$160.3	$178.0		
152	Changes in Working Capital	$694.7	($798.0)	($799.0)	($42.0)	($269.3)	($296.2)	($328.8)		
153	Cash from Operating Activities	$3,164.2	$1,722.0	$1,899.0	$3,027.0	$3,136.5	$3,455.1	$3,834.9		
154										
155				*(12) Sum of Cash Provided By Operations items* *Enter =SUM(B147:B152) and copy across*						
156	**Cash from Investing Activities**									
157	Capital Expenditures	($335.1)	($432.0)	($597.0)	($636.0)	($619.5)	($681.5)	($756.4)		
158	Other Investing Cash Flow Item	($932.4)	($589.0)	$1,111.0	($431.0)	($329.2)	($362.1)	($401.9)		
159	Cash from Investing Activities	($1,267.5)	($1,021.0)	$514.0	($1,067.0)	($948.7)	($1,043.6)	($1,158.4)		
160										
161				*(13) Sum of Cash Provided by Investing items* *Enter =SUM(B157:B158) and copy across*						
162	**Cash from Financing Activities**									
163	Financing Cash Flow Items	$58.5	$64.0	$115.0	$72.0	$96.8	$106.5	$118.2		
164	Total Cash Dividends Paid	($505.4)	($555.0)	($619.0)	($703.0)	($748.2)	($823.0)	($913.6)		
165	Inssuance (Ret) of Stock, Net	($376.7)	($1,514.0)	($1,346.0)	($1,361.0)	($1,424.6)	($1,567.1)	($1,739.4)		
166	Inssuance (Ret) of Debt, Net	($237.6)	$33.0	($268.0)	$952.0	$105.3	$115.8	$128.6		
167	Cash from Financing Activities	($1,061.2)	($1,972.0)	($2,118.0)	($1,040.0)	($1,970.7)	($2,167.8)	($2,406.3)		
168										
169	Foreign Exchange Effects	($47.5)	$57.0	$67.0	$100.0	$49.4	$54.3	$60.3		
170	Net Change in Cash	$788.0	($1,214.0)	$362.0	$1,020.0	$266.5	$298.0	$330.6		
171										
172	Cash and Equiv. Beg of Year	$1,388.1	$3,079.1	$1,955.0	$2,317.0	$3,337.0	$3,603.5	$3,901.5		
173	Cash and Equiv. End of Year	$2,176.1	$1,865.1	$2,317.0	$3,337.0	$3,603.5	$3,901.5	$4,232.1		
174	*(14) Sum of Cash Provided by Financing items* *Enter =SUM(B163:B166) and copy across*				*(15) Cash From Op + Cash From Invest + Cash From Financing + For Exch Eff* *Enter =B153+B159+B167+B169 and copy across*					
175										
176										

Excel 2013

FIGURE 17.16 Historical and Forecasted Cash Flow Statement Percent of Sales for Nike, Inc.

	A	B	C	D	E	F	G	H	I	J
1	**CORPORATE FINANCIAL PLANNING**				**Full-Scale Estimation**					
2	**Nike, Inc.**	5/31/2010	5/31/2011	5/31/2012	5/31/2013	5/31/2014	5/31/2015	5/31/2016	Ave. %	
3	**Financial Plan**	Actual	Actual	Actual	Actual	Forecast	Forecast	Forecast	of Sales	
176										
177	(16) (Each Cash Flow Statement item) / Sales				(17) Average of historical (actual) Percent of Sales					
178	Enter =B147/B$14 and copy to the range B183:H207				Enter =AVERAGE(B183:E183) and copy to range I183:I207					
179	Delete ranges that should be blank (B190:H191, etc.)				Delete cells that should be blank (I190, I191, etc.)					
180	(done for you)				(done for you)					
181	**Cash Flow Statement (% of Sales)**									
182	**Cash from Operating Activities**									
183	Net Income	10.0%	10.6%	9.5%	9.8%	10.0%	10.1%	10.1%	10.0%	
184	Depreciation	1.7%	1.7%	1.6%	1.7%	1.7%	1.7%	1.7%	1.7%	
185	Amortization	0.4%	0.1%	0.1%	0.3%	0.2%	0.2%	0.2%	0.2%	
186	Deferred Taxes	0.0%	-0.4%	-0.3%	0.1%	-0.1%	-0.1%	-0.1%	-0.1%	
187	Non-Cash Items	0.8%	0.5%	0.6%	0.2%	0.5%	0.5%	0.5%	0.5%	
188	Changes in Working Capital	3.7%	-4.0%	-3.4%	-0.2%	-1.0%	-1.0%	-1.0%	-1.0%	
189	Cash from Operating Activities	16.6%	8.6%	8.1%	12.0%	11.4%	11.4%	11.4%	11.3%	
190										
191	**Cash from Investing Activities**									
192	Capital Expenditures	-1.8%	-2.1%	-2.6%	-2.5%	-2.2%	-2.2%	-2.2%	-2.2%	
193	Other Investing Cash Flow Item	-4.9%	-2.9%	4.8%	-1.7%	-1.2%	-1.2%	-1.2%	-1.2%	
194	Cash from Investing Activities	-6.7%	-5.1%	2.2%	-4.2%	-3.4%	-3.4%	-3.4%	-3.4%	
195										
196	**Cash from Financing Activities**									
197	Financing Cash Flow Items	0.3%	0.3%	0.5%	0.3%	0.4%	0.4%	0.4%	0.4%	
198	Total Cash Dividends Paid	-2.7%	-2.8%	-2.7%	-2.8%	-2.7%	-2.7%	-2.7%	-2.7%	
199	Issuance (Ret) of Stock, Net	-2.0%	-7.5%	-5.8%	-5.4%	-5.2%	-5.2%	-5.2%	-5.2%	
200	Issuance (Ret) of Debt, Net	-1.2%	0.2%	-1.1%	3.8%	0.4%	0.4%	0.4%	0.4%	
201	Cash from Financing Activities	-5.6%	-9.8%	-9.1%	-4.1%	-7.1%	-7.1%	-7.1%	-7.1%	
202										
203	Foreign Exchange Effects	-0.2%	0.3%	0.3%	0.4%	0.2%	0.2%	0.2%	0.2%	
204	Net Change in Cash	4.1%	-6.0%	1.6%	4.0%	1.0%	1.0%	1.0%	0.9%	
205										
206	Cash and Equiv. Beg of Year	7.3%	15.3%	8.4%	9.2%	12.1%	11.9%	11.6%	10.0%	
207	Cash and Equiv. End of Year	11.4%	9.3%	9.9%	13.2%	13.1%	12.9%	12.6%	11.0%	

Excel 2013

FIGURE 17.17 Historical and Forecasted Financial Ratios for Nike, Inc.

	A	B	C	D	E	F	G	H	I
1	CORPORATE FINANCIAL PLANNING				Full-Scale Estimation				
2	Nike, Inc.	5/31/2010	5/31/2011	5/31/2012	5/31/2013	5/31/2014	5/31/2015	5/31/2016	Ave. %
3	Financial Plan	Actual	Actual	Actual	Actual	Forecast	Forecast	Forecast	of Sales
208									
209	**Financial Ratios**	(18) (Current Portion of L.T. Debt + Notes Payable + Long-term Debt) / (Total Assets) Enter =(B53+B54+B60)/B49 and copy across							
210	**Profitability**								
211	Return On Sales (ROS)	13.2%	14.2%	13.0%	12.9%	13.3%	13.3%	13.3%	
212	Return On Assets (ROA)		19.5%	19.9%	19.8%	19.6%	19.3%	19.5%	
213	Return On Equity (ROE)		21.8%	22.0%	23.1%	22.4%	21.5%	21.7%	
214									
215	**Asset Turnover**								
216	Receivables Turnover		7.0	7.4	8.1	8.0	7.6	7.6	
217	Inventory Turnover		4.6	4.4	4.3	4.4	4.5	4.5	
218	Asset Turnover		1.4	1.5	1.5	1.5	1.5	1.5	
219									
220	**Financial Leverage**								
221	Debt	12.8%	12.9%	12.2%	16.9%	12.0%	11.9%	11.9%	
222	Times Interest Earned	#DIV/0!	#DIV/0!	#DIV/0!	#DIV/0!	431.6	1383.6	1281.2	
223									
224	**Liquidity**								
225	Current	325.8%	285.4%	305.1%	347.1%	318.8%	317.6%	315.9%	
226	Quick	170.3%	128.7%	140.4%	164.4%	154.7%	153.5%	151.8%	
227									
228	**Market Value**								
229	Price to Earnings	18.4	18.6	21.6	22.2	21.00	21.00	21.00	
230	Market to Book	359.2%	402.3%	461.5%	494.1%	429.2%	431.2%	433.4%	

The percentage of sales method does a good job for most purposes. Additional refinements would increase accuracy of the forecast. For example, some items may be better projected as a trend, rather than an average. Other items, such as the Accounting Change, may have unique patterns. The bottom line of this forecast is steady growth in Earnings Per Share from $4.07 to $4.31 to $4.63.

Problems

1. Given historical financial statements for **Global Impact P2P** on the **Problems** tab, forecast their financial statements for the next three years. Then explore the company's needs for additional financing as expressed by the following *choice variables*: debt and equity (paid-in capital under shareholder's equity).

2. Given historical and forecasted Income Statements and Balance Sheets for **Global Impact P2P**, create the historical and forecasted Cash Flow Statement.

3. Given historical and forecasted financial statements for **Global Impact P2P**, create the historical and forecasted financial ratios.

4. Select a company with publicly traded stock. Locate the historical 10K financial statements for that company over the past few years. Forecast your company's financial statements over the next three years.

Excel 2013

FIGURE 17.18 Historical Assumptions and Income Statement for Global Impact P2P

	A	B	C	D	E	F
1	**CORPORATE FINANCIAL PLANNING**				**Problems**	
2	**Global Impact P2P**	2010	2011	2012	2013	
3	**Financial Plan**	Actual	Actual	Actual	Actual	
4	**Key Assumptions**					
5	Sales Growth Rate			21.4%	19.3%	
6	Tax Rate	40.5%	38.8%	38.2%	36.0%	
7	Int Rate on Short-Term Debt	6.3%	6.3%	6.4%	6.5%	
8	Int Rate on Long-Term Debt	7.4%	7.4%	7.5%	7.6%	
9	Dividend Payout Rate	26.1%	25.9%	26.8%	24.4%	
10	Price / Earnings	8.6	8.4	8.7	9.3	
11						
12	**Income Statement (Mil.$)**					
13	Sales	$185.76	$194.29	$235.84	$281.38	
14	Cost of Goods Sold	$109.81	$112.25	$138.97	$171.57	
15	Gross Margin	$75.95	$82.04	$96.87	$109.81	
16						
17	Selling, Gen & Adm Expenses	$12.73	$13.54	$16.87	$19.94	
18	Depreciation	$11.66	$12.39	$14.58	$18.37	
19	EBIT	$51.56	$56.11	$65.42	$71.50	
20						
21	Interest Expense	$14.23	$15.69	$23.88	$24.55	
22	Taxes	$15.12	$15.68	$15.87	$16.92	
23	Net Income	$22.21	$24.74	$25.67	$30.03	
24	Shares Outstanding (Millions)	2.03	2.10	2.15	2.44	
25	Earnings Per Share	$10.94	$11.78	$11.94	$12.31	
26						
27	Allocation of Net Income:					
28	Dividends	$5.80	$6.41	$6.87	$7.33	
29	Change in Equity	$16.41	$18.33	$18.80	$22.70	

Excel 2013

FIGURE 17.19 Historical Balance Sheet for Global Impact P2P

	A	B	C	D	E	F
1	**CORPORATE FINANCIAL PLANNING**				**Problems**	
2	**Global Impact P2P**	2010	2011	2012	2013	
3	**Financial Plan**	Actual	Actual	Actual	Actual	
31	**Balance Sheet (Mil.$)**					
32	**Assets**					
33	Current Assets					
34	Cash & Equivalents	$8.56	$13.97	$15.34	$17.75	
35	Receivables	$41.63	$49.52	$57.37	$68.91	
36	Inventories	$52.11	$60.94	$73.49	$86.32	
37	Total Current Assets	$102.30	$124.43	$146.20	$172.98	
38						
39	Property, Plant & Equip. (PPE	$663.29	$846.39	$910.34	$958.31	
40	Accumulated Depreciation	$189.20	$201.59	$216.17	$234.54	
41	Net PPE	$474.09	$644.80	$694.17	$723.77	
42						
43	Total Assets	$576.39	$769.23	$840.37	$896.75	
44						
45	**Liabilities and Shareholders' Equity**					
46	Current Liabilities					
47	Accounts Payable	$62.46	$90.48	$134.32	$174.57	
48	Short-term Debt	$202.12	$307.87	$304.96	$312.85	
49	Total Current Liabilities	$264.58	$398.35	$439.28	$487.42	
50						
51	Long-term Debt	$40.00	$55.74	$62.15	$17.69	
52	Total Liabilities	$304.58	$454.09	$501.43	$505.11	
53						
54	Shareholders' Equity					
55	Paid-in Capital	$180.00	$205.00	$210.00	$240.00	
56	Retained Earnings	$91.81	$110.14	$128.94	$151.64	
57	Total Shareholders' Equity	$271.81	$315.14	$338.94	$391.64	
58						
59	Total Liab. & Share. Equity	$576.39	$769.23	$840.37	$896.75	
60						
61	Debt / (Debt + Equity)	47.1%	53.6%	52.0%	45.8%	
62	Market Price / Share	$94.58	$99.12	$103.47	$114.95	
63	External Funds Needed		$146.49	$8.50	($6.57)	

Chapter 18 Du Pont System Of Ratio Analysis

18.1 Basics

Problem. A company's Net Profit is $170, Pretax Profit is $260, EBIT is $470, Sales are $4,600, Assets are $4,200, and Equity is $4,300. Calculate the company's ROE and decompose the ROE into its components using the Du Pont System.

Excel 2013 **FIGURE 18.1 Excel Model of Du Pont System of Ratio Analysis - Basics.**

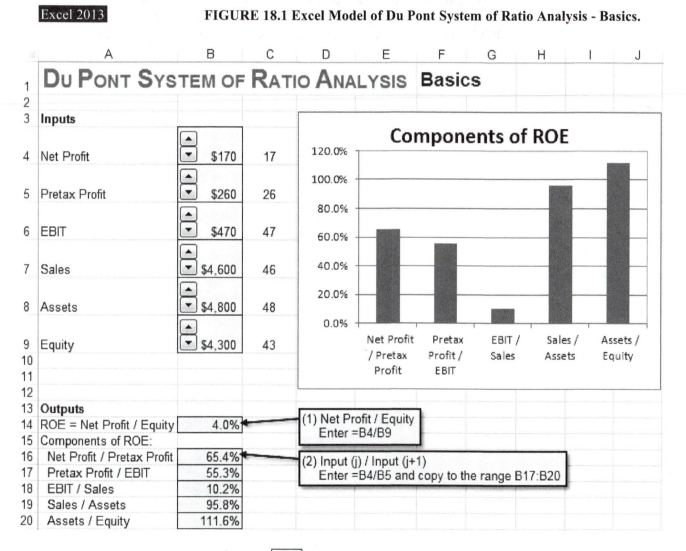

The ROE = 4.0%. The decomposition helps us see where this comes from. Here is an intuitive interpretation of the components:

- Net Profit / Pretax = 65.4% is a tax-burden ratio.
- Pretax Profits / EBIT = 55.3% is an interest-burden ratio.
- EBIT / Sales = 10.2% is the profit margin.
- Sales / Assets = 109.5% is the asset turnover.

- Asset / Equity = 97.7% is the leverage ratio.

Problems

1. A company's Net Profit is $82, Pretax Profit is $153, EBIT is $583, Sales is $3,740, Assets is $5,460, and Equity is $7,230. Calculate the company's ROE and decompose the ROE into its components using the Du Pont System.

2. A company's Net Profit is $265, Pretax Profit is $832, EBIT is $1,045, Sales is $5,680, Assets is $7,620, and Equity is $9,730. Calculate the company's ROE and decompose the ROE into its components using the Du Pont System.

Chapter 19 Life-Cycle Financial Planning

19.1 Taxable Vs. Traditional Vs. Roth Savings

Problem. Suppose that you are currently ⃞30 years old and expect to earn a constant salary of ⃞$80,000. You are planning to retire at age ⃞70 and expect to die at age ⃞95. You save at a ⃞15.0% rate. Your current tax rate is ⃞20.0% and you expect your retirement years tax rate to be ⃞25.0%. You plan to invest your money in a risky portfolio that might have a long-run low return of ⃞3.0%, medium return of ⃞7.0%, and a high return of ⃞11.0%. What would be your annual retirement income in the low, medium, and high return scenarios when saving with a taxable plan, a traditional IRA or 401(k) plan, or a Roth IRA or 401(k) plan?

Solution Strategy. For each of the three types of savings plans, calculate the cumulative savings at retirement and the annual retirement income under the low, medium, and high return scenarios.

FIGURE 19.1 Life-Cycle Financial Planning – Savings – Roth is Best.

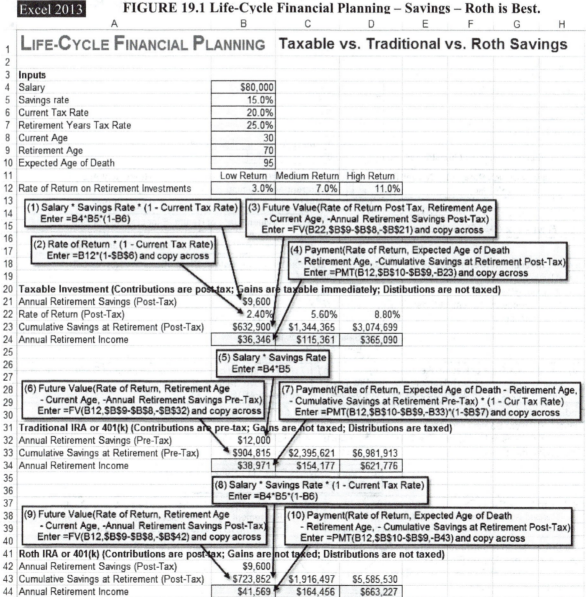

Under all three return scenarios, a Roth plan does better than a Traditional plan and both do better than a Taxable plan. For example under the medium return scenario, a Roth plan yields an annual retirement income of $164,456 vs. $154,177 under Traditional vs. $115,361 under Taxable.

The low return and high return scenarios provide a perspective on how risky the underlying investment is. Under a Roth plan, the low return scenario yields an annual retirement income of $41,569 vs. $663,227 in the high return scenario.

The dominance of the Roth plan is driven by your current tax rate being *lower* than your retirement years tax rate, as is true of many young people who are at the low-end of their lifetime income tax rates. Now consider the opposite case.

Second Problem. Keep everything else the same, but suppose that your current tax rate is 25.0% and your expected retirement years tax rate is 20.0%.

Excel 2013

FIGURE 19.2 Life-Cycle Financial Planning – Savings – Traditional is Best.

	A	B	C	D	E F G H
1	**LIFE-CYCLE FINANCIAL PLANNING Taxable vs. Traditional vs. Roth Savings**				
2					
3	**Inputs**				
4	Salary	$80,000			
5	Savings rate	15.0%			
6	Current Tax Rate	25.0%			
7	Retirement Years Tax Rate	20.0%			
8	Current Age	30			
9	Retirement Age	70			
10	Expected Age of Death	95			
11		Low Return	Medium Return	High Return	
12	Rate of Return on Retirement Investments	3.0%	7.0%	11.0%	

13-14-15: (1) Salary * Savings Rate * (1 - Current Tax Rate) Enter =B4*B5*(1-B6)

(3) Future Value(Rate of Return Post Tax, Retirement Age - Current Age, -Annual Retirement Savings Post-Tax) Enter =FV(B22,$B$9-$B$8,-$B$21) and copy across

16-17-18-19: (2) Rate of Return * (1 - Current Tax Rate) Enter =B12*(1-$B$6) and copy across

(4) Payment(Rate of Return, Expected Age of Death - Retirement Age, -Cumulative Savings at Retirement Post-Tax) Enter =PMT(B12,$B$10-$B$9,-B23) and copy across

	A	B	C	D
20	**Taxable Investment (Contributions are post-tax; Gains are taxable immediately; Distibutions are not taxed)**			
21	Annual Retirement Savings (Post-Tax)	$9,000		
22	Rate of Return (Post-Tax)	2.25%	5.25%	8.25%
23	Cumulative Savings at Retirement (Post-Tax)	$574,076	$1,155,866	$2,490,499
24	Annual Retirement Income	$32,968	$99,185	$295,722

25-26-27: (5) Salary * Savings Rate Enter =B4*B5

28-29-30: (6) Future Value(Rate of Return, Retirement Age - Current Age, -Annual Retirement Savings Pre-Tax) Enter =FV(B12,$B$9-$B$8,-$B$32) and copy across

(7) Payment(Rate of Return, Expected Age of Death - Retirement Age, - Cumulative Savings at Retirement Pre-Tax) * (1 - Cur Tax Rate) Enter =PMT(B12,$B$10-$B$9,-B33)*(1-$B$7) and copy across

	A	B	C	D
31	**Traditional IRA or 401(k) (Contributions are pre-tax; Gains are not taxed; Distributions are taxed)**			
32	Annual Retirement Savings (Pre-Tax)	$12,000		
33	Cumulative Savings at Retirement (Pre-Tax)	$904,815	$2,395,621	$6,981,913
34	Annual Retirement Income	$41,569	$164,456	$663,227

35-36-37: (8) Salary * Savings Rate * (1 - Current Tax Rate) Enter =B4*B5*(1-B6)

38-39-40: (9) Future Value(Rate of Return, Retirement Age - Current Age, -Annual Retirement Savings Post-Tax) Enter =FV(B12,$B$9-$B$8,-$B$42) and copy across

(10) Payment(Rate of Return, Expected Age of Death - Retirement Age, - Cumulative Savings at Retirement Post-Tax) Enter =PMT(B12,$B$10-$B$9,-B43) and copy across

	A	B	C	D
41	**Roth IRA or 401(k) (Contributions are post-tax; Gains are not taxed; Distributions are not taxed)**			
42	Annual Retirement Savings (Post-Tax)	$9,000		
43	Cumulative Savings at Retirement (Post-Tax)	$678,611	$1,796,716	$5,236,435
44	Annual Retirement Income	$38,971	$154,177	$621,776

Under all three return scenarios, the Traditional plan does better than the Roth plan and both do better than a Taxable Investment plan. The dominance of the Traditional plan is driven by your current tax rate being *higher* than your retirement years' tax rate, as is true of many middle-aged people who are at the high-end of their lifetime income tax rates.

19.2 Basic Life-Cycle Planning

Problem. Suppose that you are currently 30 years old and expect to earn a constant real salary of $80,000 starting next year. You are planning to retire at age 70. You currently have $0 in financial capital. You are limited to investing in the riskfree asset. The real riskfree rate is 1.0%. Develop a financial plan for real savings and real consumption over your lifetime.

Solution Strategy. Develop a financial plan on a year-by-year basis over an entire lifetime. During your working years, divide your salary each year between current consumption and savings to provide for consumption during your retirement years. Put savings in a retirement fund that is invested at the riskfree rate. During your retirement years, your salary is zero, but you are able to consume each year by withdrawing money from your retirement fund. Calculate a constant level of real consumption that can be sustained in both working years and retirement years. Since there is substantial uncertainty about how long you will actually live and since it's not a good idea to run out of money, calculate real consumption based on an infinite annuity. This level of real consumption can be sustained indefinitely. Finally, analyze human capital, financial capital, and total wealth over your lifetime.

Life Expectancy. How long should you expect to live? Here is the latest life expectancy data for the US:

Current Age	30	40	50	60	70	80	90
Remaining Years	50.0	40.5	31.4	23.1	15.5	9.1	4.6

These numbers aren't fixed. Life expectancy at birth increased by approximately 1 year over the prior 5 years due to medical and health progress. Furthermore, medical and health progress is likely to accelerate in the future, rather than just maintain the current rate of improvement.

Your individual life expectancy is influenced by many individual factors. The most important things that you can do to live longer are: (1) don't smoke, (2) exercise, (3) get seven to eight hours of sleep per night, (4) maintain a healthy diet and a desirable weight, (5) have an annual medical exam to catch cancer and other health problems early, (6) take a daily aspirin to reduce fatal heart attacks, (7) prevent high blood pressure, (8) get immunized against pneumonia and influenza, and (9) avoid heavy alcohol consumption.

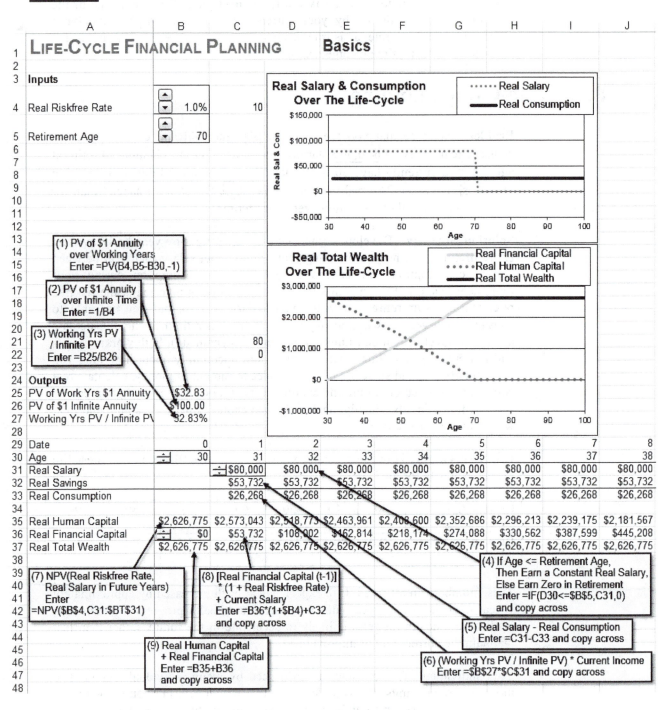

FIGURE 19.3 Excel Model of Life-Cycle Financial Planning - Basics.

Excel 2013 **FIGURE 19.4 Transition from Working Years to Retirement Years.**

	A	AN	AO	AP	AQ	AR
29	Date	38	39	40	41	42
30	Age	68	69	70	71	72
31	Real Salary	$80,000	$80,000	$80,000	$0	$0
32	Real Savings	$53,732	$53,732	$53,732	-$26,268	-$26,268
33	Real Consumption	$26,268	$26,268	$26,268	$26,268	$26,268
34						
35	Real Human Capital	$157,632	$79,208	$0	$0	$0
36	Real Financial Capital	$2,469,143	$2,547,567	$2,626,775	$2,626,775	$2,626,775
37	Real Total Wealth	$2,626,775	$2,626,775	$2,626,775	$2,626,775	$2,626,775

From the first graph, we see that your Real Salary from working years only is used to support a constant level of Real Consumption over an "infinite" lifetime. By using this approach, the same level of Real Consumption can be sustained even if you end up living much longer than originally anticipated. From the second graph, we see that Real Total Wealth is constant over a lifetime. At date 0, Real Total Wealth comes entirely from Real Human Capital, which is the present value of all future Real Salary. Over time Real Human Capital declines and Real Financial Capital builds up. After retirement, Real Total Wealth comes entirely from Real Financial Capital.

19.3 Full-Scale Life-Cycle Planning

Problem. Suppose that you are currently 30 years old and expect to earn a constant real salary of $80,000 starting next year. You are planning to retire at age 70. You currently have $0 in financial capital. You can invest in the riskfree asset or a broad stock portfolio. The inflation rate is 1.5% and the real riskfree rate is 0.0%. A broad stock portfolio offers an average real return of 6.0% and a standard deviation of 17.0%. Suppose that federal income taxes have six brackets with the following rates: 10.0%, 15.0%, 25.0%, 28.0%, 33.0%, and 35.0%. For the current year, the upper cutoffs on the first five brackets are $8,925, $36,250, $87,850, $183,250, and $398,350, and these cutoffs are indexed to inflation. The state tax rate is 3.4%, federal FICA-SSI tax rate on salary up to $113,700 is 6.2%, and the federal FICA-Medicare tax rate on any level of salary is 1.45%. The current level of Social Security benefits is $34,368 per year and this is indexed to inflation. Develop a financial plan for real savings and real consumption over your lifetime.

Solution Strategy. The full-scale Excel model of life-cycle financial planning adds consideration of inflation, taxes, social security, and the opportunity to invest in a broad stock index. It is assumed that your savings are put in a tax-deferred retirement fund. You pay zero taxes on contributions to the retirement fund during your working years. But you have to pay taxes on withdrawals from the retirement fund during your retirement years. This Excel model includes several *choice variables*. You need to choose your Real Growth Rate in Salary. You need to choose your Taxable Income / Total Wealth. Specifying taxable income as a percentage of total wealth indirectly determines your consumption and savings as a percentage of total wealth. You also need to choose your Asset Allocation: Stock Portfolio %, that is, what percentage of your savings to invest in the broad stock portfolio. Investing in the broad stock portfolio will give you higher average returns than the riskfree asset, but also more risk. The balance of your savings will be invested in the riskfree asset and will grow at the riskfree rate.

Excel 2013

FIGURE 19.5 Excel Model of Life-Cycle Fin Plan – Full-Scale Estimation.

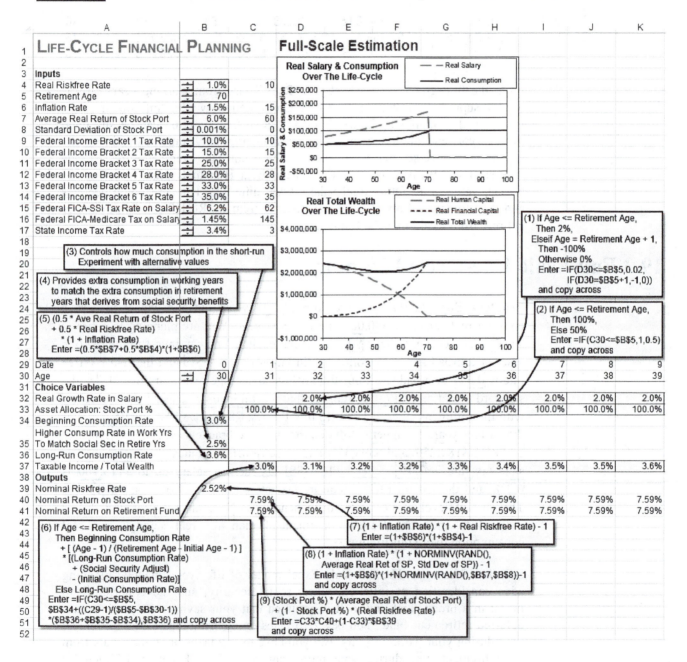

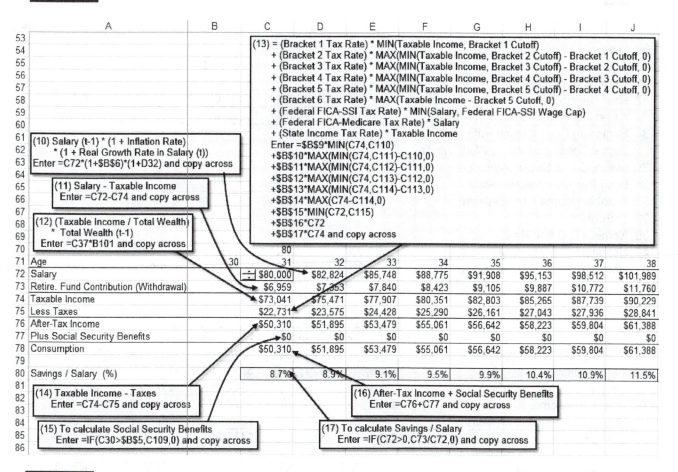

FIGURE 19.6 Excel Model of Life-Cycle Fin Plan – Full-Scale Estimation.

FIGURE 19.7 Excel Model of Life-Cycle Fin Plan – Full-Scale Estimation.

Excel 2013	FIGURE 19.8 Transition From Working To Retirement Years.

A	AN	AO	AP	AQ	AR
29 Date	38	39	40	41	42
30 Age	68	69	70	71	72
31 **Choice Variables**					
32 Real Growth Rate in Salary	2.0%	2.0%	2.0%	-100.0%	0.0%
33 Asset Allocation: Stock Port %	100.0%	100.0%	100.0%	50.0%	50.0%
34 Beginning Consumption Rate					
Higher Consump Rate in Work Yrs To					
35 Match Social Sec in Retire Yrs					
36 Long-Run Consumption Rate					
37 Taxable Income / Total Wealth	5.9%	6.0%	6.1%	3.6%	3.6%
38 **Outputs**					
39 Nominal Riskfree Rate					
40 Nominal Return on Stock Port	7.59%	7.59%	7.59%	7.59%	7.59%
41 Nominal Return on Retirement Fund	7.59%	7.59%	7.59%	5.05%	5.05%
42					
70					
71 Age	68	69	70	71	72
72 Salary	$288,762	$298,955	$309,508	$0	$0
73 Retire. Fund Contribution (Withdrawal)	$52,120	$50,545	$48,406	-$159,226	-$161,615
74 Taxable Income	$236,642	$248,410	$261,103	$159,226	$161,615
75 Less Taxes	$79,096	$82,948	$87,096	$37,724	$38,290
76 After-Tax Income	$157,546	$165,462	$174,007	$121,502	$123,325
77 Plus Social Security Benefits	$0	$0	$0	$62,344	$63,279
78 Consumption	$157,546	$165,462	$174,007	$183,846	$186,604
79					
80 Savings / Salary (%)	18.0%	16.9%	15.6%	0.0%	0.0%
81					
97					
98 Age	68	69	70	71	72
99 Human Capital	$374,830	$193,075	$0	$0	$0
100 Financial Capital	$3,783,194	$4,120,891	$4,482,085	$4,549,318	$4,617,572
101 Total Wealth	$4,158,024	$4,313,966	$4,482,085	$4,549,318	$4,617,572
102					
103 Real Salary	$163,995	$167,275	$170,620	$0	$0
104 Real Consumption	$89,474	$92,581	$95,924	$99,850	$99,850
105 Real Human Capital	$212,875	$108,031	$0	$0	$0
106 Real Financial Capital	$2,148,568	$2,305,767	$2,470,804	$2,470,806	$2,470,813
107 Real Total Wealth	$2,361,442	$2,413,799	$2,470,804	$2,470,806	$2,470,813
108					
109 Social Security Benefit Level	$59,621	$60,515	$61,423	$62,344	$63,279
110 Federal Income Tax Bracket 1 Cutoff	$15,715	$15,951	$16,190	$16,433	$16,679
111 Federal Income Tax Bracket 2 Cutoff	$63,829	$64,786	$65,758	$66,745	$67,746
112 Federal Income Tax Bracket 3 Cutoff	$154,686	$157,006	$159,362	$161,752	$164,178
113 Federal Income Tax Bracket 4 Cutoff	$322,666	$327,506	$332,419	$337,405	$342,466
114 Federal Income Tax Bracket 5 Cutoff	$701,414	$711,935	$722,614	$733,453	$744,455
115 Federal FICA-SSI Wage Cap	$200,203	$203,206	$206,254	$209,348	$212,488

As you adapt this model to your own situation, it is not necessary to go from full-time work to zero work. You could consider retiring to part-time work and then gradually tapering off. For example, you could drop to half-time work by setting your Real Growth in Salary to **-50%** in your first retirement year and then set your Real Growth in Salary to **-100.0%** in the year that you stop working entirely.

It is assumed that the Real Return on Broad Stock Portfolio is normally distributed with the average return given in cell **B7** and the standard deviation given in cell **B8**. The Excel function **RAND()** generates a random variable with a uniform distribution over the interval from 0 to 1 (that is, with an equal chance of getting any number between 0 and 1). To transform this uniformly distributed random variable into a normally distributed one, just place **RAND()** inside the Excel function **NORMINV**.[8]

The Human Capital computation makes a fairly rough adjustment for taxes, but the year-by-year cash flow analysis has a more sophisticated calculation of taxes. The reason for doing it this way (as opposed to taking the present value of the After-Tax Income row) is that this approach avoids generating circular references.

It doesn't make any sense to live like a king in your working years and then live in poverty in your retirement years. Similarly, it doesn't make sense to live in poverty in your working years and live like a king in your retirement years. The key idea is that you want to have a smooth pattern of real consumption over the life-cycle. Setting Taxable Income as a percentage of Total Wealth does a good job of delivering a smooth pattern. The only tricky part is when Social Security kicks in. Looking at the graph of Real Consumption, you should see a smooth pattern with no jump up or down at your retirement date. Notice that Taxable Income / Total Wealth is 7.0% in cell **AP37** and 4.5% the next year in cell **AQ37**, which is an adjustment of 2.5%. In other words, the drop in Taxable Income is offset by addition of Social Security Benefits (which are NOT taxable). Notice that Real Consumption transitions smoothly from $119,874 in cell **AP104** to $120,022 in cell **AQ104**. The Higher Consumption in Working Years of 2.5% in cell **B35** works well for the default input values of this Excel model. When you change input values, you may need to change the adjustment. Manually adjust the value in cell **B35** in small increments until the graph of Real Consumption shows a smooth pattern with no jump at the retirement date.

Since the standard deviation (risk) in cell **B8** is virtually zero, the results we see in the two graphs are based on *average returns*. Starting with the second graph, we see that Real Human Capital starts at $1.7 million and declines smoothly to

---

[8] The "Transformation Method" for converting a uniform random variable x into some other random variable y based on a cumulative distribution F is $y(x) = F^{-1}(x)$. See Press, W., B. Flannery, S. Teukolsky, and W. Vetterling, 1987, *Numerical Recopies: The Art of Scientific Computing*, Cambridge University Press, chapter on Random Numbers, subsection on the Transformation Method, page 201.

$0 at retirement. Real Financial Capital starts at $0, rises smoothly to $2.7 million at retirement, and then stays constant at that level. Turning to the first graph, Real Consumption starts at $33,234, rises smoothly to $120,022 at retirement, and then stays constant at that level.

How much saving does it take to reach such a comfortable lifestyle? Savings starts at 36.6% of salary at age 31 and gradually tapers off. Clearly, a lot of saving is required to live so well in retirement.

Now let's consider the risk involved. Change the standard deviation to a realistic figure. Enter **17.000%** in cell **B8**. The random variables in rows **40** and **41** spring to life and the graph of real consumption over the life-cycle reflect the high or low realizations of the broad stock portfolio. Press the function key **F9** and the Excel model is recalculated. You see a new realization of real consumption on the first graph. The three figures below show: (a) a low real consumption case due to low stock returns, (b) a medium real consumption case due to medium stock returns, and (c) a high real consumption case due to high stock returns.

Excel 2013   **FIGURE 19.9 Low Real Consumption Due To Low Stock Returns.**

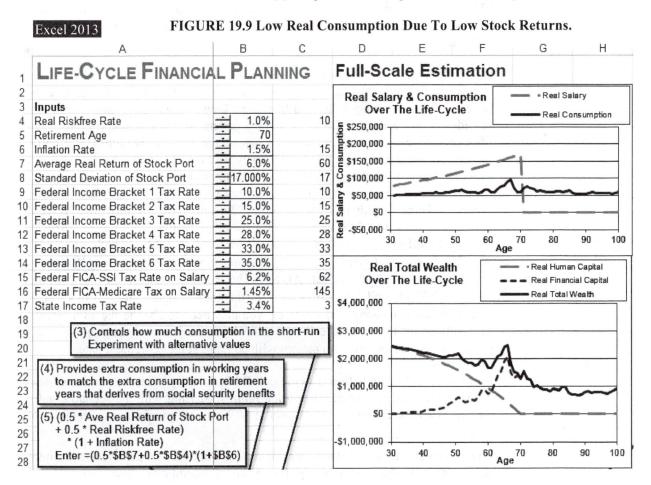

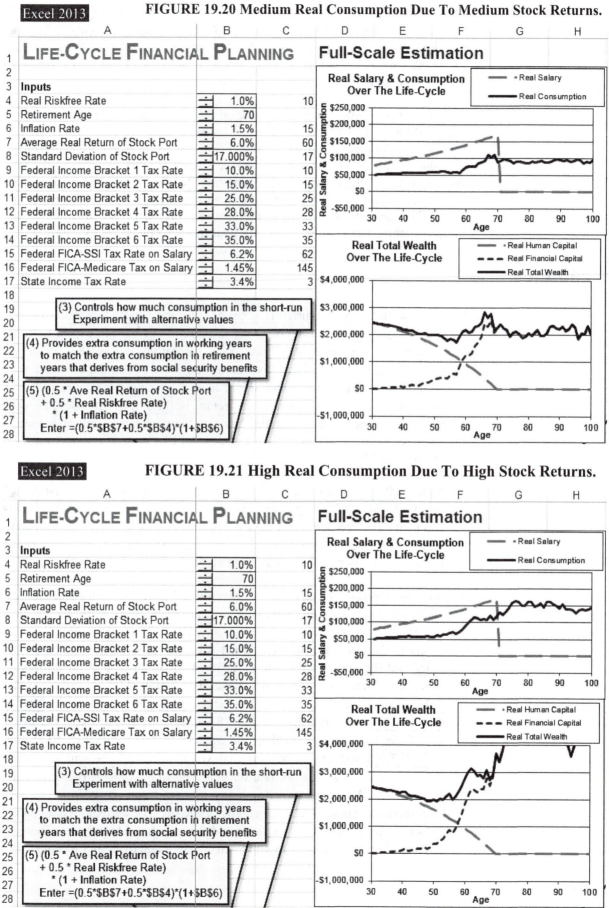

FIGURE 19.20 Medium Real Consumption Due To Medium Stock Returns.

FIGURE 19.21 High Real Consumption Due To High Stock Returns.

These three graphs are "representative" of the risk you face from being heavily invested in the broad stock portfolio. Real consumption drops to about $50,000 with low stock returns, $100,000 with medium returns, between $150,000 and $200,000 with high returns. Clearly, there is substantial risk from being so heavily exposed to the broad stock portfolio.

Now it is time for you to explore. Click on the spin buttons to change the inputs and/or edit the values of the choice variables and see the implications for lifetime real consumption and real total wealth. For example, if you are uncomfortable with the amount of risk above, try reduce stock exposure in retirement years. Play around with the Beginning Consumption Rate in cell **B34**. A higher value will tilt consumption towards working years and away from retirement years. Lower this value and it will tilt in the opposite direction. Play around with the choice variables and have fun exploring your lifetime opportunities. Enjoy!

Problems

1. Suppose that you are currently 25 years old and expect to earn a constant salary of $50,000. You are planning to retire at age 65 and expect to die at age 85. You save at a 10.0% rate. Your current tax rate is 18.0% and you expect your retirement years tax rate to be 23.0%. You plan to invest your money in a risky portfolio that might have a long-run low return of 1.0%, medium return of 5.0%, and a high return of 12.0%. What would be your annual retirement income in the low, medium, and high return scenarios when saving with a taxable plan, a traditional IRA or 401(k) plan, or a Roth IRA or 401(k) plan?

2. Suppose that you are currently 28 years old and expect to earn a constant real salary of $64,000 starting next year. You are planning to work for 32 years and then retire. You currently have $0 in financial capital. You are limited to investing in the riskfree asset. The real riskfree rate is 2.8%. Develop a financial plan for real savings and real consumption over your lifetime.

3. Suppose that you are currently 32 years old and expect to earn a constant real salary of $85,000 starting next year. You are planning to work for 25 years and then retire. You currently have $10,000 in financial capital. You can invest in the riskfree asset or a broad stock portfolio. The inflation rate is 3.4% and the real riskfree rate is 2.5%. A broad stock portfolio offers an average real return of 7.3% and a standard deviation of 25.0%. Suppose that federal income taxes have six brackets with the following rates: 10.0%, 15.0%, 27.0%, 30.0%, 35.0%, and 38.6%. For the current year, the upper cutoffs on the first five brackets are $6,000, $27,950, $67,700, $141,250, and $307,050 and these cutoffs are indexed to inflation. The state tax rate is 4.5%, federal FICA-SSI tax rate on salary up to $87,000 is 6.2%, and the federal FICA-Medicare tax rate on any level of salary is 1.45%. You will start receiving Social Security benefits at age 66. The current level of social security benefits is $24,204 per year and this is indexed to inflation. Develop a financial plan for real savings and real consumption over your lifetime.

PART 6 INTERNATIONAL CORPORATE FINANCE

Chapter 20 International Parity

20.1 System of Four Parity Conditions

Problem. Suppose the Euro/Dollar Exchange Rate is €1 = $1.3640, the annual US riskfree rate is 4.47%, the US inflation rate is 2.69%, and the annual Eurozone riskfree rate is 4.27%. What is the one-year Forward Euro/Dollar Exchange Rate, the one-year ahead Expected Spot Euro/Dollar Exchange Rate, and Eurozone inflation rate? What is the Percent Difference in:

- the Eurozone Riskfree Rate vs. US Riskfree Rate,
- the Forward Euro/Dollar Exchange Rate vs. the Spot Rate,
- the Expected Spot Euro/Dollar Exchange Rate vs. the Spot Rate, and
- the Eurozone Inflation Rate vs. the US Inflation Rate?

Solution Strategy. Use Interest Rate Parity to determine the one-year Forward Euro/Dollar Exchange Rate. Then use the Expectations Theory of Exchange Rates to determine the one-year ahead Expected Spot Euro/Dollar Exchange Rate. Then use Purchase Power Parity to determine the Eurozone inflation rate. Finally, use the International Fisher Effect to confirm the Eurozone riskfree rate. Compute the four percent differences. Under the four international parity condition, the four percent differences should be identical.

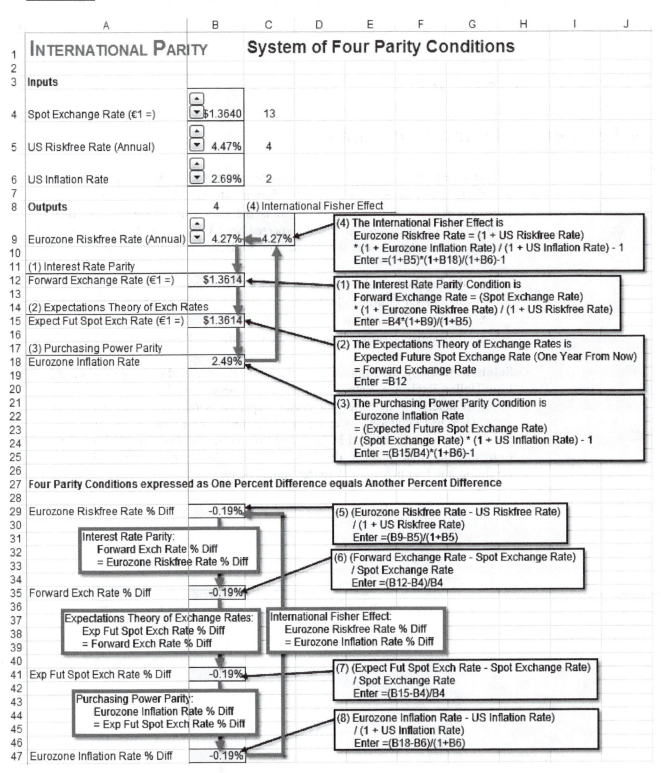

FIGURE 20.1 International Parity – System of Four Parity Conditions.

In theory, the four international parity conditions are tightly connected to each other.

20.2 Estimating Future Exchange Rates

Problem. Suppose the Euro/Dollar Exchange Rate is €1 = $1.3640, the annual US riskfree rate is 4.47%, the US inflation rate is 2.69%, the annual Eurozone riskfree rate is 4.27%, the Eurozone inflation rate is 1.90%, and the one-year Forward Euro/Dollar Exchange Rate is €1 = $1.3739. What will the Euro/Dollar Exchange Rate be in one-year, two-years, three-years, four-years, and five-years?

Excel 2013

FIGURE 20.2 International Parity – Estimating Future Exchange Rates.

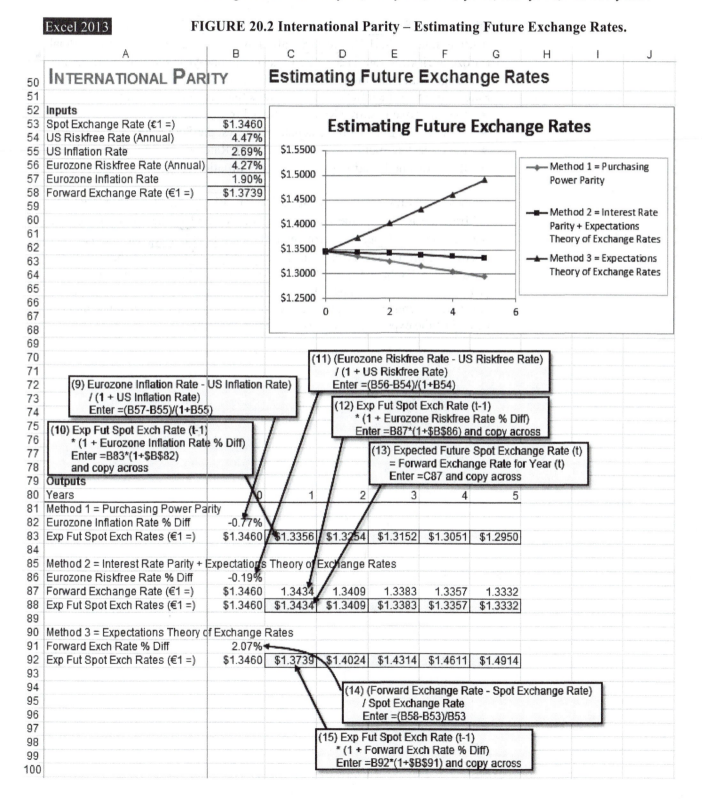

Solution. Use three different methods for forecasting future exchange rates: (1) Purchasing Power Parity, (2) Interest Rate Parity + Expectations Theory of Exchange Rates, and (3) Only the Expectations Theory of Exchange Rates.
In practice, when you use real data, the various international parity conditions yield very different forecasts of future exchange rates.

Problems

1. Suppose the Euro/Dollar Exchange Rate is €1 = $1.283, the annual US riskfree rate is 3.61%, the US inflation rate is 2.69%, and the annual Eurozone riskfree rate is 5.39%. What is the one-year Forward Euro/Dollar Exchange Rate, the one-year ahead Expected Spot Euro/Dollar Exchange Rate, and Eurozone inflation rate? What is the Percent Difference in:
   - the Eurozone Riskfree Rate vs. US Riskfree Rate,
   - the Forward Euro/Dollar Exchange Rate vs. the Spot Rate,
   - the Expected Spot Euro/Dollar Exchange Rate vs. the Spot Rate, and
   - the Eurozone Inflation Rate vs. the US Inflation Rate?

2. Suppose the Euro/Dollar Exchange Rate is €1 = $1.7271, the annual US riskfree rate is 6.31%, the US inflation rate is 4.52%, the annual Eurozone riskfree rate is 3.15%, the Eurozone inflation rate is 2.65%, and the one-year Forward Euro/Dollar Exchange Rate is €1 = $1.8241. What will the Euro/Dollar Exchange Rate be in one-year, two-years, three-years, four-years, and five-years under three forecast methods: (1) purchasing power parity, (2) interest rate parity + expectations theory of exchange rates, and (3) using just the expectations theory of exchange rates?

PART 7 OPTIONS AND CORPORATE FINANCE

Chapter 21 Binomial Option Pricing

21.1 Estimating Volatility

The binomial option pricing model can certainly be used to price European calls and puts, but it can do much more. The Binomial Tree / Risk Neutral method can be extended to price *any* type of derivative security (European, American, etc.) on any underlying asset(s), with any underlying dividends or cash flows, with any derivative payoffs at maturity and/or payoffs before maturity. It is one of the most popular techniques on Wall Street for pricing and hedging derivatives.

Problem. What is the annual standard deviation of Facebook stock based on continuous returns?

Solution Strategy. Download three months of Facebook (FB) daily stock prices. Then calculate continuous returns. Finally, calculate the annual standard deviation of the continuous returns.

Excel 2013   **FIGURE 21.1 Binomial Option Pricing - Estimating Volatility.**

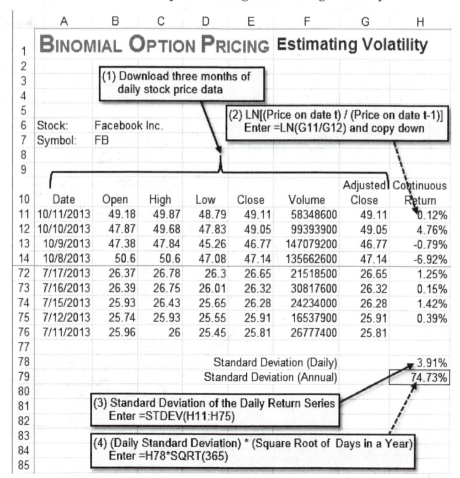

We find that Facebook's annual standard deviation is 74.73%.

21.2 Single Period

Problem. At the close of trading on October 11, 2013, the stock price of Facebook (FB) was $49.11, the standard deviation of daily returns is 74.73%, the yield on a six-month U.S. Treasury Bill was 0.12%, the exercise price of an March 45 call on Facebook was $45.00, the exercise price of an March 45 put on Facebook was $45.00, and the time to maturity for both March 22, 2014 maturity options was 0.4472 years. The dividend yield is 1.00%. What is the price of a March 45 call and a March 45 put on Facebook?

Excel 2013 **FIGURE 21.2 Binomial Option Pricing - Single Period - Call Option.**

Solution Strategy. First, calculate the binomial tree parameters: time / period, riskfree rate / period, up movement / period, and down movement / period. Second, calculate the date 1, maturity date items: stock up price, stock down price, and the corresponding call and put payoffs. Third, calculate the shares of stock and money borrowed to create a replicating portfolio that replicates the option payoff at maturity. Finally, calculate the price now of the replicating portfolio and, in the absence of arbitrage, this will be the option price now.

Results. We see that the Binomial Option Pricing model predicts a one-period European call price of $13.49. The put price (below) is valued at $9.56.

Excel 2013 | **FIGURE 21.3 Excel Model of Binomial Option Pricing - Single Period - Put**

	A	B	C	D	E	F	G	H	I	J
1	**BINOMIAL OPTION PRICING**			**Single Period**			**Put**			
2										
3	**Inputs**	Option Type								
4	Option Type	○ Call ● Put	2							
5	Underlying Asset Type	○ Stock ○ Stock Index ○ Futures ● Foreign Currency					4			
6	Spot Exch Rate Now	$49.11	49	**Outputs**						
7	Standard Dev (Annual)	74.73%	74	Time / Period		0.447				
8	Riskfree Rate (Annual)	0.12%	1	(Riskfree Rate - Under. Asset Yield) / Period		-0.39%				
9	Exercise Price	$45.00	45	Up Movement / Period		64.83%				
10	Time To Maturity (Years)	0.4472	4	Down Movement/Period		-39.33%				
11	Underlying Asset Yield is Foreign Riskfree Rate	1.00%	1							
12	Number of Periods	1								
13		**Now**	**Maturity**							
14	**Period**	0	1							
15	**Time**	0.000	0.447							
16										
17	**Stock**	$49.11	$80.95							
18			$29.79							
19										
20	**Put**	$9.56	$0.00							
21			$15.21							
22										
23	**Replicating Portfolio**									
24										
25	**Stock Shares Bought (Sold)**									
26		(0.297)								
27										
28	**Money Lent (Borrowed)**									
29		$24.16								

(1) (Time to Maturity) / (Number of Periods) Enter =$B10/B12

(2) Exp [(Riskfree Rate - Underlying Asset Yield) * (Time / Period)] - 1 Enter =EXP(($B8-$B11)*F7)-1

(3) Exp [(Standard Deviation) * Square Root (Time / Period)] - 1 Enter =EXP($B7*SQRT(F7))-1

(4) Exp [- (Standard Deviation) * Square Root (Time / Period)] - 1 Enter =EXP(-$B7*SQRT(F7))-1

(5) Time to Maturity * (Period / Number of Periods) Enter =$B$10*(B14/$B$12) and copy across

(6) Stock Price Now Enter =B6

(7) (Stock Price (t-1)) * (1 + Up Movement / Period) Enter =B17*(1+F9)

(8) (Stock Price (t-1)) * (1 + Down Movement / Period) Enter =B17*(1+F10)

(9) If Option Type = Call, Then Call Payoff at Maturity = Max (Stock Price at Maturity - Exercise Price, 0) Else Put Payoff at Maturity = Max (Exercise Price - Stock Price at Maturity, 0) Enter =IF($C$4=1,MAX(C17-$B$9,0),MAX($B$9-C17,0)) and copy down

(10) (Option Up Payoff - Option Down Payoff) / (Stock Up Price - Stock Down Price) Enter =(C20-C21)/(C17-C18)

(11) (Call Down Payoff - Hedge Ratio * Stock Down Price) / (1 + Riskfree Rate / Period) Enter =(C21-B26*C18)/(1+F8)

(12) Replicating Portfolio Price Now = Number of Shares of Stock * Stock Price Now + Money Borrowed Enter =B26*B17+B29

The model can handle three additional types of underlying asset (see **row 5**): (1) stock index, (2) futures, and (3) foreign currency. Then the underlying asset yield (see **row 11**) becomes: (1) the stock index dividend yield, (2) the riskfree rate, and (3) the foreign riskfree rate, respectively.

Excel 2013

FIGURE 21.4 Binomial - Single Period – 3 Alternative Underlying Assets

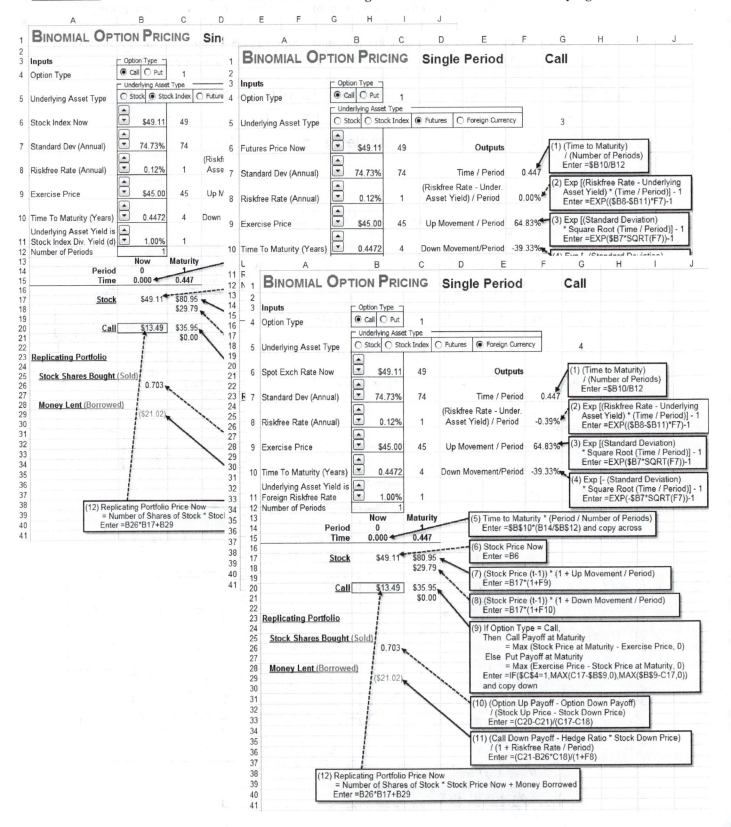

21.3 Multi-Period

Problem. Same as before, except we will use an eight-period model to evaluate it. At the close of trading on October 11, 2013, the stock price of Facebook (FB) was $49.11, the standard deviation of daily returns is 74.73%, the yield on a six-month U.S. Treasury Bill was 0.12%, the exercise price of an March 45 call on Facebook was $45.00, the exercise price of an March 45 put on Facebook was $45.00, and the time to maturity for both March 22, 2014 maturity options was 0.4472 years. The dividend yield is 1.00%. What is the price of a March 45 call and a March 45 put on Facebook?

Excel 2013   **FIGURE 21.5 Binomial Option Pricing - Multi-Period - Call.**

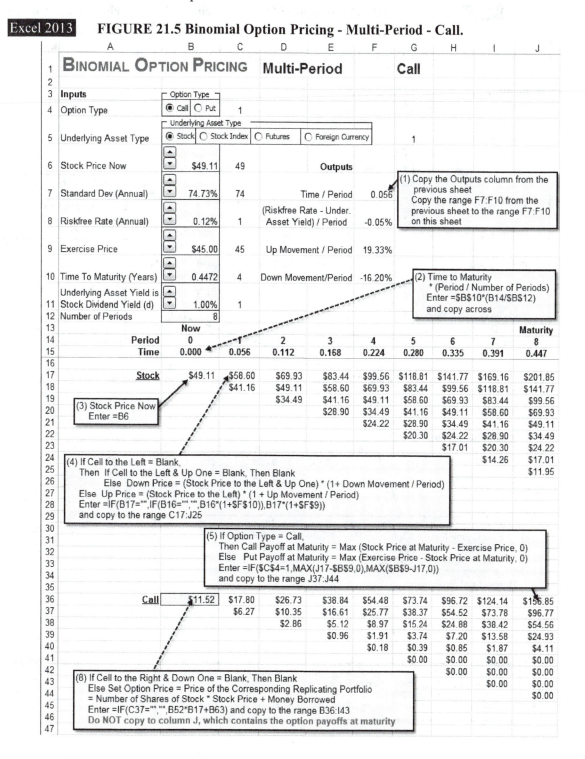

Solution Strategy. First, copy the binomial tree parameters from the single-period model. Second, build a multi-period tree of stock prices. Third, calculate call and put payoffs at maturity. Fourth, build the multi-period trees of the shares of stock and money borrowed to create a replicating portfolio that replicates the option period by period. Finally, build a multi-period tree of the value of the replicating portfolio and, in the absence of arbitrage, this will be the value of the option.

Results. We see that the Binomial Option Pricing model predicts an eight-period European call price of $11.52.

Excel 2013	**FIGURE 21.6 Binomial Option Pricing - Multi-Period - Call (Continued).**

	A	B	C	D	E	F	G	H	I	J
1	**BINOMIAL OPTION PRICING**			**Multi-Period**			**Call**			
2										
3	Inputs	Option Type								
4	Option Type	◉ Call ○ Put	1							
5	Underlying Asset Type	Underlying Asset Type ◉ Stock ○ Stock Index ○ Futures ○ Foreign Currency					1			
6	Stock Price Now	$49.11	49		**Outputs**					
7	Standard Dev (Annual)	74.73%	74		Time / Period	0.056				
8	Riskfree Rate (Annual)	0.12%	1	(Riskfree Rate - Under. Asset Yield) / Period		-0.05%				
9	Exercise Price	$45.00	45		Up Movement / Period	19.33%				
10	Time To Maturity (Years)	0.4472	4		Down Movement/Period	-16.20%				
11	Underlying Asset Yield is Stock Dividend Yield (d)	1.00%	1							
12	Number of Periods	8								
13		**Now**								**Maturity**
14	Period	0	1	2	3	4	5	6	7	8
15	Time	0.000	0.056	0.112	0.168	0.224	0.280	0.335	0.391	0.447
48										
49	**Replicating Portfolio**									
50										
51	**Stock Shares Bought (Sold)**									
52		0.661	0.787	0.895	0.969	1.000	1.000	1.000	1.000	
53			0.513	0.659	0.807	0.931	1.000	1.000	1.000	
54				0.339	0.483	0.660	0.850	1.000	1.000	
55					0.169	0.273	0.434	0.671	1.000	
56						0.045	0.083	0.153	0.281	
57							0.000	0.000	0.000	
58								0.000	0.000	
59									0.000	

(6) If Corresponding Option Down Price = Blank, Then Blank
  Else Hedge Ratio = (Option Up Price - Option Down Price)
    / (Stock Up Price - Stock Down Price)
  Enter =IF(C37="","",(C36-C37)/(C17-C18)) and copy to the range B52:I59

	A	B	C	D	E	F	G	H	I	J
62	**Money Lent (Borrowed)**									
63		($20.97)	($28.30)	($35.83)	($41.98)	($45.09)	($45.07)	($45.04)	($45.02)	
64			($14.84)	($22.00)	($30.68)	($39.35)	($45.07)	($45.04)	($45.02)	
65				($8.85)	($14.76)	($23.42)	($34.55)	($45.04)	($45.02)	
66					($3.92)	($7.52)	($14.13)	($25.77)	($45.02)	
67						($0.91)	($2.01)	($4.41)	($9.70)	
68							$0.00	$0.00	$0.00	
69								$0.00	$0.00	
70									$0.00	

(7) If Corresponding Option Down Price = Blank, Then Blank
  Else (Option Down Price - Hedge Ratio * Stock Down Price)
    / (1 + Riskfree Rate / Period)
  Enter =IF(C37="","",(C37-B52*C18)/(1+$F$8)) and copy in range B63:I70

Callout boxes:
(1) Copy the Outputs column from the previous sheet
Copy the range F7:F10 from the previous sheet to the range F7:F10 on this sheet

(2) Time to Maturity
* (Period / Number of Periods)
Enter =$B$10*(B14/$B$12) and copy across

Now let's check the put.

Excel 2013 **FIGURE 21.7 Binomial Option Pricing - Multi-Period - Put.**

We see that the Binomial Option Pricing model predicts an eight-period European put price of $7.58.

FIGURE 21.8 Binomial Option Pricing - Multi-Period - Put (Continued).

	A	B	C	D	E	F	G	H	I	J
1	**BINOMIAL OPTION PRICING**			**Multi-Period**			**Put**			
2										
3	**Inputs**	Option Type								
4	Option Type	○ Call ● Put	2							
5	Underlying Asset Type	● Stock ○ Stock Index ○ Futures ○ Foreign Currency					1			
6	Stock Price Now	$49.11	49		**Outputs**					
7	Standard Dev (Annual)	74.73%	74		Time / Period	0.056				
8	Riskfree Rate (Annual)	0.12%	1	(Riskfree Rate - Under. Asset Yield) / Period	-0.05%					
9	Exercise Price	$45.00	45		Up Movement / Period	19.33%				
10	Time To Maturity (Years)	0.4472	4		Down Movement/Period	-16.20%				
11	Underlying Asset Yield is Stock Dividend Yield (d)	1.00%	1							
12	Number of Periods	8								
13		**Now**								**Maturity**
14	**Period**	**0**	**1**	**2**	**3**	**4**	**5**	**6**	**7**	**8**
15	**Time**	**0.000**	**0.056**	**0.112**	**0.168**	**0.224**	**0.280**	**0.335**	**0.391**	**0.447**
48										
49	**Replicating Portfolio**									
50										
51	**Stock Shares Bought (Sold)**									
52		(0.339)	(0.213)	(0.105)	(0.031)	0.000	0.000	0.000	0.000	
53			(0.487)	(0.341)	(0.193)	(0.069)	0.000	0.000	0.000	
54				(0.661)	(0.517)	(0.340)	(0.150)	0.000	0.000	
55					(0.831)	(0.727)	(0.566)	(0.329)	0.000	
56						(0.955)	(0.917)	(0.847)	(0.719)	
57							(1.000)	(1.000)	(1.000)	
58								(1.000)	(1.000)	
59									(1.000)	
62	**Money Lent (Borrowed)**									
63		$24.21	$16.85	$9.30	$3.13	$0.00	$0.00	$0.00	$0.00	
64			$30.32	$23.13	$14.43	$5.74	$0.00	$0.00	$0.00	
65				$36.28	$30.36	$21.67	$10.52	$0.00	$0.00	
66					$41.19	$37.57	$30.94	$19.27	$0.00	
67						$44.18	$43.06	$40.63	$35.32	
68							$45.07	$45.04	$45.02	
69								$45.04	$45.02	
70									$45.02	

Excel 2013

(1) Copy the Outputs column from the previous sheet
Copy the range F7:F10 from the previous sheet to the range F7:F10 on this sheet

(2) Time to Maturity
* (Period / Number of Periods)
Enter =$B$10*(B14/$B$12)
and copy across

(6) If Corresponding Option Down Price = Blank, Then Blank
Else Hedge Ratio = (Option Up Price - Option Down Price)
/ (Stock Up Price - Stock Down Price)
Enter =IF(C37="","",(C36-C37)/(C17-C18)) and copy to the range B52:I59

(7) If Corresponding Option Down Price = Blank, Then Blank
Else (Option Down Price - Hedge Ratio * Stock Down Price)
/ (1 + Riskfree Rate / Period)
Enter =IF(C37="","",(C37-B52*C18)/(1+$F$8)) and copy in range B63:I70

As in the single period case, replicating a Call option requires **Buying** Shares of Stock and **Borrowing** Money, whereas a Put option requires **Selling** Shares of Stock and **Lending** Money. Notice that the quantity of Money Borrowed or Lent and the quantity of Shares Bought or Sold changes over time and differs for up nodes vs. down nodes. This process of changing the replicating portfolio every period based on the realized up or down movement in the underlying stock price is called dynamic replication.

Price accuracy can be increased by subdividing the option's time to maturity into more periods (15, 30, etc.). Typically, from 50 to 100 periods are required in order to achieve price accuracy to the penny.

21.4 Risk Neutral

The previous Excel model, **Binomial Option Pricing Multi-Period**, determined the price of an option by constructing a replicating portfolio, which combines a stock and a bond to replicate the payoffs of the option. An alternative way to price an option is the Risk Neutral method. Both techniques give you the same answer. The main advantage of the Risk Neutral method is that it is faster and easier to implement. The Replicating Portfolio method required the construction of four trees (stock prices, shares of stock **bought (sold)**, money **lent (borrowed)**, and option prices). The Risk Neutral method will only require two trees (stock prices and option prices).

Problem. Same as before, except we will use the risk neutral method to evaluate it. At the close of trading on October 11, 2013, the stock price of Facebook (FB) was $49.11, the standard deviation of daily returns is 74.73%, the yield on a six-month U.S. Treasury Bill was 0.12%, the exercise price of an March 45 call on Facebook was $45.00, the exercise price of an March 45 put on Facebook was $45.00, and the time to maturity for both March 22, 2014 maturity options was 0.4472 years. The dividend yield is 1.00%. What is the price of a March 45 call and a March 45 put on Facebook?

Solution Strategy. First, copy the binomial tree parameters, stock price tree, and option payoffs at maturity from the multi-period model. Second, calculate the risk neutral probability. Finally, build a option value tree using the risk neutral probability.

Results. We see that the Risk Neutral method predicts an eight-period European call price of $11.52. This is identical to previous section's Replicating Portfolio Price. Next let's check the put.

Excel 2013   **FIGURE 21.9 Binomial Option Pricing – Risk Neutral - Call.**

	A	B	C	D	E	F	G	H	I	J
1	**BINOMIAL OPTION PRICING**			**Risk Neutral**			**Call**			
2										
3	**Inputs**	Option Type								
4	Option Type	◉ Call ○ Put	1							
5	Underlying Asset Type	Underlying Asset Type ◉ Stock ○ Stock Index	○ Futures	○ Foreign Currency			1			
6	Stock Price Now	▲▼ $49.11	49		**Outputs**					
7	Standard Dev (Annual)	▲▼ 74.73%	74		Time / Period	0.056				
8	Riskfree Rate (Annual)	▲▼ 0.12%	1	(Riskfree Rate - Under. Asset Yield) / Period		-0.05%				
9	Exercise Price	▲▼ $45.00	45	Up Movement / Period		19.33%				
10	Time To Maturity (Years)	▲▼ 0.4472	4	Down Movement/Period		-16.20%				
11	Underlying Asset Yield is Stock Dividend Yield (d)	▲▼ 1.00%	1	Risk Neutral Probability		45.46%				
12	Number of Periods	8								
13		**Now**								**Maturity**
14	Period	0	1	2	3	4	5	6	7	8
15	Time	0.000	0.056	0.112	0.168	0.224	0.280	0.335	0.391	0.447
16										
17	**Stock**	$49.11	$58.60	$69.93	$83.44	$99.56	$118.81	$141.77	$169.16	$201.85
18			$41.16	$49.11	$58.60	$69.93	$83.44	$99.56	$118.81	$141.77
19				$34.49	$41.16	$49.11	$58.60	$69.93	$83.44	$99.56
20					$28.90	$34.49	$41.16	$49.11	$58.60	$69.93
21						$24.22	$28.90	$34.49	$41.16	$49.11
22							$20.30	$24.22	$28.90	$34.49
23								$17.01	$20.30	$24.22
24									$14.26	$17.01
25										$11.95
26										
27										
28										
29										
30										
31										
32										
33										
34										
35										
36	**Call**	$11.52	$17.80	$26.73	$38.84	$54.48	$73.74	$96.72	$124.14	$156.85
37			$6.27	$10.35	$16.61	$25.77	$38.37	$54.52	$73.78	$96.77
38				$2.86	$5.12	$8.97	$15.24	$24.88	$38.42	$54.56
39					$0.96	$1.91	$3.74	$7.20	$13.58	$24.93
40						$0.18	$0.39	$0.85	$1.87	$4.11
41							$0.00	$0.00	$0.00	$0.00
42								$0.00	$0.00	$0.00
43									$0.00	$0.00
44										$0.00
45										
46										
47										
48										
49										
50										
51										

(1) Copy the Outputs column from the previous sheet
Copy the range F7:F10 from the previous sheet to the range F7:F10 on this sheet

(2) (Riskfree Rate / Period
- Down Movement / Period)
/ (Up Movement / Period
- Down Movement / Period)
Enter =(F8-F10)/(F9-F10)

(3) Copy the Stock Price Tree from the previous sheet
Copy the range B17:J25 from the previous sheet
to the range B17:J25 on this sheet

(4) Copy the Payoffs at Maturity from the previous sheet
Copy the range J36:J44 from the previous sheet
to the range J36:J44 on this sheet

(5) If Cell to the Right & Down One = Blank, Then Blank
Else Expected Value of Option Price Next Period (using the Risk Neutral Probability)
Discounted at the Riskfree Rate
= [(Risk Neutral Probability) * (Stock Up Price) + (1 - Risk Neutral Probability) * (Stock Down Price)]
/ (1+ Riskfree Rate / Period)
Enter =IF(C37="","",($F$11*C36+(1-$F$11)*C37)/(1+$F$8)) and copy to the range B36:I43
Do **NOT** copy to column J, which contains the option payoffs at maturity

FIGURE 21.10 Binomial Option Pricing – Risk Neutral - Put.

Excel 2013

	A	B	C	D	E	F	G	H	I	J
1	BINOMIAL OPTION PRICING			Risk Neutral			Put			
2										
3	Inputs	Option Type								
4	Option Type	○ Call ● Put	2							
5	Underlying Asset Type	● Stock ○ Stock Index ○ Futures ○ Foreign Currency				1				
6	Stock Price Now	$49.11	49		Outputs					
7	Standard Dev (Annual)	74.73%	74		Time / Period	0.056				
8	Riskfree Rate (Annual)	0.12%	1	(Riskfree Rate - Under. Asset Yield) / Period		-0.05%				
9	Exercise Price	$45.00	45	Up Movement / Period		19.33%				
10	Time To Maturity (Years)	0.4472	4	Down Movement/Period		-16.20%				
11	Underlying Asset Yield is Stock Dividend Yield (d)	1.00%	1	Risk Neutral Probability		45.46%				
12	Number of Periods		8							
13		Now								Maturity
14	Period	0	1	2	3	4	5	6	7	8
15	Time	0.000	0.056	0.112	0.168	0.224	0.280	0.335	0.391	0.447
16										
17	Stock	$49.11	$58.60	$69.93	$83.44	$99.56	$118.81	$141.77	$169.16	$201.85
18			$41.16	$49.11	$58.60	$69.93	$83.44	$99.56	$118.81	$141.77
19				$34.49	$41.16	$49.11	$58.60	$69.93	$83.44	$99.56
20					$28.90	$34.49	$41.16	$49.11	$58.60	$69.93
21						$24.22	$28.90	$34.49	$41.16	$49.11
22							$20.30	$24.22	$28.90	$34.49
23								$17.01	$20.30	$24.22
24									$14.26	$17.01
25										$11.95
36	Put	$7.58	$4.36	$1.94	$0.51	$0.00	$0.00	$0.00	$0.00	$0.00
37			$10.26	$6.37	$3.12	$0.93	$0.00	$0.00	$0.00	$0.00
38				$13.50	$9.08	$4.95	$1.71	$0.00	$0.00	$0.00
39					$17.17	$12.51	$7.65	$3.13	$0.00	$0.00
40						$21.04	$16.55	$11.40	$5.73	$0.00
41							$24.77	$20.82	$16.12	$10.51
42								$28.03	$24.72	$20.78
43									$30.76	$27.99
44										$33.05

(1) Copy the Outputs column from the previous sheet
Copy the range F7:F10 from the previous sheet to the range F7:F10 on this sheet

(2) (Riskfree Rate / Period - Down Movement / Period) / (Up Movement / Period - Down Movement / Period)
Enter =(F8-F10)/(F9-F10)

(3) Copy the Stock Price Tree from the previous sheet Copy the range B17:J25 from the previous sheet to the range B17:J25 on this sheet

(4) Copy the Payoffs at Maturity from the previous sheet Copy the range J36:J44 from the previous sheet to the range J36:J44 on this sheet

(5) If Cell to the Right & Down One = Blank, Then Blank
Else Expected Value of Option Price Next Period (using the Risk Neutral Probability)
Discounted at the Riskfree Rate
= [(Risk Neutral Probability) * (Stock Up Price) + (1 - Risk Neutral Probability) * (Stock Down Price)]
/ (1+ Riskfree Rate / Period)
Enter =IF(C37="","",($F$11*C36+(1-$F$11)*C37)/(1+$F$8)) and copy to the range B36:I43
Do NOT copy to column J, which contains the option payoffs at maturity

We see that the Risk Neutral method predicts an eight-period European put price of $7.58. This is identical to previous section's Replicating Portfolio Price. Again, we get the same answer either way. The advantage of the Risk Neutral method is that we only have to construct two trees, rather than four trees.

21.5 Average of N and N-1

Problem. Same as before, except we will use the average of N and N-1 method to evaluate it. At the close of trading on October 11, 2013, the stock price of Facebook (FB) was $49.11, the standard deviation of daily returns is 74.73%, the yield on a six-month U.S. Treasury Bill was 0.12%, the exercise price of an March 45 call on Facebook was $45.00, the exercise price of an March 45 put on Facebook was $45.00, and the time to maturity for both March 22, 2014 maturity options was 0.4472 years. The dividend yield is 1.00%. What is the price of a March 45 call and a March 45 put on Facebook?

Excel 2013 **FIGURE 21.11 Binomial Option Pricing – Ave of N and N-1 - Call.**

	A	B	C	D	E	F	G	H	I	J
1	BINOMIAL OPTION PRICING				Average of N and N-1				Call	
2										
3	**Inputs**	Option Type					(1) Copy the Outputs column from the previous sheet Copy the range F7:F11 from the previous sheet to the range F7:G11 on this sheet			
4	Option Type	⦿ Call ◯ Put	1							
5	Underlying Asset Type	Underlying Asset Type ⦿ Stock ◯ Stock Index ◯ Futures ◯ Foreign Currency					1			
6	Stock Price Now	$49.11	49		**Outputs**	N Periods	N-1 Periods			
7	Standard Dev (Annual)	74.73%	74		Time / Period	0.056	0.064			
8	Riskfree Rate (Annual)	0.12%	1		(Riskfree Rate - Under. Asset Yield) / Period	-0.05%	-0.06%			
9	Exercise Price	$45.00	45		Up Movement / Period	19.33%	20.79%			
10	Time To Maturity (Years)	0.4472	4		Down Movement/Period	-16.20%	-17.21%			
11	Underlying Asset Yield is Stock Dividend Yield (d)	1.00%	1		Risk Neutral Probability	45.46%	45.14%			
12	Number of Periods	8	7							
13		Now								Maturity
14	Period	0	1	2	3	4	5	6	7	8
15	Time	0.000	0.056	0.112	0.168	0.224	0.280	0.335	0.391	0.447
16										
17	**N Period Stock**	$49.11	$58.60	$69.93	$83.44	$99.56	$118.81	$141.77	$169.16	$201.85
18			$41.16	$49.11	$58.60	$69.93	$83.44	$99.56	$118.81	$141.77
19				$34.49	$41.16	$49.11	$58.60	$69.93	$83.44	$99.56
20	(2) Copy the Stock Price Tree from the previous sheet Copy the range B17:J25 from the previous sheet to the range B17:J25 on this sheet				$28.90	$34.49	$41.16	$49.11	$58.60	$69.93
21						$24.22	$28.90	$34.49	$41.16	$49.11
22							$20.30	$24.22	$28.90	$34.49
23								$17.01	$20.30	$24.22
24									$14.26	$17.01
25										$11.95
26										
27										
28										
29										
30										
31										
32										
33										
34										
35										
36	**N Period Call**	$11.52	$17.80	$26.73	$38.84	$54.48	$73.74	$96.72	$124.14	$156.85
37			$6.27	$10.35	$16.61	$25.77	$38.37	$54.52	$73.78	$96.77
38				$2.86	$5.12	$8.97	$15.24	$24.88	$38.42	$54.56
39	(3) Copy the Call Price Tree from the previous sheet Copy the range B36:J44 from the previous sheet to the range B36:J44 on this sheet				$0.96	$1.91	$3.74	$7.20	$13.58	$24.93
40						$0.18	$0.39	$0.85	$1.87	$4.11
41							$0.00	$0.00	$0.00	$0.00
42								$0.00	$0.00	$0.00
43									$0.00	$0.00
44										$0.00

Solution Strategy. First, copy the 8-period binomial model from the prior section. Second, create an analogous 7-period binominal model. Finally, compute the average derivate price from the 8-period price and 7-period price.

FIGURE 21.12 Binomial Option Pricing – Ave of N and N-1 - Call.

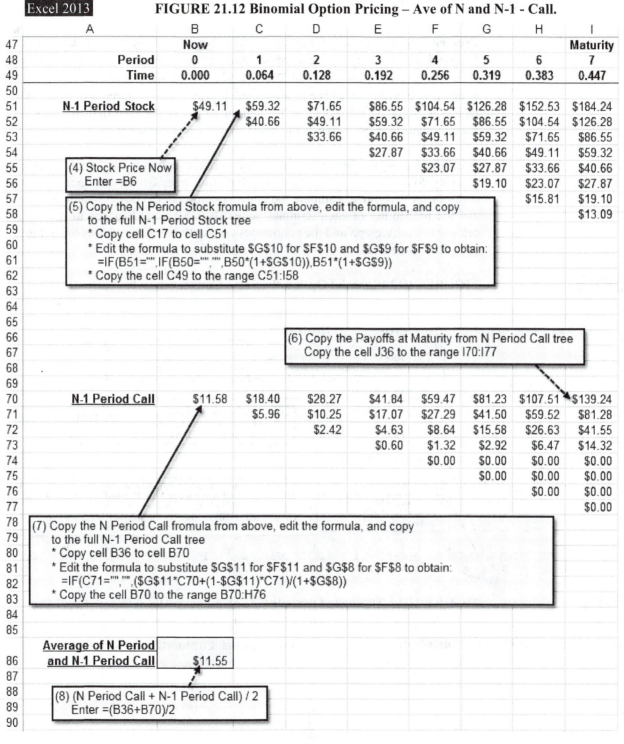

Results. The 8-period price is $13.32 and the 7-period price is $13.88. The average of these two prices is $11.55. This is a much more accurate estimate of the true option price, because the binomial model alternates between overshooting the true price and undershooting the true price as additional periods are added.

21.6 Convergence to Normal

Problem. At the close of trading on October 11, 2013, the stock price of Facebook was $49.11, the standard deviation of daily returns is 74.73%, and the option time to maturity was 0.4472 years. Show what happens to the stock price at maturity distribution of the binomial stock price tree as the number of periods increases. Show what happens to the continuous cumulative return distribution of the binomial stock price tree as the number of periods increases.

Solution Strategy. Given a number of periods, compute the stock price at maturity for each terminal node of the binomial tree. Given the stock price at maturity for each node, compute the corresponding continuous cumulative return and the probability of each terminal node. Then see what happens to the stock price at maturity graph and the continuous cumulative return graph as the number of periods increases.

Excel 2013   **FIGURE 21.13 Binomial Option Pricing – Convergence To Normal.**

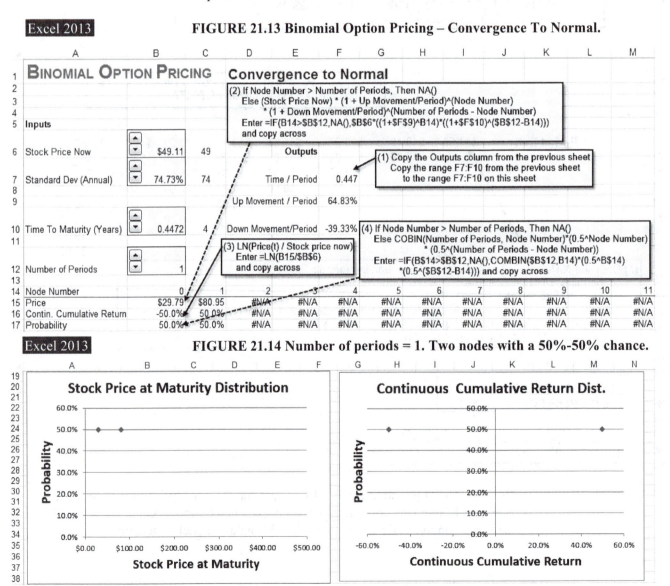

Excel 2013   **FIGURE 21.14 Number of periods = 1. Two nodes with a 50%-50% chance.**

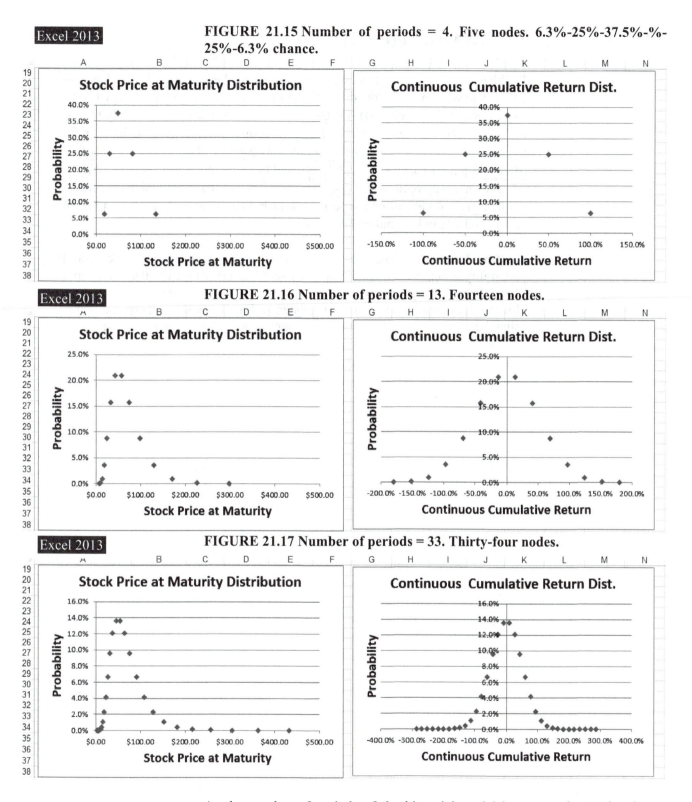

FIGURE 21.15 Number of periods = 4. Five nodes. 6.3%-25%-37.5%-%-25%-6.3% chance.

FIGURE 21.16 Number of periods = 13. Fourteen nodes.

FIGURE 21.17 Number of periods = 33. Thirty-four nodes.

As the number of periods of the binomial model increases, the stock price at maturity converges to a left-skewed, lognormal distribution and the continuous cumulative return converges to the normal distribution.

21.7 American With Discrete Dividends

Problem. Same as before, except we will value American options where the underlying stock pays dividends. At the close of trading on October 11, 2013, the stock price of Facebook (FB) was $49.11, the standard deviation of daily returns is 74.73%, the yield on a six-month U.S. Treasury Bill was 0.12%, the exercise price of an March 45 call on Facebook was $45.00, the exercise price of an March 45 put on Facebook was $45.00, and the time to maturity for both March 22, 2014 maturity options was 0.4472 years. Assume that Facebook pays certain, riskfree $1.00 dividends on the periods show below. What is the price of a March 45 call and a March 45 put on Facebook?

Solution Strategy. First, copy the binomial tree parameters, the risk neutral probability, stock price tree, and option payoffs at maturity from the risk neutral model. Second, calculate the total stock price as the sum of the risky stock price plus the discounted value of future dividends. Finally, build a option value tree using the risk neutral probability and accounting for optimal early exercise.

Excel 2013 **FIGURE 21.18 Binomial – American With Discrete Dividends – Call.**

	A	B	C	D	E	F	G	H	I	J
1	**BINOMIAL OPTION PRICING**			**American With Discrete Dividends**						**Call**
2										
3	**Inputs**		Option Type				Early Exercise			
4	Option Type		◉ Call ○ Put	1		Early Exercise	○ European ◉ American	2		
5	Underlying Asset Type		Underlying Asset Type ◉ Stock ○ Stock Index ○ Futures ○ Foreign Currency				1			
6	Stock Price Now	▲▼ $49.11	49			**Outputs**				
7	Standard Dev (Annual)	▲▼ 74.73%	74		Time / Period	0.056				
8	Riskfree Rate (Annual)	▲▼ 0.12%	1	(Riskfree Rate - Under. Asset Yield) / Period	-0.05%				
9	Exercise Price	▲▼ $45.00	45	Up Movement / Period	19.33%				
10	Time To Maturity (Years)	▲▼ 0.4472	4	Down Movement/Period	-16.20%				
11	Underlying Asset Yield is Stock Dividend Yield (d)	▲▼ 1.00%	1	Risk Neutral Probability	45.46%				
12	Number of Periods	8								
13		**Now**								**Maturity**
14	Period	**0**	**1**	**2**	**3**	**4**	**5**	**6**	**7**	**8**
15	Time	**0.000**	**0.056**	**0.112**	**0.168**	**0.224**	**0.280**	**0.335**	**0.391**	**0.447**
16										
17	**Risky Part of the Stock**	$49.11	$58.60	$69.93	$83.44	$99.56	$118.81	$141.77	$169.16	$201.85
18			$41.16	$49.11	$58.60	$69.93	$83.44	$99.56	$118.81	$141.77
19				$34.49	$41.16	$49.11	$58.60	$69.93	$83.44	$99.56
20					$28.90	$34.49	$41.16	$49.11	$58.60	$69.93
21						$24.22	$28.90	$34.49	$41.16	$49.11
22							$20.30	$24.22	$28.90	$34.49
23								$17.01	$20.30	$24.22
24									$14.26	$17.01
25										$11.95
26										
27	**Riskfree Dividends**		$0.00	$0.00	$0.00	$1.00	$0.00	$0.00	$1.00	$0.00
28										
29	**Cum. Pres Value Factor**	100.00%	100.05%	100.10%	100.15%	100.20%	100.25%	100.30%	100.34%	100.39%
30										
31	**Total Stock Price**	$51.12	$60.61	$71.93	$85.44	$100.57	$119.81	$142.77	$169.16	$201.85
32			$43.16	$51.11	$60.60	$70.93	$84.44	$100.56	$118.81	$141.77
33				$36.49	$43.16	$50.11	$59.60	$70.93	$83.44	$99.56
34					$30.91	$35.49	$42.16	$50.11	$58.60	$69.93
35						$25.22	$29.91	$35.49	$41.16	$49.11
36							$21.30	$25.22	$28.90	$34.49
37								$18.01	$20.30	$24.22
38									$14.26	$17.01
39										$11.95

Annotations:

(1) Copy the Outputs column (including the Risk Neutral Probability) from the previous sheet Copy the range F7:F11 from the previous sheet to the range F7:F11 on this sheet

(2) Copy the Stock Price Tree from the previous sheet Copy the range B17:J25 from the previous sheet to the range B17:J25 on this sheet

(3) 1 / ((1 + (Riskfree Rate / Period)) ^ Period) Enter =1/((1+$F$8)^C14) and copy across

(4) If corresponding cell on Risky Part of Stock tree is blank, Then blank, Else Risky Part of Stock + SUMPRODUCT(Riskfree Dividends Range, Cum. Pres Value Factor Range) / (Cum. Pres Value Factor(t)) Enter =IF(B17="","",B17+SUMPRODUCT(C$27:$J$27,C$29:$J$29)/B$29) and copy to the range B31:I38 Do NOT copy to column J, which contains a different formula

(5) Risky Part of the Stock Tree Enter =J17 and copy down

Excel 2013   **FIGURE 21.19 Binomial – American With Discrete Dividends - Call.**

	A	B	C	D	E	F	G	H	I	J
1	BINOMIAL OPTION PRICING				American With Discrete Dividends					Call
2										
3	Inputs	Option Type				Early Exercise				
4	Option Type	◉ Call ○ Put	1		Early Exercise	○ European ◉ American	2			
5	Underlying Asset Type	Underlying Asset Type ◉ Stock ○ Stock Index ○ Futures ○ Foreign Currency					1			
6	Stock Price Now	$49.11	49		Outputs					
7	Standard Dev (Annual)	74.73%	74		Time / Period	0.056				
8	Riskfree Rate (Annual)	0.12%	1		(Riskfree Rate - Under. Asset Yield) / Period	-0.05%				
9	Exercise Price	$45.00	45		Up Movement / Period	19.33%				
10	Time To Maturity (Years)	0.4472	4		Down Movement/Period	-16.20%				
11	Underlying Asset Yield is Stock Dividend Yield (d)	1.00%	1		Risk Neutral Probability	45.46%				
12	Number of Periods	8								
13		Now								Maturity
14	Period	0	1	2	3	4	5	6	7	8
15	Time	0.000	0.056	0.112	0.168	0.224	0.280	0.335	0.391	0.447

(1) Copy the Outputs column (including the Risk Neutral Probability) from the previous sheet Copy the range F7:F11 from the previous sheet to the range F7:F11 on this sheet

(6) Copy the Payoffs at Maturity from the previous sheet Copy the range J36:J44 from the previous sheet to the range J50:J58 on this sheet

	A	B	C	D	E	F	G	H	I	J
50	American Call	$11.87	$18.40	$27.71	$40.44	$55.57	$74.81	$97.77	$124.16	$156.85
51			$6.41	$10.62	$17.08	$26.52	$39.44	$55.56	$73.81	$96.77
52				$2.90	$5.22	$9.19	$15.72	$25.93	$38.44	$54.56
53					$0.97	$1.91	$3.74	$7.21	$13.60	$24.93
54						$0.18	$0.39	$0.85	$1.87	$4.11
55							$0.00	$0.00	$0.00	$0.00
56								$0.00	$0.00	$0.00
57									$0.00	$0.00
58										$0.00

(7) If Cell to the Right & Down One = Blank, Then Blank
  Else Max{ Not Exercised Value, Exercised Value}
where: Not Exercised Value = [(Risk Neutral Probability) * (Stock Up Price)
          + (1 - Risk Neutral Probability) * (Stock Down Price)]
          / (1+ Riskfree Rate / Period),
  Exercised Value = If Early Exercise = European, Then 0,
          Else If (Option Type = Call, 1, -1)
          * (Total Stock Price - Exercise Price) }
Enter =IF(C51="","",MAX(($F$11*C50+(1-$F$11)*C51)/(1+$F$8),
          IF($H$4=1,0,IF($C$4=1,1,-1)*(B31-$B$9))))

Optionally, use Conditional Formatting to highlight Early Exercise cells:
  click on Home | Styles | Conditional Formatting | New Rule
  click on "use a formula to determine which cells to format"
  enter the rule: =AND($H$4=2,B50=IF($C$4=1,1,-1)*(B31-$B$9))
  click on the Format button, click on the Fill tab,
  click on the color of your choice, click on OK, click on OK

Then copy to the range B50:I57

The purple-shading highlights the periods and call prices where it is optimal to exercise the American call early. Notice that it is optimal to exercise an American call early just before a dividend is paid, which will reduce the value of the underlying stock and thus reduce the value of an unexercised call option. We see that the model predicts an eight-period American call price of $11.87.

Excel 2013   **FIGURE 21.20 American With Discrete Dividends - Put.**

	A	B	C	D	E	F	G	H	I	J
1	**BINOMIAL OPTION PRICING**				**American With Discrete Dividends**					**Put**
2										
3	Inputs	Option Type				Early Exercise				
4	Option Type	○ Call ◉ Put	2		Early Exercise	○ European ◉ American	2			
5	Underlying Asset Type	◉ Stock ○ Stock Index ○ Futures ○ Foreign Currency					1			
6	Stock Price Now	$49.11	49		**Outputs**					
7	Standard Dev (Annual)	74.73%	74		Time / Period	0.056				
8	Riskfree Rate (Annual)	0.12%	1	(Riskfree Rate - Under. Asset Yield) / Period		-0.05%				
9	Exercise Price	$45.00	45		Up Movement / Period	19.33%				
10	Time To Maturity (Years)	0.4472	4		Down Movement/Period	-16.20%				
11	Underlying Asset Yield is Stock Dividend Yield (d)	1.00%	1		Risk Neutral Probability	45.46%				
12	Number of Periods	8								
13		**Now**								**Maturity**
14	Period	0	1	2	3	4	5	6	7	8
15	Time	0.000	0.056	0.112	0.168	0.224	0.280	0.335	0.391	0.447

(1) Copy the Outputs column (including the Risk Neutral Probability) from the previous sheet Copy the range F7:F11 from the previous sheet to the range F7:F11 on this sheet

(6) Copy the Payoffs at Maturity from the previous sheet Copy the range J36:J44 from the previous sheet to the range J50:J58 on this sheet

	A	B	C	D	E	F	G	H	I	J
46										
47										
48										
49										
50	**American Put**	$7.58	$4.36	$1.94	$0.51	$0.00	$0.00	$0.00	$0.00	$0.00
51			$10.26	$6.37	$3.12	$0.93	$0.00	$0.00	$0.00	$0.00
52				$13.50	$9.08	$4.95	$1.71	$0.00	$0.00	$0.00
53					$17.17	$12.51	$7.65	$3.13	$0.00	$0.00
54						$21.04	$16.55	$11.40	$5.73	$0.00
55							24.77	$20.82	$16.12	$10.51
56								$28.03	$24.72	$20.78
57									$30.76	$27.99
58										$33.05

(7) If Cell to the Right & Down One = Blank, Then Blank
    Else Max{ Not Exercised Value, Exercised Value}
where: Not Exercised Value = [(Risk Neutral Probability) * (Stock Up Price)
        + (1 - Risk Neutral Probability) * (Stock Down Price)]
        / (1+ Riskfree Rate / Period),
    Exercised Value = If Early Exercise = European, Then 0,
        Else If (Option Type = Call, 1, -1)
        * (Total Stock Price - Exercise Price) }
Enter =IF(C51="","",MAX(($F$11*C50+(1-$F$11)*C51)/(1+$F$8),
    IF($H$4=1,0,IF($C$4=1,1,-1)*(B31-$B$9))))

Optionally, use Conditional Formatting to highlight Early Exercise cells:
    click on Home | Styles | Conditional Formatting | New Rule
    click on "use a formula to determine which cells to format"
    enter the rule: =AND($H$4=2,B50=IF($C$4=1,1,-1)*(B31-$B$9))
    click on the Format button, click on the Fill tab,
    click on the color of your choice, click on OK, click on OK

Then copy to the range B50:I57
Do NOT copy to column J, which contains the option payoffs at maturity

The purple-shading highlights the periods and call prices where it is optimal to exercise the American put early. Notice that it is optimal to exercise an American put early just when a dividend is paid, which will reduce the value of the underlying stock and thus increases the value of the put option. We see that the model predicts an eight-period American put price of $7.58.

21.8 Full-Scale

Problem. Same as before, except we will use a fifty-period model to evaluate it in order to increase accuracy. At the close of trading on October 11, 2013, the stock price of Facebook (FB) was $49.11, the standard deviation of daily returns is 74.73%, the yield on a six-month U.S. Treasury Bill was 0.12%, the exercise price of an March 45 call on Facebook was $45.00, the exercise price of an March 45 put on Facebook was $45.00, and the time to maturity for both March 22, 2014 maturity options was 0.4472 years. Assume that Facebook pays certain, riskfree $1.00 dividends on the periods show below. What is the price of a March 45 call and a March 45 put on Facebook?

Excel 2013 | **FIGURE 21.21 Binomial Option Pricing - Full-Scale - Call.**

	A	B	C	D	E	F	G	H
1	**BINOMIAL OPTION PRICING**			**Full-Scale**			**American Call**	
2								
3	**Inputs**	Option Type				Early Exercise		
4	Option Type	◉ Call ○ Put	1		Early Exercise	○ European	◉ American	2
5	Underlying Asset Type	Underlying Asset Type ◉ Stock ○ Stock Index ○ Futures ○ Foreign Currency					1	
6	Risky Part of Stock	$49.11	49		**Outputs**			
7	Standard Dev (Annual)	74.73%	74		Time / Period	0.009		
8	Riskfree Rate (Annual)	0.12%	1	(Riskfree Rate - Under. Asset Yield) / Period	0.00%			
9	Exercise Price	$45.00	45		Up Movement / Period	7.32%		
10	Time To Maturity (Years)	0.4472	4		Down Movement/Period	-6.82%		
11	Underlying Asset Yield is Stock Dividend Yield (d)	0.00%	0		Risk Neutral Probability	48.24%		
12	Number of Periods	50						
13		**Now**						
14	Period	0	1	2	3	4	5	6
15	Time	0.000	0.009	0.018	0.027	0.036	0.045	0.054
16								
17	**Risky Part of the Stock**	$49.11	$52.71	$56.57	$60.71	$65.15	$69.93	$75.05
18			$45.76	$49.11	$52.71	$56.57	$60.71	$65.15
19				$42.64	$45.76	$49.11	$52.71	$56.57
20					$39.73	$42.64	$45.76	$49.11
21						$37.02	$39.73	$42.64
22							$34.49	$37.02
23								$32.14

(1) Risky Part of Stock Now
    Enter =B6

(2) Copy the Stock Price fomula from the previous sheet and expand it to a larger range
Copy the cell C17 from the previous sheet
to the range C17:AZ67 on this sheet

Solution Strategy. First, copy the binomial tree parameters, the risk neutral probability, stock price tree, and option payoffs at maturity from the risk neutral model. Second, calculate the total stock price as the sum of the risky stock price plus the discounted value of future dividends. Finally, build an option value tree using the risk neutral probability and accounting for optimal early exercise.

Excel 2013 **FIGURE 21.22 Binomial Option Pricing - Full-Scale - Call (Continued).**

	A	B	C	D	E	F	G	H
1	**BINOMIAL OPTION PRICING**			**Full-Scale**			**American Call**	
2								
3	**Inputs**	Option Type				Early Exercise		
4	Option Type	◉ Call ○ Put		1	Early Exercise	○ European	◉ American	2
5	Underlying Asset Type	◉ Stock ○ Stock Index ○ Futures ○ Foreign Currency					1	
6	Risky Part of Stock	$49.11	49		**Outputs**			
7	Standard Dev (Annual)	74.73%	74	Time / Period		0.009		
8	Riskfree Rate (Annual)	0.12%	1	(Riskfree Rate - Under. Asset Yield) / Period		0.00%		
9	Exercise Price	$45.00	45	Up Movement / Period		7.32%		
10	Time To Maturity (Years)	0.4472	4	Down Movement/Period		-6.82%		
11	Underlying Asset Yield is Stock Dividend Yield (d)	0.00%	0	Risk Neutral Probability		48.24%		
12	Number of Periods	50						
13		**Now**						
14	**Period**	0	1	2	3	4	5	6
15	**Time**	0.000	0.009	0.018	0.027	0.036	0.045	0.054
64								
65	(3) (Cum. Pres Value Factor(t-1)) * EXP(- (Riskfree Rate / Period)) Enter =B71*EXP(-$F$8) and copy across							
66								
67								
68								
69	**Riskfree Dividends**		$0.00	$0.00	$0.00	$0.00	$1.00	$0.00
70								
71	**Cum. Pres Value Factor**	100.000%	99.999%	99.998%	99.997%	99.996%	99.995%	99.994%
72								
73	**Total Stock Price**	$52.11	$55.71	$59.57	$63.71	$68.15	$71.93	$77.05
74			$48.76	$52.11	$55.71	$59.57	$62.71	$67.15
75				$45.64	$48.76	$52.11	$54.71	$58.57
76					$42.73	$45.64	$47.76	$51.11
77						$40.02	$41.73	$44.64
78	(4) If corresponding cell on Risky Part of Stock tree is blank,						$36.49	$39.02
79	Then blank,							$34.14
80	Else Risky Part of Stock							
81	+ SUMPRODUCT(Riskfree Dividends Range,							
82	Cum. Pres Value Factor Range)							
83	/ (Cum. Pres Value Factor(t))							
84	Enter =IF(B17="","",B17+SUMPRODUCT(C$69:$AZ$69,C$71:$AZ$71)/B$71)							
85	and copy to the range B73:AY122							
86	Do NOT copy to column AZ, which contains a different formula							

The up movement / period and down movement / period are calibrated to correspond to the stock's annual standard deviation. It is not necessary to calibrate them to the stock's expected return.[9]

Excel 2013 **FIGURE 21.23 Binomial Option Pricing - Full-Scale - Call (Continued).**

	AU	AV	AW	AX	AY	AZ
13						**Maturity**
14	45	46	47	48	49	50
15	0.402	0.411	0.420	0.429	0.438	0.447
64			$1.77	$1.90	$2.04	$2.19
65				$1.65	$1.77	$1.90
66					$1.54	$1.65
67						$1.43
68						
69	$0.00	$0.00	$0.00	$0.00	$0.00	$0.00
70						
71	99.952%	99.951%	99.950%	99.948%	99.947%	99.946%
72						
73	$1,181.34	$1,267.85	$1,360.69	$1,460.34	$1,567.28	$1,682.06
74	$1,025.62	$1,100.73	$1,181.34	$1,267.85	$1,360.69	$1,460.34
75	$890.43	$955.64	$1,025.62	$1,100.73	$1,181.34	$1,267.85

(5) Risky Part of the Stock Tree
Enter =AZ17 and copy down

Excel 2013 **FIGURE 21.24 Binomial Option Pricing - Full-Scale - Call (Continued).**

	AR	AS	AT	AU	AV	AW	AX	AY	AZ
13									**Maturity**
14	42	43	44	45	46	47	48	49	50
15	0.376	0.385	0.394	0.402	0.411	0.420	0.429	0.438	0.447
120						$1.77	$1.90	$2.04	$2.19
121							$1.65	$1.77	$1.90
122								$1.54	$1.65
123									$1.43
124									
125									
126									
127	$910.64	$980.62	$1,055.73	$1,136.34	$1,222.85	$1,315.70	$1,415.34	$1,522.28	$1,637.06
128	$784.68	$845.43	$910.64	$980.62	$1,055.73	$1,136.34	$1,222.85	$1,315.69	$1,415.34
129	$675.31	$728.06	$784.67	$845.43	$910.64	$980.62	$1,055.73	$1,136.34	$1,222.85

(6) If Option Type = Call,
Then Call Payoff at Maturity = Max (Stock Price at Maturity - Exercise Price, 0)
Else   Put Payoff at Maturity = Max (Exercise Price - Stock Price at Maturity, 0)
Enter =IF($C$4=1,MAX(AZ73-$B$9,0),MAX($B$9-AZ73,0))
and copy to the range AZ128:AZ177

---

[9] At full-scale (50 periods), the binomial option price is very insensitive to the expected return of the stock. For example, suppose that you calibrated this Facebook case to an annual expected return of 10%. Just add **.1*F7** to the formulas for the up and down movements / period. So the up movement / period in cell **F9** would become **=EXP(.1*F7+B7*SQRT(F7))-1** and the down movement / period in cell **F10** would become **=EXP(.1*F7-B7*SQRT(F7))-1**. This changes the option price by less than 1/100th of one penny! In the (Black-Scholes) limit as the number of (sub)periods goes to infinity, the option price becomes totally insensitive to the expected return of the stock. Because of this insensitivity, the conventions for calculating the up movement / period and down movement / period ignore the expected return of the stock.

Excel 2013   **FIGURE 21.25 Binomial Option Pricing - Full-Scale - Call (Continued).**

	A	B	C	D	E	F	G	H
1	**BINOMIAL OPTION PRICING**			**Full-Scale**			**American Call**	
2								
3	**Inputs**	Option Type				Early Exercise		
4	Option Type	◉ Call ○ Put	1		Early Exercise	○ European ◉ American		2
5	Underlying Asset Type	Underlying Asset Type ◉ Stock ○ Stock Index ○ Futures ○ Foreign Currency					1	
6	Risky Part of Stock	$49.11	49		**Outputs**			
7	Standard Dev (Annual)	74.73%	74		Time / Period	0.009		
8	Riskfree Rate (Annual)	0.12%	1	(Riskfree Rate - Under. Asset Yield) / Period		0.00%		
9	Exercise Price	$45.00	45	Up Movement / Period		7.32%		
10	Time To Maturity (Years)	0.4472	4	Down Movement/Period		-6.82%		
11	Underlying Asset Yield is Stock Dividend Yield (d)	0.00%	0	Risk Neutral Probability		48.24%		
12	Number of Periods	50						
13		**Now**						
14	**Period**	**0**	**1**	**2**	**3**	**4**	**5**	**6**
15	**Time**	**0.000**	**0.009**	**0.018**	**0.027**	**0.036**	**0.045**	**0.054**
126								
127	**American Call**	$11.73	$14.19	$17.03	$20.29	$23.99	$28.16	$32.82
128			$9.44	$11.54	$14.00	$16.84	$20.10	$23.82
129				$7.49	$9.25	$11.35	$13.80	$16.64
130					$5.84	$7.31	$9.06	$11.15
131						$4.47	$5.67	$7.12
132							$3.36	$4.32
133								$2.47

(7) If Cell to the Right & Down One = Blank, Then Blank
    Else Max{ Not Exercised Value, Exercised Value}
where: Not Exercised Value = [(Risk Neutral Probability) * (Stock Up Price)
                    + (1 - Risk Neutral Probability) * (Stock Down Price)]
        / (1+ Riskfree Rate / Period),
    Exercised Value = If Early Exercise = European, Then 0,
                Else If (Option Type = Call, 1, -1)
                    * (Total Stock Price - Exercise Price) }
Enter =IF(C128="","",MAX(($F$11*C127+(1-$F$11)*C128)/(1+$F$8),
                IF($H$4=1,0,IF($C$4=1,1,-1)*(B73-$B$9))))

Optionally, use Conditional Formatting to highlight Early Exercise cells:
        click on Home | Styles | Conditional Formatting | New Rule
        click on "use a formula to determine which cells to format"
        enter the rule: =AND($H$4=2,B127=IF($C$4=1,1,-1)*(B73-$B$9))
        click on the Format button, click on the Fill tab,
        click on the color of your choice, click on OK, click on OK

Then copy to the range B127:AY176
Do NOT copy to column AZ, which contains the option payoffs at maturity

Again, optimal early exercise for an American call occurs just before a dividend is paid. We see that the Full-Scale model predicts an American call price of $11.73. Now let's check the put.

Excel 2013

FIGURE 21.26 Binomial Option Pricing - Full-Scale - Put Option.

	AJ	AK	AL	AM	AN	AO	AP
14	**34**	**35**	**36**	**37**	**38**	**39**	**40**
15	**0.304**	**0.313**	**0.322**	**0.331**	**0.340**	**0.349**	**0.358**
68							
69	$0.00	$1.00	$0.00	$0.00	$0.00	$0.00	$0.00
70							
151	$26.74	$25.40	$23.97	$22.43	$20.78	$19.02	$17.13
152	$29.15	$27.99	$26.74	$25.40	$23.97	$22.43	$20.78
153	$31.24	$30.23	$29.15	$27.99	$26.74	$25.40	$23.97
154	$33.05	$32.18	$31.24	$30.23	$29.15	$27.99	$26.74
155	$34.63	$33.87	$33.05	$32.18	$31.24	$30.23	$29.15
156	$35.99	$35.33	$34.63	$33.87	$33.05	$32.18	$31.24
157	$37.18	$36.61	$35.99	$35.33	$34.63	$33.87	$33.05
158	$38.21	$37.71	$37.18	$36.61	$35.99	$35.33	$34.63
159	$39.11	$38.67	$38.21	$37.71	$37.18	$36.61	$35.99
160	$39.88	$39.51	$39.11	$38.67	$38.21	$37.71	$37.18
161	$40.56	$40.23	$39.88	$39.51	$39.11	$38.67	$38.21
162		$40.86	$40.56	$40.23	$39.88	$39.51	$39.11
163			$41.14	$40.86	$40.56	$40.23	$39.88
164				$41.41	$41.14	$40.86	$40.56
165					$41.65	$41.41	$41.14
166						$41.88	$41.65
167							$42.09

Optimal early exercise for an American put often occurs on the date that the dividend is paid. More generally, it is optimal to exercise an American put option when the underlying stock price is very low for a given amount of time to maturity.

Excel 2013

FIGURE 21.27 Binomial Option Pricing - Full-Scale - Put (Continued).

	A	B	C	D	E	F	G	H
1	**BINOMIAL OPTION PRICING**			**Full-Scale**			**American Put**	
2								
3	**Inputs**	┌ Option Type ┐				┌ Early Exercise ┐		
4	Option Type	○ Call ◉ Put	2		Early Exercise	○ European	◉ American	2
5	Underlying Asset Type	┌ Underlying Asset Type ─────┐ ◉ Stock ○ Stock Index ○ Futures ○ Foreign Currency					1	
6	Risky Part of Stock	▲ ▼ $49.11	49		**Outputs**			
7	Standard Dev (Annual)	▲ ▼ 74.73%	74	Time / Period		0.009		
8	Riskfree Rate (Annual)	▲ ▼ 0.12%	1	(Riskfree Rate - Under. Asset Yield) / Period		0.00%		
9	Exercise Price	▲ ▼ $45.00	45	Up Movement / Period		7.32%		
10	Time To Maturity (Years)	▲ ▼ 0.4472	4	Down Movement/Period		-6.82%		
11	Underlying Asset Yield is Stock Dividend Yield (d)	▲ ▼ 0.00%	0	Risk Neutral Probability		48.24%		
12	Number of Periods	50						
13		**Now**						
14	**Period**	0	1	2	3	4	5	6
15	**Time**	0.000	0.009	0.018	0.027	0.036	0.045	0.054
126								
127	**American Put**	$7.40	$6.19	$5.09	$4.11	$3.24	$2.50	$1.88
128			$8.52	$7.22	$6.01	$4.91	$3.94	$3.08

We see that the Full-Scale model predicts an American put price of $7.40.

Problems

1. Download three months of daily stock price for any stock that has listed options on it. What is the annual standard deviation of your stock based on continuous returns?

2. Lookup the current stock price of your stock, use the standard deviation of daily returns you computed, lookup the yield on a six-month U.S. Treasury Bill, lookup the exercise price of a call on your stock that matures in approximately six months, lookup the exercise price of a put on your stock that matures in approximately six months, and compute the time to maturity for both options in fractions of a year. For the call and put that you identified on your stock, determine the replicating portfolio and the price of the call and put using a single-period, replicating portfolio model.

3. For the same inputs as problem 2, determine the replicating portfolio and the price of the call and put using an eight-period, replicating portfolio model.

4. For the same inputs as problem 3, determine the price of the call and put using an eight-period, risk neutral model.

5. For the same inputs as problem 4 determine the price of the call and put using the average of N and N-1 method to evaluate them.

6. For the same inputs as problem 4, show what happens to the stock price at maturity distribution of the binomial stock price tree as the number of periods increases. Show what happens to the continuous cumulative return distribution of the binomial stock price tree as the number of periods increases.

7. Use the same inputs as problem 4. Further, forecast the dividends that you stock pays or make an assumption about the dividends that your stock pays. What is the price of an American call and an American put using an eight-period, risk neutral model of American options with discrete dividends?

8. For the same inputs as problem 7, determine the price of an American call and an American put using a fifty-period, risk neutral model of American options with discrete dividends?

9. For the same inputs as problem 7, determine the price of an American call and an American put using a fifty-period, risk neutral model of American options with discrete dividends?Extend the Binomial Option Pricing model to analyze Digital Options. The only thing which needs to be changed is the option's payoff at maturity.
   (a.) For a Digital Call, the Payoff At Maturity
       = $1.00 When Stock Price At Mat > Exercise Price
       Or $0.00 Otherwise.
   (b.) For a Digital Put, the Payoff At Maturity
       = $1.00 When Stock Price At Mat < Exercise Price
       Or $0.00 Otherwise.

10. Extend the Binomial Option Pricing – Full-Scale Estimation model to determine how fast the binomial option price converges to the price in the Black-Scholes Option Pricing – Basics model. Reduce the Full-Scale model to a 10 period model and to a 20 period model. Increase the 50 period model to a 100 period model. Then for the same inputs, compare call and put prices of the 10 period, 20 period, 50 period, 100 period, and Black-Scholes models.

11. Extend the Binomial Option Pricing – Full-Scale Estimation model to determine how fast the binomial option price with averaging of adjacent odd and even numbers of periods converges to the price in the Black-Scholes Option Pricing – Basics model. As you increase the number of periods in the binomial model, it oscillates between overshooting and undershooting the true price. A simple technique to increase price efficiency is to average adjacent odd and even numbers of periods. For example, average the 10 period call price and the 11 period call price. Reduce the Full-Scale model to a 10 period, 11 period, 20 period, and 21 period model. Increase the 50 period model to a 51 period, 100 period, and 101 period model. Then for the same inputs, compare call and put prices of the average of the 10 and 11 period models, 20 and 21 period models, 50 and 51 period models, 100 and 101 period models, and Black-Scholes model.

Chapter 22 Real Options

22.1 Option To Abandon

Problem. The static project value, defined as the net present value of future project cash flows ignoring any real options, is $146 million right now. The standard deviation of static project value is 63.0%, the riskfree rate is 0.00%, the project can be abandoned at any time for a salvage value of $95.0 million, the time to project completion is 2.4 years, and an 8 period binomial model will be used. The flexible project value is defined as the static project value plus the value of any real options. When should the project be abandoned? What is the flexible project value? What is the value of the option to abandon?

Solution Strategy. Start by copying the output formulas and stock price tree from Chapter 21 Binomial Option Pricing in Section 4 Risk Neutral. Calculate the flexible project value at maturity. Then build the flexible project value tree over all periods. Calculate the value of the option to abandon as the difference between the flexible project value and the static project value.

Excel 2013   **FIGURE 22.1 Real Options – Option to Abandon.**

	A	B	C	D	E	F	G	H	I	J	K
1	**REAL OPTIONS**			**Options to Abandon, Expand, Contract, and Choose**							
2											
3	**Inputs**										
4	Expansion Rate	75.0%	75		Contraction Rate		55.0%	55			
5	Expansion Cost	$130.0	130		Contraction Savings		$75.0	75			
6	Static Project Value Now	$146.0	146		**Outputs**						
7	Standard Dev (Annual)	63.0%	63		Time / Period	0.300	(1) Copy the Outputs column from Chapter 21 Binomial Option Pricing, Risk Neutral sheet Copy the range F7:F11 from sheet 21.4 to the range F7:F11 on this sheet				
8	Riskfree Rate (Annual)	0.00%	0		(Riskfree Rate) / Period	0.00%					
9	Salvage Value	$95.0	95		Up Movement / Period	41.21%					
10	Time To Maturity (Years)	2.4	24		Down Movement/Period	-29.18%					
11					Risk Neutral Probability	41.46%					
12	Number of Periods	8									
13		**Now**								**Maturity**	
14	Period	0	1	2	3	4	5	6	7	8	
15	Time	0.000	0.300	0.600	0.900	1.200	1.500	1.800	2.100	2.400	
16											
17	**Static Project Value**	$146.0	$206.2	$291.1	$411.1	$580.5	$819.7	$1,157.5	$1,634.5	$2,308.0	
18			$103.4	$146.0	$206.2	$291.1	$411.1	$580.5	$819.7	$1,157.5	
19				$73.2	$103.4	$146.0	$206.2	$291.1	$411.1	$580.5	
20	(2) Copy the Stock Price Tree from Chapter 21				$51.9	$73.2	$103.4	$146.0	$206.2	$291.1	
21	Binomial Option Pricing, Risk Neutral sheet					$36.7	$51.9	$73.2	$103.4	$146.0	
22	Copy the range B17:J25 from sheet 21.4						$26.0	$36.7	$51.9	$73.2	
23	to the range B17:J25 on this sheet							$18.4	$26.0	$36.7	
24									$13.0	$18.4	
25										$9.2	

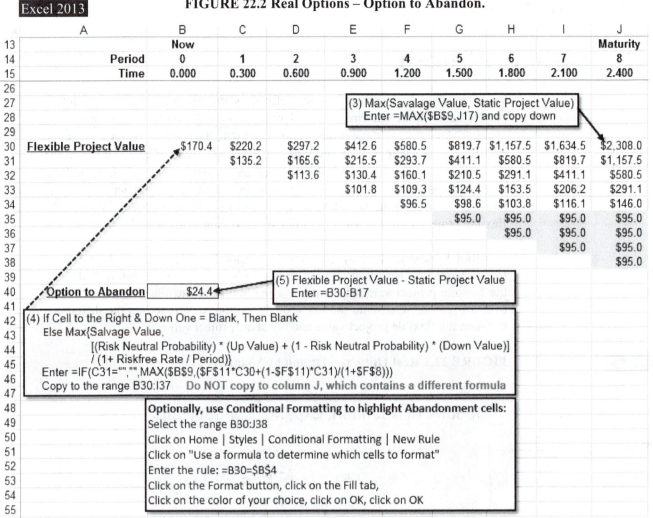

FIGURE 22.2 Real Options – Option to Abandon.

	A	B	C	D	E	F	G	H	I	J
		Now								Maturity
13										
14	Period	0	1	2	3	4	5	6	7	8
15	Time	0.000	0.300	0.600	0.900	1.200	1.500	1.800	2.100	2.400
30	Flexible Project Value	$170.4	$220.2	$297.2	$412.6	$580.5	$819.7	$1,157.5	$1,634.5	$2,308.0
31			$135.2	$165.6	$215.5	$293.7	$411.1	$580.5	$819.7	$1,157.5
32				$113.6	$130.4	$160.1	$210.5	$291.1	$411.1	$580.5
33					$101.8	$109.3	$124.4	$153.5	$206.2	$291.1
34						$96.5	$98.6	$103.8	$116.1	$146.0
35							$95.0	$95.0	$95.0	$95.0
36								$95.0	$95.0	$95.0
37									$95.0	$95.0
38										$95.0
40	Option to Abandon	$24.4								

(3) Max(Savalage Value, Static Project Value)
Enter =MAX($B$9,J17) and copy down

(5) Flexible Project Value - Static Project Value
Enter =B30-B17

(4) If Cell to the Right & Down One = Blank, Then Blank
    Else Max{Salvage Value,
           [(Risk Neutral Probability) * (Up Value) + (1 - Risk Neutral Probability) * (Down Value)]
           / (1+ Riskfree Rate / Period)}
    Enter =IF(C31="","",MAX($B$9,($F$11*C30+(1-$F$11)*C31)/(1+$F$8)))
    Copy to the range B30:I37   Do NOT copy to column J, which contains a different formula

Optionally, use Conditional Formatting to highlight Abandonment cells:
Select the range B30:J38
Click on Home | Styles | Conditional Formatting | New Rule
Click on "Use a formula to determine which cells to format"
Enter the rule: =B30=$B$4
Click on the Format button, click on the Fill tab,
Click on the color of your choice, click on OK, click on OK

The project should be abandoned (highlighted cells) under bad conditions. The flexible project value is $170.4 million. So the option to abandon is worth $24.4 million.

22.2 Option to Expand

Problem. Same as before, except that the project has the option to expand. The static project value now is $146 million, the standard deviation of static project value is 63.0%, the riskfree rate is 0.00%, the project can be expanded by 75% at any time for an expansion cost of $130.0 million, the time to project completion is 2.4 years, and an 8 period binomial model will be used. When should the project be expanded? What is the flexible project value? What is the value of the option to expand?

Solution Strategy. Calculate the flexible project value at maturity. Then build the flexible project value tree over all periods. Calculate the value of the option to expand as the difference between the flexible and static project values.

FIGURE 22.3 Real Options – Option to Expand.

Excel 2013

	A	B	C	D	E	F	G	H	I	J
13		**Now**								**Maturity**
14	Period	**0**	**1**	**2**	**3**	**4**	**5**	**6**	**7**	**8**
15	Time	**0.000**	**0.300**	**0.600**	**0.900**	**1.200**	**1.500**	**1.800**	**2.100**	**2.400**

(6) Max(Static Project Value*(1+Expansion Rate) - Expansion Cost, Static Project Value)
Enter =MAX(J17*(1+$B$4)-$B$5,J17) and copy down

	A	B	C	D	E	F	G	H	I	J
60	**Flexible Project Value**	$181.7	$270.1	$402.6	$599.6	$888.3	$1,304.5	$1,895.6	$2,730.29	$3,909.0
61			$119.1	$176.3	$263.2	$395.1	$593.5	$885.9	$1,304.5	$1,895.6
62				$78.6	$114.8	$169.8	$254.6	$386.5	$589.4	$885.9
63					$52.9	$75.8	$109.7	$161.2	$242.8	$379.5
64						$36.7	$51.9	$73.2	$103.4	$146.0
65							$26.0	$36.7	$51.9	$73.2
66								$18.4	$26.0	$36.7
67									$13.0	$18.4
68										$9.2

(8) Flexible Project Value - Static Project Value
Enter =B60-B17

	A	B
70	**Option to Expand**	$35.7

(7) If Cell to the Right & Down One = Blank, Then Blank
Else Max{Static Project Value*(1+Expansion Rate) - Expansion Cost,
    [(Risk Neutral Probability) * (Up Value) + (1 - Risk Neutral Probability) * (Down Value)]
    / (1+ Riskfree Rate / Period)}
Enter =IF(C61="","",MAX(B17*(1+$B$4)-$B$5,($F$11*C60+(1-$F$11)*C61)/(1+$F$8)))
Copy to the range B60:I67   Do NOT copy to column J, which contains a different formula

Optionally, use Conditional Formatting to highlight Expansion cells:
Select the range B60:J68
Click on Home | Styles | Conditional Formatting | New Rule
Click on "Use a formula to determine which cells to format"
Enter the rule: =B60=B17*(1+$B$4)-$B$5
Click on the Format button, click on the Fill tab,
Click on the color of your choice, click on OK, click on OK

The project should be expanded (highlighted cells) under good conditions. The flexible project value is $181.7 million. So the option to expand is worth $35.7 million.

22.3 Option to Contract

Problem. Same as before, except that the project has the option to contract. The static project value now is $146 million, the standard deviation of static project value is 63.0%, the riskfree rate is 0.00%, the project can be contracted by 55% at any time for contraction savings of $75.0 million, the time to project completion is 2.4 years, and an 8 period binomial model will be used. When should the project be contracted? What is the flexible project value? What is the value of the option to contract?

Solution Strategy. Calculate the flexible project value at maturity. Then build the flexible project value tree over all periods. Calculate the value of the option to contract as the difference between the flexible and static project values.

FIGURE 22.4 Real Options – Option to Contract.

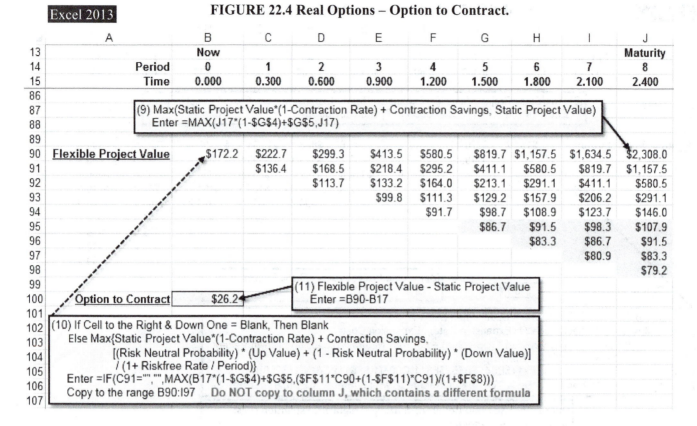

The project should be contracted (highlighted cells) under bad conditions. The flexible project value is $172.2 million. So the option to contract is worth $26.2 million.

22.4 Option To Choose

Problem. Same as before, except that the project has the option to choose among all three alternatives: (1) abandonment, (2) expansion, or (3) contraction. The static project value now is $146 million, the standard deviation of static project value is 63.0%, the riskfree rate is 0.00%, the project can be abandoned at any time for a salvage value of $95.0 million, the project can be expanded by 75% at any time for an expansion cost of $130.0 million, the project can be contracted by 55% at any time for contraction savings of $75.0 million, the time to project completion is 2.4 years, and an 8 period binomial model will be used. When should the project be abandoned, expanded, or contracted? What is the flexible project value? What is the value of the option to choose?

Solution Strategy. Calculate the flexible project value at maturity. Then build the flexible project value tree over all periods. Calculate the value of the option to choose as the difference between the flexible and static project values.

Excel 2013

FIGURE 22.5 Real Options – Option to Choose.

	A	B	C	D	E	F	G	H	I	J
13		**Now**								**Maturity**
14	**Period**	0	1	2	3	4	5	6	7	8
15	**Time**	0.000	0.300	0.600	0.900	1.200	1.500	1.800	2.100	2.400

115										
116		(12) Max(Salvage Value, Static Project Value*(1+Expansion Rate) - Expansion Cost,								
117		Static Project Value*(1-Contraction Rate) + Contraction Savings, Static Project Value)								
118		Enter =MAX($B$9,J17*(1+$B$4)-$B$5,J17*(1-$G$4)+$G$5,J47)								
119										
120	**Flexible Project Value**	$208.4	$285.8	$409.3	$600.7	$887.6	$1,304.5	$1,895.6	$2,730.3	$3,909.0
121			$153.6	$198.4	$273.8	$397.4	$592.4	$885.9	$1,304.5	$1,895.6
122				$121.9	$144.9	$186.3	$259.3	$384.7	$589.4	$885.9
123					$105.6	$115.6	$134.6	$170.5	$239.7	$379.5
124						$98.5	$102.2	$109.1	$121.5	$140.7
125							$95.9	$97.2	$100.4	$107.9
126								$95.0	$95.0	$95.0
127									$95.0	$95.0
128										$95.0
129										
130	Option to Choose	$62.4		(14) Flexible Project Value - Static Project Value						
131				Enter =B120-B17						

(13) If Cell to the Right & Down One = Blank, Then Blank
    Else Max{Salvage Value, Static Project Value*(1+Expansion Rate) - Expansion Cost,
        Static Project Value*(1-Contraction Rate) + Contraction Savings,
        [(Risk Neutral Probability) * (Up Value) + (1 - Risk Neutral Probability) * (Down Value)]
        / (1+ Riskfree Rate / Period)}
    Enter =IF(C121="","",MAX($B$9,B17*(1+$B$4)-$B$5,B17*(1-$G$4)+$G$5,
        ($F$11*C120+(1-$F$11)*C121)/(1+$F$8)))
Copy to the range B120:I127   Do NOT copy to column J, which contains a different formula

Optionally, use Conditional Formatting to highlight Contraction cells:
Select the range B120:J128
Click on Home | Styles | Conditional Formatting | New Rule
Click on "Use a formula to determine which cells to format"
Enter the rule: =B120=$B$4
Click on the Format button, click on the Fill tab,
Click on the color of your choice, click on OK, click on OK

Click on Home | Styles | Conditional Formatting | New Rule
Click on "Use a formula to determine which cells to format"
Enter the rule: =B120=B17*(1-$G$4)+$G$5
Click on the Format button, click on the Fill tab,
Click on the color of your choice, click on OK, click on OK

Click on Home | Styles | Conditional Formatting | New Rule
Click on "Use a formula to determine which cells to format"
Enter the rule: =B120=B17*(1-$G$4)+$G$5
Click on the Format button, click on the Fill tab,
Click on the color of your choice, click on OK, click on OK

Here we see that each of the three choices are made some of the time. The project should be expanded (orange highlighted cells) under good conditions, contracted (blue highlighted cells) under moderately bad conditions, and abandoned (purple highlighted cells) under very bad conditions. The flexible project value is $208.4 million. So the option to choose is worth $62.4 million.

If we sum of the value of the separate options from above we get $24.4 million + $35.7 million + $26.2 million = $86.3 million. So the value of the option to choose is *not equal* to the sum of the value of the three options separately. This is because the three options interact with each other. For example, under very bad conditions (the lower right part of the tree) the separate option to contract would contract, but the separate option to abandon would abandon. But it is impossible to both contract and abandon as the same time. The option to choose forces you to pick the *single* most valuable action under any condition.

22.5 Compound Option

Problem. A project requires two sequential investments, each of which takes time to implement, before the project cash flows are generated. This is a compound option, because it is an option to make the phase 1 investment on top of an option to make the phase 2 investment. The phase 1 investment cost is $53.0 million and takes 2 periods to implement. The phase 2 investment cost is $76.0 million and takes 1 period to implement. After both investments have been made and implemented, the project will generate cash flows whose present value now is $146 million. This static cash flow value will fluctuate in the future with a standard deviation of 63.0%. The riskfree rate is 0.00%, The project is only available for 2.4 years and an 8 period binomial model will be used. When should the phase 1 investment be made? When should the phase 2 investment be made? What is the static project value? What is the flexible project value? What is the value of the compound option?

Solution Strategy. Start by copying the output formulas and value tree from the prior sheet and calculating the static project value. The compound option is analyzed in reverse order, by considering the phase 2 investment first and then working backwards to the phase 1 investment. This is called dynamic programming. So start with the phase 2 investment decision. Calculate the flexible phase 2 value (net of making the phase 2 investment) at maturity. Then build the flexible phase 2 value tree (net of making the phase 2 investment) over all periods. Then work backwards to the phase 1 investment decision. Calculate the flexible project value (net of making the phase 1 investment) at maturity. Then build the flexible project value tree (net of making the phase 1 investment) over all periods. Calculate the value of the compound option as the difference between the flexible project value and the static project value.

FIGURE 22.6 Real Options – Compound Option – Static Cash Flow Value.

	A	B	C	D	E	F	G	H	I	J
1	**REAL OPTIONS**			**Compound Option**						
2										
3	**Inputs**									
4	Phase 1 Cost	$53.0	53	Phase 1 Periods		2	2			
5	Phase 2 Cost	$76.0	76	Phase 2 Periods		1	1			
6	Static C. F. Value Now	$146.0	146	**Outputs**						
7	Standard Dev (Annual)	64.0%	64	Time / Period		0.300				
8	Riskfree Rate (Annual)	0.00%	0	(Riskfree Rate) / Period		0.00%				
9				Up Movement / Period		41.98%				
10	Time To Maturity (Years)	2.4	24	Down Movement/Period		-29.57%				
11				Risk Neutral Probability		41.33%				
12	Number of Periods	8								
13		**Now**								**Maturity**
14	Period	0	1	2	3	4	5	6	7	8
15	Time	0.000	0.300	0.600	0.900	1.200	1.500	1.800	2.100	2.400
16										
17	**Static Cash Flow Value**	$146.0	$207.3	$294.3	$417.9	$593.3	$842.5	$1,196.1	$1,698.3	$2,411.4
18			$102.8	$146.0	$207.3	$294.3	$417.9	$593.3	$842.5	$1,196.1
19				$72.4	$102.8	$146.0	$207.3	$294.3	$417.9	$593.3
20					$51.0	$72.4	$102.8	$146.0	$207.3	$294.3
21						$35.9	$51.0	$72.4	$102.8	$146.0
22							$25.3	$35.9	$51.0	$72.4
23								$17.8	$25.3	$35.9
24									$12.6	$17.8
25										$8.8
26	**Static Project Value**	$17.0								
27										
28										

(1) Copy the Outputs column from the prior sheet
Copy the range F7:F11 from the prior sheet to the range F7:F11 on this sheet

(2) Copy the Static Project Value Tree from the prior sheet
Copy the range B17:J25 from the prior sheet to the range B17:J25 on this sheet

(3) Static Cash Flow Value - Phase 1 Cost - Phase 2 Cost
Enter =B17-B4-B5

We analyze the compound option in reverse order by considering the phase 2 investment first. In other words, we are supposing that the phase 1 investment has already been made and so the only remaining decision is whether to make the phase 2 investment.

The phase 2 investment takes one period to implement, so it would provide the static cash flow value one period from now. If it is currently period 8, then it is too late to make the phase 2 investment and so the flexible phase 2 value in period 8 is zero.

In earlier periods, we compute the value of exercising the phase 2 option to invest. Note that even though we will receive the static cash flow value one period into the future, the phase 2 option to invest is based on the *contemporaneous* static cash flow value because this is the present value of those one period ahead cash flows.

| Excel 2013 | **FIGURE 22.7 Real Options – Compound Option – Flexible Phase 2 Value.** |

	A	B	C	D	E	F	G	H	I	J
13		**Now**								**Maturity**
14	Period	0	1	2	3	4	5	6	7	8
15	Time	0.000	0.300	0.600	0.900	1.200	1.500	1.800	2.100	2.400
29					(4) If Number of Periods - Current Period < Phase 2 Periods, 0,					
30					Max(Static Cash Flow Value - Phase 2 Cost, 0)					
31					Enter =IF($B$12-J$14<$F$5,0,MAX(J17-$B$5,0)) and copy down					
32										
33	**Flexible Phase 2 Value**	$83.7	$137.7	$220.1	$341.9	$517.3	$766.5	$1,120.1	$1,622.3	$0.0
34			$45.7	$79.6	$134.3	$218.3	$341.9	$517.3	$766.5	$0.0
35				$21.9	$41.2	$75.0	$131.3	$218.3	$341.9	$0.0
36					$8.3	$17.3	$35.4	$70.0	$131.3	$0.0
37						$1.9	$4.6	$11.1	$26.8	$0.0
38							$0.0	$0.0	$0.0	$0.0
39								$0.0	$0.0	$0.0
40									$0.0	$0.0
41										$0.0

(5) If Cell to the Right & Down One = Blank, Then Blank
 Else If Number of Periods - Current Period < Phase 2 Periods, 0,
 Else Max{Static Cash Flow Value - Phase 2 Cost,
  [(Risk Neutral Probability) * (Up Value) + (1 - Risk Neutral Probability) * (Down Value)]
  / (1+ Riskfree Rate / Period)}
 Enter IF(C34="","",IF($B$12-B$14<$F$5,0,MAX(B17-$B$5,($F$11*C33+(1-$F$11)*C34)/(1+$F$8))))
 Copy to the range B33:I40   Do NOT copy to column J, which contains a different formula

Optionally, use Conditional Formatting to highlight Phase 2 Investment cells:
Select the range B33:J41
Click on Home | Styles | Conditional Formatting | New Rule
Click on "Use a formula to determine which cells to format"
Enter the rule: =B33=B17-$B$5
Click on the Format button, click on the Fill tab,
Click on the color of your choice, click on OK, click on OK

The phase 2 investment (highlighted cells) should be made under favorable conditions as long as there is at least one period left. The period 8 value is zero.

Now we work backwards to the phase 1 investment decision. The phase 1 investment takes two periods to implement, so it will provide the flexible phase 2 value two periods from now. If it is currently period 6 or later, then it is too late to make the phase 1 investment and so the flexible project value in period 6 or later is zero.

In earlier periods, we compute the value of exercising the phase 1 option to invest. Note that even though we will receive the flexible phase 2 value two periods into the future, the phase 1 option to invest is based on the *contemporaneous* flexible phase 2 value because this is the present value of those two periods ahead values.

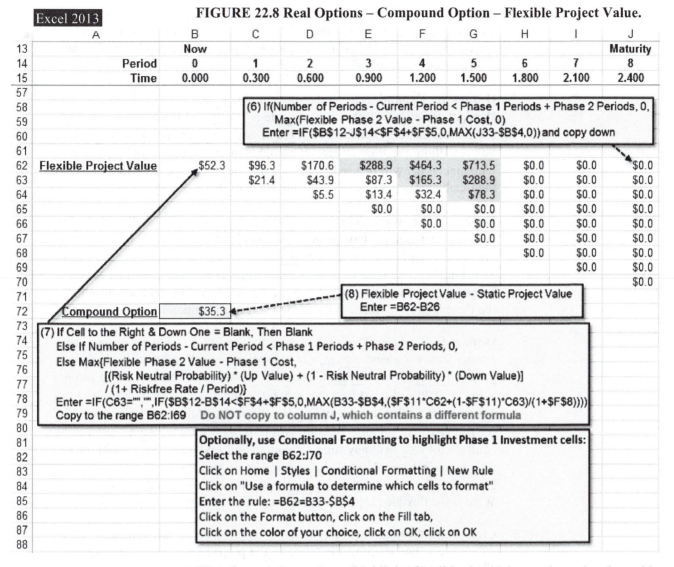

FIGURE 22.8 Real Options – Compound Option – Flexible Project Value.

The phase 1 investment (highlighted cells) should be made under favorable conditions as long as there is at least three period left (two periods for phase 1 and one period for phase 2). The period 6 and later value is zero. The flexible project value is $52.3 million. So the compound option is worth $35.3 million.

The model allows you evaluate the impact of implementation time on value. Try increasing the phase 1 time to 3 periods. The flexible project value drops to $48.7 million and the compound option value drops to $31.7 million.

Problems

1. **Option to Abandon.** The static project value, defined as the net present value of future project cash flows ignoring any real options, is $283 million right now. The standard deviation of static project value is 72.0%, the riskfree rate is 0.00%, the project can be abandoned at any time for a salvage value of $73.0 million, the time to project completion is 3.1 years, and an 8

period binomial model will be used. The flexible project value is defined as the static project value plus the value of any real options. When should the project be abandoned? What is the flexible project value? What is the value of the option to abandon?

2. **Option to Expand.** The static project value now is $318 million, the standard deviation of static project value is 59.0%, the riskfree rate is 0.00%, the project can be expanded by 47% at any time for an expansion cost of $87.0 million, the time to project completion is 4.1 years, and an 8 period binomial model will be used. When should the project be expanded? What is the flexible project value? What is the value of the option to expand?

3. **Option to Contract.** The static project value now is $482 million, the standard deviation of static project value is 87.0%, the riskfree rate is 0.00%, the project can be contracted by 42% at any time for contraction savings of $53.0 million, the time to project completion is 5.7 years, and an 8 period binomial model will be used. When should the project be contracted? What is the flexible project value? What is the value of the option to contract?

4. **Option to Choose.** The project has the option to choose among three alternatives: (1) abandonment, (2) expansion, or (3) contraction. The static project value now is $318 million, the standard deviation of static project value is 78.0%, the riskfree rate is 0.00%, the project can be abandoned at any time for a salvage value of $83.0 million, the project can be expanded by 65% at any time for an expansion cost of $109.0 million, the project can be contracted by 62% at any time for contraction savings of $61.0 million, the time to project completion is 3.4 years, and an 8 period binomial model will be used. When should the project be abandoned, expanded, or contracted? What is the flexible project value? What is the value of the option to choose?

5. **Compound Option.** A project requires two sequential investments, each of which takes time to implement, before the project cash flows are generated. This is a compound option, because it is an option to make the phase 1 investment on top of an option to make the phase 2 investment. The phase 1 investment cost is $48.0 million and takes 2 periods to implement. The phase 2 investment cost is $87.0 million and takes 1 period to implement. After both investments have been made and implemented, the project will generate cash flows whose present value now is $183 million. This static cash flow value will fluctuate in the future with a standard deviation of 71.0%. The riskfree rate is 0.00%, The project is only available for 4.3 years and an 8 period binomial model will be used. When should the phase 1 investment be made? When should the phase 2 investment be made? What is the static project value? What is the flexible project value? What is the value of the compound option?

Chapter 23 Black-Scholes Option Pricing

23.1 Basics

Problem. At the close of trading on October 11, 2013, the stock price of Facebook (FB) was $49.11, the standard deviation of daily returns is 74.73%, the yield on a six-month U.S. Treasury Bill was 0.12%, the exercise price of an March 45 call on Facebook was $45.00, the exercise price of an March 45 put on Facebook was $45.00, and the time to maturity for both March 22, 2014 maturity options was 0.4472 years. What is the price of a March 45 call and a March 45 put on Facebook?

Excel 2013

FIGURE 23.1 Excel Model for Black-Scholes Option Pricing - Basics.

	A	B	C
1	**BLACK SCHOLES OPTION PRICING**		**Basics**
5	**Inputs**		
6	Stock Price Now (S_0)	$49.11	49
7	Standard Dev - Annual (σ)	74.73%	7
8	Riskfree Rate- Annual (r)	0.12%	1
9	Exercise Price (X)	$45.00	45
10	Time To Maturity - Years (T)	0.4472	4
11			1
14	**Outputs**		
15	d_1	0.426	
16	d_2	-0.074	
17	$N(d_1)$	0.665	
18	$N(d_2)$	0.471	
19	Call Price (C_0)	$11.49	
21	$-d_1$	-0.426	
22	$-d_2$	0.074	
23	$N(-d_1)$	0.335	
24	$N(-d_2)$	0.529	
25	Put Price (P_0)	$7.36	

(1) $\left(\ln(S_0/X)+(r+\sigma^2/2)\cdot T\right)/\left(\sigma\cdot\sqrt{T}\right)$
Enter =(LN(B6/B9)+(B8+B7^2/2)*B10)/(B7*SQRT(B10))

(2) $d_1-\sigma\sqrt{T}$
Enter =B15-B7*SQRT(B10)

(3) Standard Cumulative Normal Distribution (d1)
Enter =NORMSDIST(B15)
Copy to cell B18 and copy to the range B23:B24

(4) The Black-Scholes call formula is:
$C_0 = S_0N(d_1)-Xe^{-rT}N(d_2)$
Enter =B6*B17-B9*EXP(-B8*B10)*B18

(5) -d1
Enter =-B15 and copy to cell B22

(6) The Black-Scholes put formula is:
$P_0 = -S_0N(-d_1)+Xe^{-rT}N(-d_2)$
Enter =-B6*B23+B9*EXP(-B8*B10)*B24

The Black-Scholes model predicts a call price of $11.49. This is four cents different than what the Binominal Option Pricing - Full-Scale Estimation model predicts for a *European* call with identical inputs (including no dividends). The Black-Scholes model predicts a put price of $7.36. This is four cents different than what the Binominal Option Pricing - Full-Scale Estimation model predicts for a *European* put with identical inputs (including no dividends). The advantage of the Black-Scholes model and its natural analytic extensions is that they are quick and easy to calculate. The disadvantage is that they are limited to a narrow range of derivatives (such as *European* options only, etc.).

23.2 Continuous Dividend

Problem. Suppose that Facebook paid dividends in tiny amounts on a continuous basis throughout the year at a 1.0% / year rate. What would be the new price of the call and put?

`Excel 2013`   **FIGURE 23.2 Black-Scholes – Cont Div Yield and Alt Under Assets – Call**

BLACK SCHOLES OPTION PRICING   **Continuous Dividend Yield and Alternative Underlying Assets**

	A	B	C
3	**Inputs**	Option Type	
4	Option Type	⦿ Call ○ Put	1
5	Underlying Asset Type	⦿ Stock ○ Stock Index ○ Futures ○ Foreign Currency	1
6	Stock Price Now (S(0))	$49.11	49
7	Standard Dev - Annual (σ)	74.73%	7
8	Riskfree Rate- Annual (r)	0.12%	0
9	Exercise Price (X)	$45.00	45
10	Time To Maturity - Yrs (T)	0.4472	4
11	Underlying Asset Yield is Stock Dividend Yield (d)	1.00%	1
14	**Outputs**		
15	d_1	0.417	
16	d_2	-0.083	
17	$N(d_1)$	0.662	
18	$N(d_2)$	0.467	
19	Call Price (C_0)	$11.34	
21	$-d_1$	-0.417	
22	$-d_2$	0.083	
23	$N(-d_1)$	0.338	
24	$N(-d_2)$	0.533	
25	Put Price (P_0)	$7.43	

(1) Copy the basic Black-Scholes formulas from the previous sheet Copy the range B15:B25 from the previous sheet to the range

(2) Add dividend yield (*d*) to the d_1 formula:
$$\left(\ln\left(S_0/X\right) + \left(r - d + \sigma^2/2\right) \cdot T \right) / \left(\sigma \cdot \sqrt{T}\right)$$
Enter =(LN(B6/B9)+(B8-B11+B7^2/2)*B10)/(B7*SQRT(B10))

(3) Add dividend yield (*d*) to the call formula:
$$C_0 = S_0 e^{-dT} N\left(d_1\right) - X e^{-rT} N\left(d_2\right)$$
Enter =B6*EXP(-B11*B10)*B17-B9*EXP(-B8*B10)*B18

(4) Add dividend yield (d) to the put formula:
$$P_0 = -S_0 e^{-dT} N\left(-d_1\right) + X e^{-rT} N\left(-d_2\right)$$
Enter =-B6*EXP(-B11*B10)*B23+B9*EXP(-B8*B10)*B24

Solution Strategy. Modify the basic Black-Scholes formulas from the previous sheet to include the continuous dividend.

Results. We see that the continuous dividend model predicts a call price of $11.34. This is a drop of 15 cents from the no dividend version. The continuous dividend model predicts a put price of $7.43. This is a rise of 7 cents from the no dividend version. To create a dynamic chart, we have a few more steps.

Excel 2013

FIGURE 23.3 Black-Scholes – Cont Div Yield and Alt Under Assets – Call

	A	B	C	D	E	F	G	H	I	J
28	(6) Enter the output formula		(5) Enter the input values							
29	for the Option Price.		for Stock Price Now.							
30	If Option Type = Call,		Enter $0.01, $10.00, 20.00, etc.							
31	Then Call Price, Else Put Price		in the range C35:Q35							
32	Enter =IF($C$4=1,B19,B25)									
33	Data Table: Sensitivity of Option Price to Stock Price Now									
34					Input Values for Stock Price Now (P)					
35	Output Formula:		$0.01	$5.00	$10.00	$15.00	$20.00	$25.00	$30.00	$35.00
36	Option Price	$11.34	$0.00	$0.00	$0.00	$0.06	$0.32	$0.95	$2.09	$3.79
37	Intrinsic Value									

(7) Create the option price Data Table. Select the range B35:Q36, click on Data | Data Tools | What-If Analysis | Data Table, enter B6 in the Row Input Cell, and click on OK.

Data Table

Row input cell: B6

Column input cell:

OK   Cancel

Excel 2013

FIGURE 23.4 Black-Scholes – Cont Div Yield and Alt Under Assets – Call

	N	O	P	Q	R	S	T
30							
31	(8) Lowest X-Axis Price, Excercise Price, Highest X-Axis Price						
32	Enter $100 in R35, =B9 in S35, $180.00 in T35						
33							
34							
35	$55.00	$60.00	$65.00	$70.00	$0.00	$45.00	$70.00
36	$15.46	$19.28	$23.34	$27.59			
37					$0.00	$0.00	$25.00
38							

(9) If Option Type = Call,
Then Max(Stock Price Now - Exercise Price, 0)
Else Max(Exercise Price - Stock Price Now, 0)
Enter =IF($C$4=1,MAX(R35-$B$9,0),MAX($B$9-R35,0))
and copy across

The spin buttons allow you to change Black-Scholes inputs and instantly see the impact on a graph of the option price and intrinsic value. This allows you to perform instant experiments on the Black-Scholes option pricing model. Here is a list of experiments that you might want to perform:

- What happens when the standard deviation is increased?

- What happens when the time to maturity is increased?

- What happens when the exercise price is increased?

- What happens when the riskfree rate is increased?

- What happens when the dividend yield is increased?

- What happens when the standard deviation is really close to zero?

- What happens when the time to maturity is really close to zero?

Notice that the Black-Scholes option price is usually greater than the payoff you would obtain if the option was maturing today (the "intrinsic value"). This extra value is called the "Time Value" of the option. Given your result in the last experiment above, can you explain *why* the extra value is called the "Time Value?" Now let's look at the put option.

FIGURE 23.5 Black-Scholes – Cont Div Yield and Alt Under Assets - Put

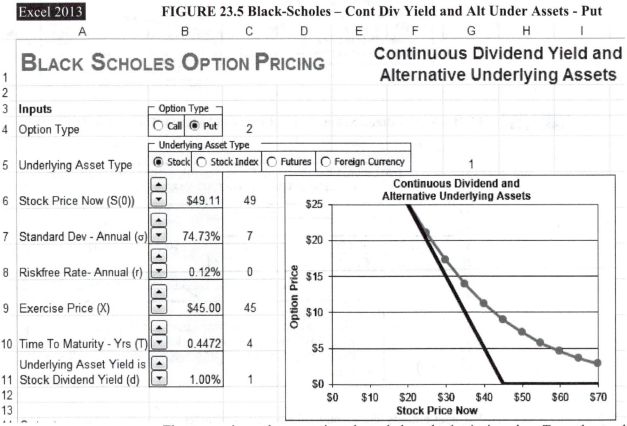

The put option value sometime drops below the intrinsic value. To understand why, try increasing the riskfree rate and see what happens. Then decrease the riskfree rate to zero and see what happens. You can perform many similar experiments on the put option.

The model can handle three additional types of underlying assets (see **row 5**): (1) stock index, (2) futures, and (3) foreign currency. Then the underlying asset yield (see **row 11**) becomes: (1) the stock index dividend yield, (2) the riskfree rate, and (3) the foreign riskfree rate, respectively.

FIGURE 23.6 Black-Scholes – Cont Div Yield and Alt Under Assets – Call

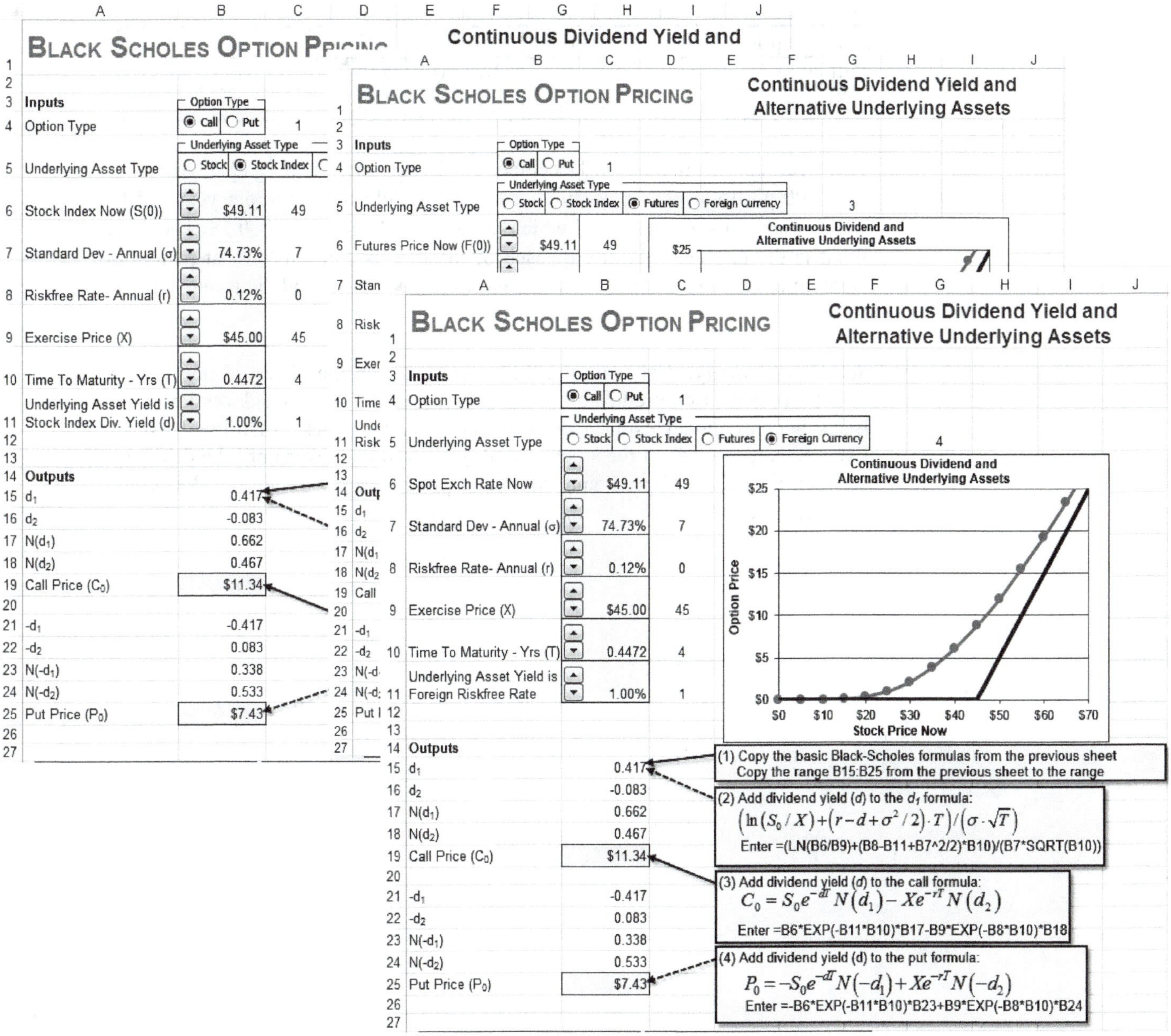

(1) Copy the basic Black-Scholes formulas from the previous sheet. Copy the range B15:B25 from the previous sheet to the range

(2) Add dividend yield (*d*) to the d_1 formula:

$$\left(\ln\left(S_0 / X \right) + \left(r - d + \sigma^2 / 2 \right) \cdot T \right) / \left(\sigma \cdot \sqrt{T} \right)$$

Enter =(LN(B6/B9)+(B8-B11+B7^2/2)*B10)/(B7*SQRT(B10))

(3) Add dividend yield (*d*) to the call formula:

$$C_0 = S_0 e^{-dT} N\left(d_1 \right) - X e^{-rT} N\left(d_2 \right)$$

Enter =B6*EXP(-B11*B10)*B17-B9*EXP(-B8*B10)*B18

(4) Add dividend yield (d) to the put formula:

$$P_0 = -S_0 e^{-dT} N\left(-d_1 \right) + X e^{-rT} N\left(-d_2 \right)$$

Enter =-B6*EXP(-B11*B10)*B23+B9*EXP(-B8*B10)*B24

23.3 Implied Volatility

Problem. At the close of trading on October 11, 2013, SPY, an Exchange Traded Fund (ETF) based on the S&P 500 index, traded at 170.30. European call and put options on SPY with the exercise prices shown below traded for the following prices:

Exercise price	160	165	170	175	180
Call price	$16.97	$13.80	$10.85	$8.37	$6.15
Put price	$9.81	$11.74	$13.91	16.18	$19.09

These call options mature on December 20, 2014, which is in 1.1917 years. The S&P 500 portfolio pays a continuous dividend yield of 1.95% per year and the annual yield on a Treasury Bill which matures on August 15th is 0.18% per year. What is the implied volatility of each of these calls and puts? What pattern do these implied volatilities follow across exercise prices and between calls vs. puts?

Solution Strategy. Calculate the difference between the observed option price and the option price predicted by the continuous dividend yield version of the Black-Scholes model using a dummy value for the stock volatility. Have the Excel Solver tool adjust the stock volatility by trial and error until the difference between the observed price and the model price is equal to zero (within a very small error tolerance).

FIGURE 23.7 Excel Model of Black-Scholes - Implied Volatility.

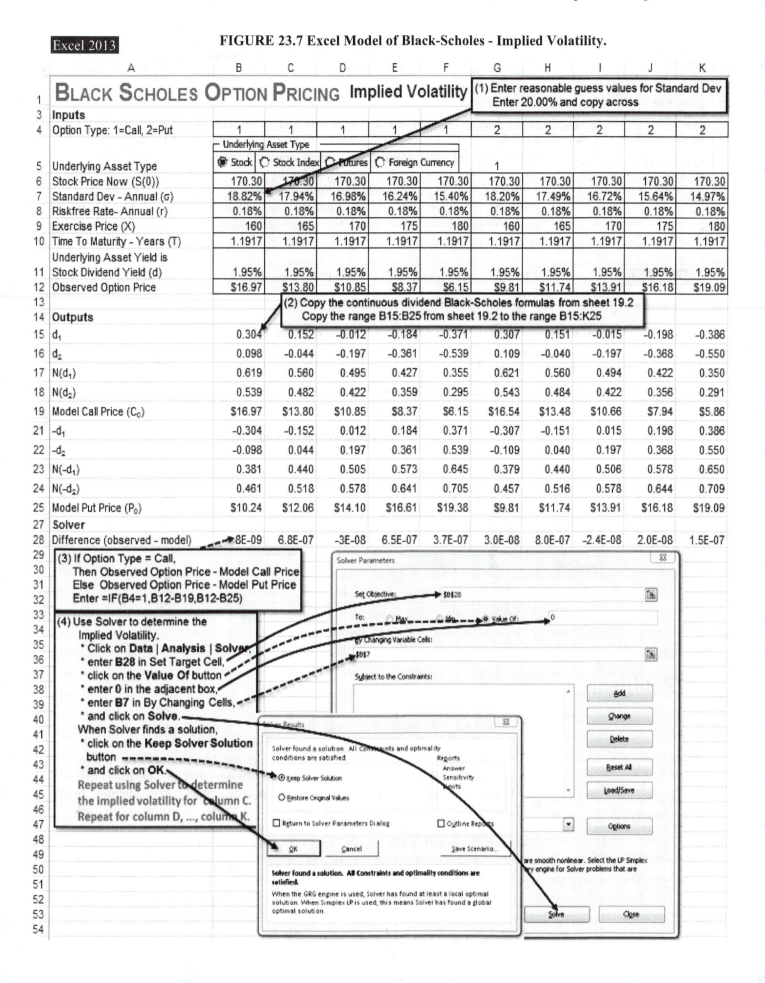

Excel 2013

	A	B	C	D	E	F	G	H	I	J	K
1	BLACK SCHOLES OPTION PRICING Implied Volatility						(1) Enter reasonable guess values for Standard Dev Enter 20.00% and copy across				
3	Inputs										
4	Option Type: 1=Call, 2=Put	1	1	1	1	1	2	2	2	2	2
5	Underlying Asset Type	● Stock ○ Stock Index ○ Futures ○ Foreign Currency					1				
6	Stock Price Now (S(0))	170.30	170.30	170.30	170.30	170.30	170.30	170.30	170.30	170.30	170.30
7	Standard Dev - Annual (σ)	18.82%	17.94%	16.98%	16.24%	15.40%	18.20%	17.49%	16.72%	15.64%	14.97%
8	Riskfree Rate- Annual (r)	0.18%	0.18%	0.18%	0.18%	0.18%	0.18%	0.18%	0.18%	0.18%	0.18%
9	Exercise Price (X)	160	165	170	175	180	160	165	170	175	180
10	Time To Maturity - Years (T)	1.1917	1.1917	1.1917	1.1917	1.1917	1.1917	1.1917	1.1917	1.1917	1.1917
11	Underlying Asset Yield is Stock Dividend Yield (d)	1.95%	1.95%	1.95%	1.95%	1.95%	1.95%	1.95%	1.95%	1.95%	1.95%
12	Observed Option Price	$16.97	$13.80	$10.85	$8.37	$6.15	$9.81	$11.74	$13.91	$16.18	$19.09
13											
14	Outputs		(2) Copy the continuous dividend Black-Scholes formulas from sheet 19.2 Copy the range B15:B25 from sheet 19.2 to the range B15:K25								
15	d_1	0.304	0.152	-0.012	-0.184	-0.371	0.307	0.151	-0.015	-0.198	-0.386
16	d_2	0.098	-0.044	-0.197	-0.361	-0.539	0.109	-0.040	-0.197	-0.368	-0.550
17	$N(d_1)$	0.619	0.560	0.495	0.427	0.355	0.621	0.560	0.494	0.422	0.350
18	$N(d_2)$	0.539	0.482	0.422	0.359	0.295	0.543	0.484	0.422	0.356	0.291
19	Model Call Price (C_0)	$16.97	$13.80	$10.85	$8.37	$6.15	$16.54	$13.48	$10.66	$7.94	$5.86
21	$-d_1$	-0.304	-0.152	0.012	0.184	0.371	-0.307	-0.151	0.015	0.198	0.386
22	$-d_2$	-0.098	0.044	0.197	0.361	0.539	-0.109	0.040	0.197	0.368	0.550
23	$N(-d_1)$	0.381	0.440	0.505	0.573	0.645	0.379	0.440	0.506	0.578	0.650
24	$N(-d_2)$	0.461	0.518	0.578	0.641	0.705	0.457	0.516	0.578	0.644	0.709
25	Model Put Price (P_0)	$10.24	$12.06	$14.10	$16.61	$19.38	$9.81	$11.74	$13.91	$16.18	$19.09
27	Solver										
28	Difference (observed - model)	8E-09	6.8E-07	-3E-08	6.5E-07	3.7E-07	3.0E-08	8.0E-07	-2.4E-08	2.0E-08	1.5E-07

(3) If Option Type = Call,
Then Observed Option Price - Model Call Price
Else Observed Option Price - Model Put Price
Enter =IF(B4=1,B12-B19,B12-B25)

(4) Use Solver to determine the
Implied Volatility.
* Click on **Data | Analysis | Solver**
* enter B28 in Set Target Cell,
* click on the **Value Of** button
* enter 0 in the adjacent box,
* enter B7 in By Changing Cells,
* and click on **Solve**.
When Solver finds a solution,
* click on the **Keep Solver Solution**
button
* and click on **OK**.
Repeat using Solver to determine
the implied volatility for column C.
Repeat for column D, ..., column K.

Solver Parameters

Set Objective: $B$28

To: ○ Max ○ Min ● Value Of: 0

By Changing Variable Cells:
$B$7

Subject to the Constraints:

Add
Change
Delete
Reset All
Load/Save
Options

Solver Results

Solver found a solution. All Constraints and optimality conditions are satisfied.

Reports
Answer
Sensitivity
Limits

● Keep Solver Solution
○ Restore Original Values

☐ Return to Solver Parameters Dialog   ☐ Outline Reports

OK   Cancel   Save Scenario...

are smooth nonlinear. Select the LP Simplex
ry engine for Solver problems that are

Solver found a solution. All Constraints and optimality conditions are satisfied.
When the GRG engine is used, Solver has found at least a local optimal solution. When Simplex LP is used, this means Solver has found a global optimal solution.

Solve   Close

Excel 2007 Equivalent

To install Solver in Excel 2007, click on 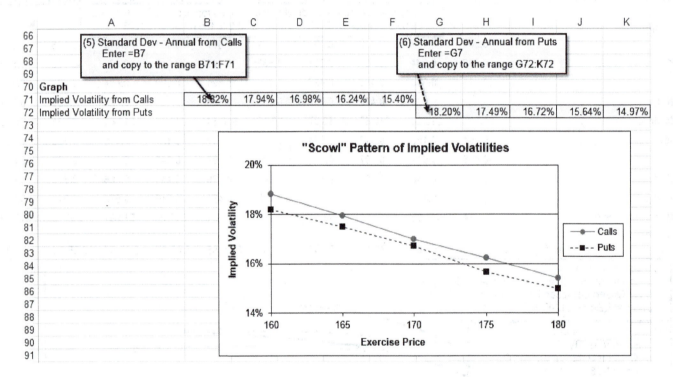, click on **Excel Options** at the bottom of the drop-down window, click on **Add-Ins**, highlight **Solver** in the list of Inactive Applications, click on **Go**, check **Solver**, and click on **OK**.

To install Solver, click on **File**, click on **Options**, click on **Add-Ins**, highlight **Solver** in the list of Inactive Applications, click on **Go**, check **Solver**, and click on **OK**.

If the market's belief about the distribution of returns of the S&P 500 Index matched the theoretical distribution of returns assumed by the Black-Scholes model, then all of the implied volatilities would be the same. From the graph we see this is not the case. The implied volatility pattern declines sharply with the exercise price and puts have lower implied volatilities than calls. In the '70s and '80s, the typical implied volatility pattern was a U-shaped, "Smile" pattern. In the '90s and 2000s, it is more typical to see a downward-sloping, "Scowl" pattern.

Excel 2013

FIGURE 23.8 Graph of the "Scowl" Pattern of Implied Volatilities.

Problems

1. Download three months of daily stock prices for any stock that has listed options on it and compute the standard deviation of daily returns. Lookup the current stock price of your stock, use the standard deviation of daily returns you just computed, lookup the yield on a six-month U.S. Treasury Bill, lookup the exercise price of a call on your stock that matures in approximately six months, lookup the exercise price of a put on your stock that matures in approximately six months, and compute the time to maturity for both options in fractions of a year. For the call and put that you identified on your stock, determine the price of the call and put using the Black-Scholes basics model.

2. Use the same inputs as problem 1. Forecast the continuous dividend that your stock pays or make an assumption about the continuous dividend that your stock pays. Determine the price of the call and put using the Black-Scholes continuous dividend model.

3. Perform instant experiments on whether changing various inputs causes an increase or decrease in the Call Price and in the Put Price and by how much.

   (a.) What happens when the standard deviation is increased?
   (b.) What happens when the time to maturity is increased?
   (c.) What happens when the exercise price is increased?
   (d.) What happens when the riskfree rate is increased?
   (e.) What happens when the dividend yield is increased?
   (f.) What happens when the standard deviation is really close to zero?
   (g.) What happens when the time to maturity is really close to zero?

4. The S&P 500 index closes at 2000. European call and put options on the S&P 500 index with the exercise prices shown below trade for the following prices:

Exercise price	1,950	1,975	2,000	2,025	2,050
Call price	$88	$66	$47	$33	$21
Put price	$25	$26	$32	$44	$58

All options mature in 88 days. The S&P 500 portfolio pays a continuous dividend yield of 1.56% per year and the annual yield on a Treasury Bill which matures on the same day as the options is 4.63% per year. Determine what is the implied volatility of each of these calls and puts. What pattern do these implied volatilities follow across exercise prices and between calls vs. puts?

Chapter 24 Debt And Equity Valuation

24.1 Two Methods

Problem. The Value of the Firm (V) is $340 million, the Face Value of the Debt (B) is $160 million, the time to maturity of the debt (t) is 2.00 years, the riskfree rate (k_{RF}) is 5.0%, and the standard deviation of the return on the firm's assets (σ) is 50.0%. There are two different methods for valuing the firm's equity and risky debt based in an option pricing framework. Using both methods, what is the firm's Equity Value (E) and Risky Debt Value (D)? Do both methods produce the same result?

Solution Strategy. In the first method, equity is considered to be a call option. Thus, E = Call Price. For this call option, the underlying asset is the Value of the Firm (V) and the exercise price is the face value of the debt (B). Hence, the call price is calculated from the Black-Scholes call formula by substituting V for P and B for X. The rationale is that if V > B, then the equityholders gain the net profit V-B. However, if V < B, then the equityholders avoid the loss by declaring bankruptcy, turning V over to the debtholders, and walking away with zero rather than owing money. Thus, the payoff to equityholders is Max (V - B, 0), which has the same payoff form as a call option. Further, we can use the fact that Debt plus Equity equals Total Value of Firm (D + E = V) and obtain the value of debt D = V - E = V - Call.

In the second method, Risky Debt is considered to be Riskfree Debt minus a Put option. Thus, D = Riskfree Debt - Put. For this put option, the underlying asset is also the Value of the Firm (V) and the exercise price is also the face value of the debt (B). Hence, the put price is calculated from the Black-Scholes put formula by substituting V for P and B for X. The rationale is that the put option is a *Guarantee* against default in repaying the face value of the debt (B). Specifically, if V > B, then the equityholders repay the face value B in full and the value of the guarantee is zero. However, if V < B, then the equityholders only pay V and default on the rest, so the guarantee must pay the balance B - V. Thus, the payoff on the guarantee is Max (B - V, 0), which has the same payoff form as a put option. Further, we can use the fact that Debt plus Equity equals Total Value of Firm (D + E = V) and obtain E = V - Risky Debt = V - (Riskfree Debt - Put).

FIGURE 24.1 Excel Model for Stocks and Risky Bonds.

Excel 2013

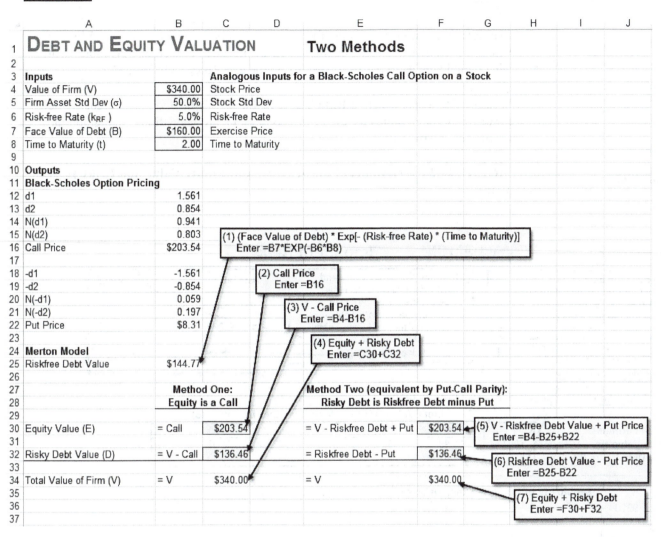

Both methods of doing the calculation find that the Equity Value (E) = $203.54 and the Risky Debt Value (D) = $136.46. We can verify that both methods should always generate the same results. Consider what we get if we equate the Method One and Method Two expressions for the Equity Value (E): **Call Price = V – Riskfree Bond Value + Put Price**. You may recognize this as an alternative version of Put-Call Parity. The standard version of Put-Call Parity is: **Call Price = Stock Price - Bond Price + Put Price**. To get the alternative version, just substitute V for the Stock Price and substitute the Riskfree Bond Value for the Bond Price. Consider what we get if we equate the Method One and Method Two expressions for the Risky Debt Value (D): **V - Call Price = Riskfree Bond - Put Price**. This is simply a rearrangement of the alternative version of Put-Call Parity. Since Put-Call Parity is always true, then both methods of valuing debt and equity will always yield the same result!

24.2 Impact of Risk

Problem. What impact does the firm's risk have upon the firm's Debt and Equity valuation? Specifically, if you increased Firm Asset Standard Deviation, then what would happen to the firm's Equity Value and Risky Debt Value?

Solution Strategy. Create a **Data Table** of Equity Value and Risky Debt Value for different input values for the Firm's Asset Standard Deviation. Then graph the results and interpret it.

Excel 2013

FIGURE 24.2 Excel Model of the Sensitivity of Equity Value and Risky Debt Value.

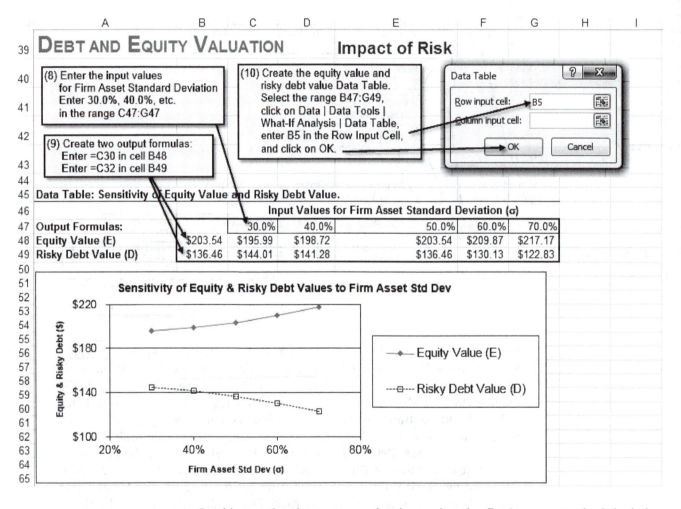

Looking at the chart, we see that increasing the firm's asset standard deviation causes a wealth transfer from debtholders to equityholders. This may seem surprising, but this is a direct consequence of equity being a call option and debt being V *minus* a call option. We know that increasing the standard deviation makes a call more valuable, so equivalently increasing the firm's asset standard deviation makes the firm's Equity Value more valuable and reduces the Risky Debt Value by the same amount.

The intuitive rationale for this is that an increase in standard deviation allows equityholders to benefit from more frequent and bigger increases in V, while not being hurt by more frequent and bigger decreases in V. In the later case, the equityholders are going to declare bankruptcy anyway so they don't care how much V drops. Debtholders are the mirror image. They do *not* benefit from more frequent and bigger increases in V since repayment is capped at B, but they are *hurt* by more frequent and bigger decreases in V. In the latter case, the size of the repayment default (B – V) increases as V drops more.

The possibility of transferring wealth from debtholders to equityholders (or visa versa) illustrates the potential for conflict between equityholders and debtholders. Equityholders would like the firm to take on riskier projects, but debtholders would like the firm to focus on safer projects. Whether the firm ultimately decides to take on risky or safe projects will determine how wealth is divided between the two groups.

Problems

1. The Value of the Firm (V) is $780 million, the Face Value of the Debt (B) is $410 million, the time to maturity of the debt (t) is 1.37 years, the riskfree rate (k_{RF}) is 3.2%, and the standard deviation of the return on the firm's assets (σ) is 43.0%. Using both methods of debt and equity valuation, what is the firm's Equity Value (E) and Risky Debt Value (D)? Do both methods produce the same result?

2. Determine what impact an increase in the Firm Asset Standard Deviation has on the firm's Equity Value and Risky Debt Value.

PART 8 EXCEL SKILLS

Chapter 25 Useful Excel Tricks

25.1 Quickly Delete The Instructions and Arrows

Task. Quickly get rid of all of the instruction boxes and arrows after you are done building the Excel model.

How To. All of the instruction boxes and arrows are *objects* and there is an easy way to select all of them at once. Click on **Home | Editing | Find & Select**

down-arrow | Select Objects. This causes the cursor to become a pointer. Then point to a **location above and to the left** of the instruction boxes and arrows, continue to hold down the left mouse button while you drag the pointer to a **location below and to the right** of the instruction boxes and arrows, and then let go of the left mouse button. This selects *all* of the instruction boxes and arrows (see example below). Then just press the **Delete** key and they are all gone!

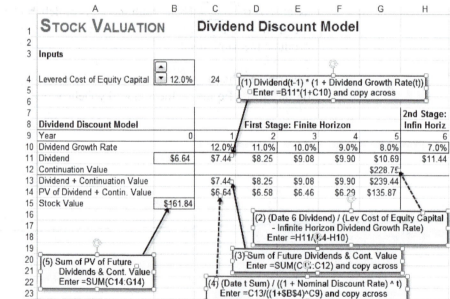

25.2 Freeze Panes

Task. Freeze column titles at the top of the columns and/or freeze row titles on the left side of the rows. This is especially useful for large spreadsheets.

How To. In the example below, suppose you want to freeze the column titles from row 8 and above (freezing Barrick over column B, Hanson over column C, etc.) and you want to freeze the row titles in column A. Select cell **B9** (as shown), because cell **B9** is just below row 8 that you want to freeze and just to the right of column A that you want to freeze.

	A	B	C	D	E	F	G	H
1	ASSET PRICING			Static CAPM Using Fama-MacBeth Method				
2								
3	**Inputs**							
4	Market Portfolio Benchmark	*Market Portfolio Benchmark* — ⦿ US S&P 500 (SPY) ○ CRSP VWMR ○ DJ World (DWG)			1			
5	Asset Type	*Asset Type* — ○ Stock ○ US FF Port ⦿ Country ETF			3			
6								
7		Stock	Stock	Stock	Stock	Stock	Stock	US FF Port
8		Barrick Gold (ABX)	IBM (IBM)	Korea Electric (KEP)	Siemens (SI)	Grupo Televisa (TV)	YPF (YPF)	Small-Growth
9	**Monthly Returns**							
10	Dec 2012	1.39%	0.78%	13.85%	5.77%	12.29%	27.97%	2.55%
11	Nov 2012	-14.25%	-1.86%	-4.81%	2.57%	4.73%	3.23%	0.75%
12	Oct 2012	-3.02%	-6.23%	3.78%	0.76%	-3.87%	-14.08%	-3.86%
13	Sep 2012	8.41%	6.47%	15.97%	6.23%	2.31%	3.92%	3.24%
14	Aug 2012	17.76%	-0.14%	-3.08%	11.32%	0.83%	9.64%	3.28%

Then click on **View | Window | Freeze Panes down-arrow | Freeze Panes**.

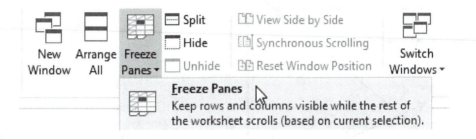

25.3 Spin Buttons and the Developer Tab

Task. Add a spin button to make an input interactive.

How To. Spin buttons and other so-called "form controls" are located on the Developer tab DEVELOPER . If the Developer tab is not visible, you can display it by clicking on File , click on Options , click on **Customize Ribbon**, check the **Developer** checkbox, and click **OK**.

Then click on **Developer | Controls | Insert down-arrow | Form Controls | Spin Button**.

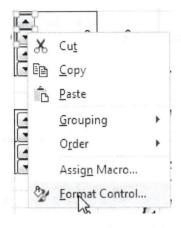

Then point the cursor crosshairs to the upper-left corner of where you want the spin button to be, click and drag to the lower-right corner, and release. You get a spin button 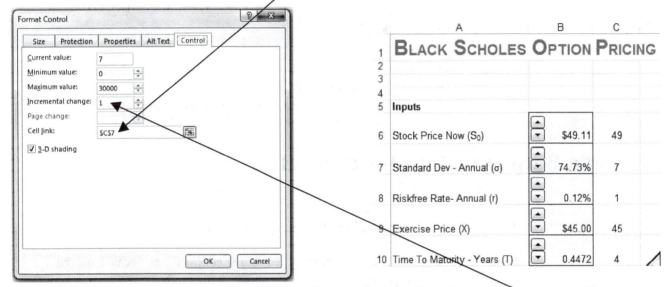. Now place the cursor over the top of the spin button, right-click, and select **Format Control** from the pop-up menu. On the **Control** tab of the **Format Control** dialog box, enter C7 in the **Cell Link** entry box, and click **OK**.

Now when you click on the spin button, the value in cell **C7** will increase or decrease by 1. For convenience, I scale the spin button output to the appropriate scale of the input. For example, in the spreadsheet below the spin button in cell **B7** is linked to the cell **C7** and creates the integer value **7**. The formula in cell B7 is **=C7/10+0.0473** and this create the value **74.73%** for the standard deviation.

	A	B	C
1	**BLACK SCHOLES OPTION PRICING**		
2			
3			
4			
5	**Inputs**		
6	Stock Price Now (S$_0$)	$49.11	49
7	Standard Dev - Annual (σ)	74.73%	7
8	Riskfree Rate- Annual (r)	0.12%	1
9	Exercise Price (X)	$45.00	45
10	Time To Maturity - Years (T)	0.4472	4

Unfortunately, Spin Buttons are only allowed to have **Incremental Changes** that are integers (1, 2, 3, etc.). It would be convenient if they could have **Incremental Changes** of any value, such as .01 or -.0043.

25.4 Option Buttons and Group Boxes

Task. Add option buttons 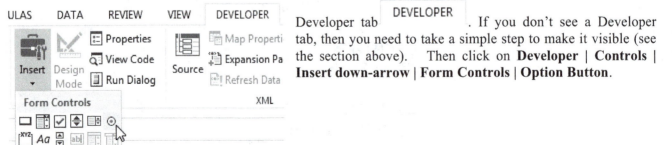 to allow input choices.

How To. Option buttons and other so-called "form controls" are located on the Developer tab DEVELOPER . If you don't see a Developer tab, then you need to take a simple step to make it visible (see the section above).   Then click on **Developer | Controls | Insert down-arrow | Form Controls | Option Button**.

Then point the cursor crosshairs to the upper-left corner of where you want the option button to be, click and drag to the lower-right corner, and release. You get

a option button [⊙]. Repeat this process to get more option buttons.

Now place the cursor over the top of the first option button, right-click, then click over the blank text area, click a second time over the blank text area, delete any unwanted text (e.g., "Option Button1"), enter a text description of the choice

(e.g., "Buy"), and then click outside the option button to finish [⊙ Buy].

Repeat this process for the other option buttons (e.g., "Sell") [⊙ Sell].

Now place the cursor over the top of the first option button, right-click, and select **Format Control** from the pop-up menu. On the **Control** tab of the **Format Control** dialog box, enter **C5** in the **Cell Link** entry box, and click **OK**.

Now when the first option button is clicked, then the cell **C5** will show a **1**, and when the second option button is clicked, then the cell **C5** will show a **2**. Optionally, you click on the **Colors and Lines** tab of **Format Control** dialog box and specify the option button's fill color, line color, etc.

If you just want to have *one set* of option buttons on a spreadsheet, then you are done. However, if you want to have two or more sets of option buttons (the example below has four sets of option buttons), then you need to use **Group Boxes** to indicate which option buttons belong to which set.

	A	B	C	D	E
1	**OPTION TRADING STRATEGIES**		**Two Assets**		
2					
3	**Inputs**	**Buying a Bullish Spread**			
4		Trade Direction		Asset Type	
5	First Asset (Lowest Exercise Price)	1st Trade Direction ⊙ Buy ○ Sell	1	1st Asset Type ⊙ Call ○ Put ○ Stock	1
6	Second Asset (Highest Exercise Price)	2nd Trade Direction ○ Buy ⊙ Sell	2	2nd Asset Type ⊙ Call ○ Put ○ Stock	1

Click on **Developer | Controls | Insert down-arrow | Form Controls | Group Box**.

Then point the cursor crosshairs above and left of the first option button, click and drag to below and right of the second option button (or last option button in the set), and release. A Group Box is created which surrounds the option buttons. Click on the title of the Group Box, delete any unwanted text (e.g., "Group Box 1"), enter a text description (e.g., "1ˢᵗ Trade Direction"). Now when you click on the Buy or Sell option button in cell **B5** of the example above, then the linked cell **C5** changes to 1 or 2. Repeat the process of creating option buttons and surrounding them by group boxes to create all of the sets of option buttons that you want.

25.5 Scroll Bar

Task. Add a scroll bar call option to make big or small changes to an input.

How To. Option buttons and other so-called "form controls" are located on the Developer tab DEVELOPER. If you don't see a Developer tab, then you need to take a simple step to make it visible (see two sections above).

Then click on **Developer | Controls | Insert down-arrow | Form Controls | Scroll Bar**.

Then point the cursor crosshairs to the upper-left corner of where you want the option button to be, click and drag to the lower-right corner, and release. You get a scroll bar.

Now place the cursor over the top of the scroll bar, right-click, and select **Format Control** from the pop-up menu.

On the **Control** tab of the **Format Control** dialog box, enter I7 in the **Cell Link** entry box, and click **OK**. Optionally, you can specify the **Page Change** amount, which is the change in the cell link when you click on the white space of the scroll bar. In this example, a **Page Change** of **12** months jumps a year ahead.

The advantage of a scroll bar is that you can make big or small changes (see example below). Clicking on the left or right arrow lowers or raises the value in cell **I7** by 1. Clicking on the white space of the scroll bar, lowers or raises the value in cell **I7** by 12 (the Page Change). Sliding the position bar allows you to rapidly scroll through the entire range of values.

	A	B	C	D	E	F	G	H	I	J	K	L	M	N	O
1	AFFINE YIELD CURVE MODELS				US Yield Curve Dynamics										
2	Inputs		Month = Nov-87		Static Features:		Shape = Upward								
3										click right arrow = ahead 1 month					
4	◀								▶	click left arrow = back 1 month					
5										click to the right the position bar = ahead 1 year					
6		Dynamic Chart of US Yield Curve Dynamics						Row		click to the left the position bar = back 1 year					
7								2		slide the position bar to jump ahead or back					

25.6 Install Solver or the Analysis ToolPak

Task. Install Solver or the Analysis ToolPak.

How To. Excel provides several special tools, such as Solver and the Analysis ToolPak, which need to be separately installed. Solver is a sophisticated, yet easy to use optimizer. The Analysis ToolPak contains advanced statistical programs and advanced functions.

To install the Analysis ToolPak, click on **File**, click on **Options**, click on **Add-Ins**, highlight the **Analysis ToolPak** Analysis ToolPak in the list of Inactive Applications, click on **Go** Go... near the bottom of the dialog box, check the **Analysis ToolPak**, and click on **OK**.

To install Solver, do the same steps except substitute **Solver** in place of **Analysis ToolPak** along the way.

25.7 Format Painter

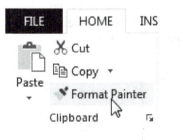

Task. Apply formatting from one cell to other cells.

How To. Select the cell(s) whose format you want to copy (e.g., select **D5:E5** in the example below). Then click on **Home | Clipboard | Format Painter** ❖ Format Painter . The cursor now includes a paint brush. Then select the range that you want to apply the formatting to (e.g., range **D6:E17** in the example below). Notice that Format Painter copies all of the formatting, including number type (percentage), number of decimals, background color, and border color.

Before

	A	B	C	D	E
1	THE YIELD CURVE	Obtaining and Using It			
2		Maturity	Time To	Yield To	Forward
3	Yield Curve Inputs	Date	Maturity	Maturity	Rates
4	Today's Date	10/11/2013			
5	One Month Treasury Bill	11/15/2013	0.09	0.021%	0.021%
6	Three Month Treasury Bill	1/9/2014	0.24	0.00061	0.00086
7	Six Month Treasury Bill	4/10/2014	0.50	0.00071	0.00081
8	One Year Treasury Strip	10/15/2014	1.01	0.00180	0.00286
9	Two Year Treasury Strip	10/15/2015	2.01	0.00350	0.00522
10	Three Year Treasury Strip	11/15/2016	3.09	0.00730	0.01439
11	Four Year Treasury Strip	11/15/2017	4.09	0.01130	0.02378
12	Five Year Treasury Strip	11/15/2018	5.09	0.01480	0.02926
13	Ten Year Treasury Strip	11/15/2023	10.09	0.02920	0.04408
14	Fifteen Year Treasury Bond	11/15/2028	15.09	0.03550	0.04834
15	Twenty Year Treasury Bond	11/15/2033	20.09	0.03820	0.04639
16	Twenty Five Year Treasury Bond	11/15/2038	25.09	0.03950	0.04474
17	Thirty Year Treasury Bond	5/15/2043	29.59	0.04010	0.04345

After

	A	B	C	D	E
1	THE YIELD CURVE	Obtaining and Using It			
2		Maturity	Time To	Yield To	Forward
3	Yield Curve Inputs	Date	Maturity	Maturity	Rates
4	Today's Date	10/11/2013			
5	One Month Treasury Bill	11/15/2013	0.09	0.021%	0.021%
6	Three Month Treasury Bill	1/9/2014	0.24	0.061%	0.086%
7	Six Month Treasury Bill	4/10/2014	0.50	0.071%	0.081%
8	One Year Treasury Strip	10/15/2014	1.01	0.180%	0.286%
9	Two Year Treasury Strip	10/15/2015	2.01	0.350%	0.522%
10	Three Year Treasury Strip	11/15/2016	3.09	0.730%	1.439%
11	Four Year Treasury Strip	11/15/2017	4.09	1.130%	2.378%
12	Five Year Treasury Strip	11/15/2018	5.09	1.480%	2.926%
13	Ten Year Treasury Strip	11/15/2023	10.09	2.920%	4.408%
14	Fifteen Year Treasury Bond	11/15/2028	15.09	3.550%	4.834%
15	Twenty Year Treasury Bond	11/15/2033	20.09	3.820%	4.639%
16	Twenty Five Year Treasury Bond	11/15/2038	25.09	3.950%	4.474%
17	Thirty Year Treasury Bond	5/15/2043	29.59	4.010%	4.345%

25.8 Conditional Formatting

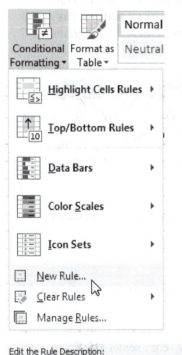

Task. Conditionally format a cell. This allows the displayed format to change based upon the results of a formula calculation.

How To. Suppose you want to use special formatting to highlight the best portfolio in constrained portfolio optimization (see example below). Select cell M166. Click on **Home | Styles | Conditional Formatting down-arrow | New Rule**. Then click on Use a formula to determine which cells to format ▶ Use a formula to determine which cells to format. In the text entry box, enter **=M166=1**. This checks whether the value of cell M166 is equal to one. Formulas for conditional fomatting must begin with an equal sign, so oddly you end up with two equal signs in the formula. Then click on the **Format** button. In the **Format Cells** dialog box, click on the **Fill** tab, select the **color** you like, click **OK**, and then click **OK** again. Finally, copy this new conditional format down the column using Format Painter. Click on **Home | Clipboard | Format Painter** ✒ Format Painter. The cursor now includes a paint brush. Then select the range **M167:M181**. In this example, the cell **M173** turns orange because it is the highest ranking (#1) portfolio. If you changed one of the problem inputs, then a different portfolio might be ranked #1 and the cell corresponding to the new #1 would be highlighted in orange.

Edit the Rule Description:

Format values where this formula is true:

Edit the Rule Description:

Format values where this formula is true:

=M166=1

Preview: No Format Set   Format...

Format Cells

Number Font Border **Fill**

Background Color: Pattern Color:
No Color Automatic

Pattern Style:

Fill Effects... More Colors...

Sample

Clear

OK Cancel

	L	M
54	Investor Utility	Portfolio Ranking
166	0.555%	15
167	0.568%	13
168	0.578%	11
169	0.587%	9
170	0.594%	7
171	0.599%	5
172	0.603%	3
173	0.604%	1
174	0.604%	2
175	0.602%	4
176	0.598%	6
177	0.593%	8
178	0.585%	10
179	0.576%	12
180	0.565%	14
181	0.552%	16

25.9 Fill Handle

Task. Fill in row 10 with integers from 0 to 8 to create the timeline (see example below). This fill technique works for wide range of patterns.

How To. Enter **0** in cell **B10** and **1** in cell **C10**. Select the range **B10:C10**, then hover the cursor over the fill handle ▬▪ (the square in the lower-right corner) of cell **C10** and the cursor turns to a plus symbol ✛. Click, drag the plus symbol to cell **J10**, and release. The range fills up with the rest the pattern from 2 to 8.

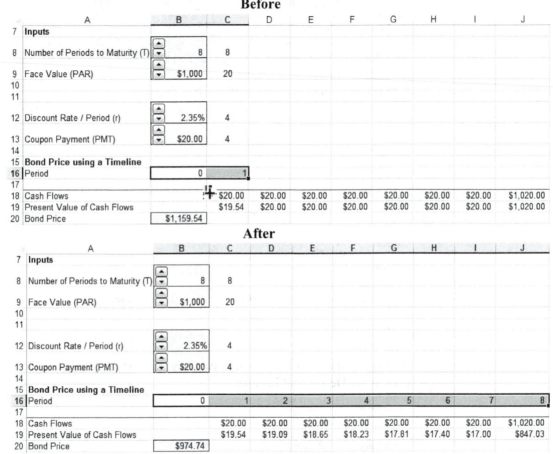

Before

	A	B	C	D	E	F	G	H	I	J
7	Inputs									
8	Number of Periods to Maturity (T)	8	8							
9	Face Value (PAR)	$1,000	20							
10										
11										
12	Discount Rate / Period (r)	2.35%	4							
13	Coupon Payment (PMT)	$20.00	4							
14										
15	**Bond Price using a Timeline**									
16	Period	0	1							
17										
18	Cash Flows		$20.00	$20.00	$20.00	$20.00	$20.00	$20.00	$20.00	$1,020.00
19	Present Value of Cash Flows		$19.54	$20.00	$20.00	$20.00	$20.00	$20.00	$20.00	$1,020.00
20	Bond Price	$1,159.54								

After

	A	B	C	D	E	F	G	H	I	J
7	Inputs									
8	Number of Periods to Maturity (T)	8	8							
9	Face Value (PAR)	$1,000	20							
10										
11										
12	Discount Rate / Period (r)	2.35%	4							
13	Coupon Payment (PMT)	$20.00	4							
14										
15	**Bond Price using a Timeline**									
16	Period	0	1	2	3	4	5	6	7	8
17										
18	Cash Flows		$20.00	$20.00	$20.00	$20.00	$20.00	$20.00	$20.00	$1,020.00
19	Present Value of Cash Flows		$19.54	$19.09	$18.65	$18.23	$17.81	$17.40	$17.00	$847.03
20	Bond Price	$974.74								

25.10 2-D Scatter Chart

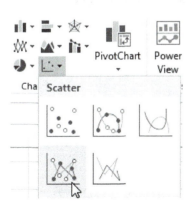

Task. Create a two-dimensional Scatter Chart.

How To. Select the range that has the data you wish to graph (e.g., select **C5:E17** in the example below). Click on **Insert | Charts | Scatter down-arrow | Scatter with Straight Lines and Markers**.

	A	B	C	D	E
1	THE YIELD CURVE	Obtaining and Using It			
2		Maturity	Time To	Yield To	Forward
3	**Yield Curve Inputs**	Date	Maturity	Maturity	Rates
4	Today's Date	10/11/2013			
5	One Month Treasury Bill	11/15/2013	0.09	0.021%	0.021%
6	Three Month Treasury Bill	1/9/2014	0.24	0.061%	0.086%
7	Six Month Treasury Bill	4/10/2014	0.50	0.071%	0.081%
8	One Year Treasury Strip	10/15/2014	1.01	0.180%	0.286%
9	Two Year Treasury Strip	10/15/2015	2.01	0.350%	0.522%
10	Three Year Treasury Strip	11/15/2016	3.09	0.730%	1.439%
11	Four Year Treasury Strip	11/15/2017	4.09	1.130%	2.378%
12	Five Year Treasury Strip	11/15/2018	5.09	1.480%	2.926%
13	Ten Year Treasury Strip	11/15/2023	10.09	2.920%	4.408%
14	Fifteen Year Treasury Bond	11/15/2028	15.09	3.550%	4.834%
15	Twenty Year Treasury Bond	11/15/2033	20.09	3.820%	4.639%
16	Twenty Five Year Treasury Bond	11/15/2038	25.09	3.950%	4.474%
17	Thirty Year Treasury Bond	5/15/2043	29.59	4.010%	4.345%

A rough version of the 2-D Scatter Chart appears.

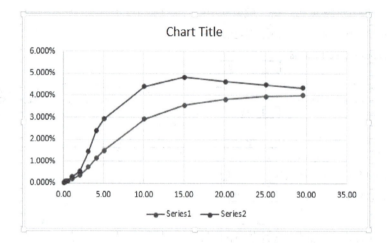

As long as the Chart is selected, two new tabs appear that provide lots of chart options for Design and Format.

CHART TOOLS

DESIGN   FORMAT

Alternatively, you can right-click on parts of the chart to get pop-up menus with formatting choices. Here is what a fully-formatted 2-D Scatter Chart looks like.

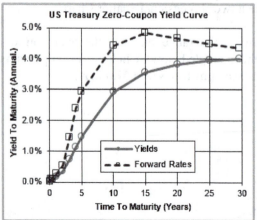

25.11 3-D Surface Chart

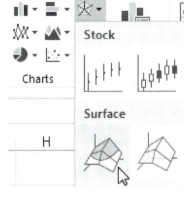

Task. Create a three-dimensional Surface Chart.

How To. Select the range that has the data you wish to graph (e.g., select **C94:G98** in the example below). Click on **Insert | Charts | Other Charts down-arrow | Surface | 3-D Surface**.

	A	B	C	D	E	F	G
1	PROJECT NPV	Sensitivity Analysis					
2	(in thousands of $)						
3		Year 0	Year 1	Year 2	Year 3	Year 4	Year 5
91	Data Table: Sensitivity of the Net	Present Value to Unit Sales and Date 0 Real Cost of Capital					
92			Input Values for Unit Sales Scale Factor				
93	Out Formula: Net Present Value	$3,180	80%	90%	100%	110%	120%
94		9.0%	($1,324)	$1,667	$4,658	$7,649	$10,640
95	Input Values for	11.0%	($2,336)	$422	$3,180	$5,938	$8,696
96	Date 0 Real Cost of Capital	13.0%	($3,246)	($698)	$1,851	$4,399	$6,947
97		15.0%	($4,065)	($1,706)	$652	$3,010	$5,369
98		17.0%	($4,804)	($2,617)	($431)	$1,755	$3,941

A rough version of the 3-D Surface Chart appears.

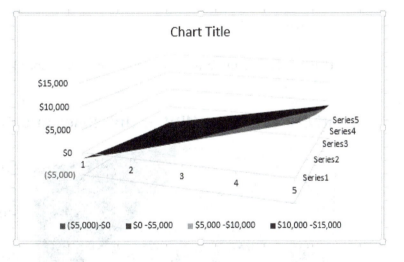

As long as the Chart is selected, two new tabs appear that provide lots of chart options for Design and Format.

CHART TOOLS

DESIGN   FORMAT

Alternatively, you can right-click on parts of the chart to get pop-up menus with formatting choices.

Fill   Outline   Floor ▼

Delete

Reset to Match Style

Change Chart Type...

Select Data...

3-D Rotation...

Format Floor...

It is often useful to rotate a 3-D chart. To do this, right-click on the main part of the graph and select 3-D Rotation. 3-D Rotation provides the ability to rotate the surface in the X-axis direction, Y-axis direction, or Z-axis direction.

Format Chart Area ▼ ✕

CHART OPTIONS ▼   TEXT OPTIONS

▷ SHADOW

▷ GLOW

▷ SOFT EDGES

▷ 3-D FORMAT

◢ 3-D ROTATION

Presets

X Rotation   20°

Y Rotation   15°

Z Rotation   0°

Perspective   15°

Here is what a fully-formatted 3-D Surface Chart looks like.

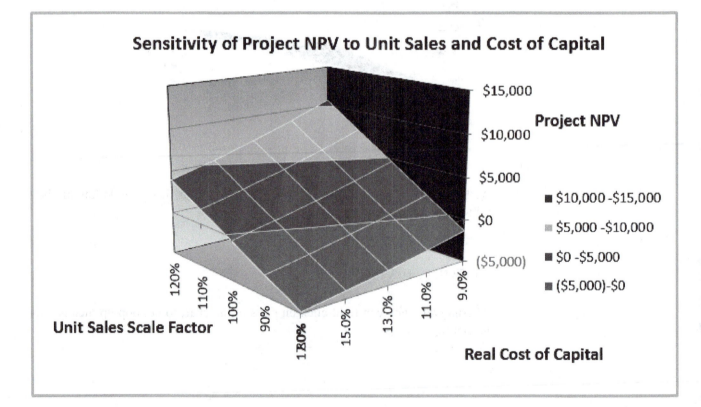

Pronouncing American English

Sounds, Stress, and Intonation

Second Edition

14, 15, 29, 30.